Charlotte Brontë's
World of Death

Charlotte Brontë's World of Death

ROBERT KEEFE

University of Texas Press, Austin & London

The publication of this book was assisted by a
grant from the Andrew W. Mellon Foundation.

Library of Congress Cataloging in Publication Data

Keefe, Robert, 1938–
    Charlotte Brontë's world of death.

    Bibliography: p.
    Includes index.
    1. Brontë, Charlotte, 1816–1855—Criticism and
interpretation. 2. Death in literature. 3. Psychology
and literature. I. Title.
PR4169.K4   823'.8   78–9853
ISBN 0–292–75043–9

Printed in the United States of America

TO JAN

*As always you were my primary audience,
the one I opened up to. Both stylistically
and intellectually, the book is the result of
your side of the conversations as well as
mine.*

Poetry destroyed? Genius banished? No!
Mediocrity, no: do not let envy prompt you
to the thought. No; they not only live, but
reign, and redeem: and without their divine
influence spread everywhere you would be in
hell—the hell of your own meanness.
    CHARLOTTE BRONTË, *Jane Eyre*

The fact that a human being does not just
cry out in formless protest against the pain
and passion of individual fate but
deliberately obeys the discipline of language
and the rules of custom seems inexplicable—
until we realize that art is the individual's
way back to the collective.
    ERNST FISCHER, *The Necessity of Art*

Contents

Introduction

This book began as an attempt to examine the Cinderella motif in *Jane Eyre*. I was struck several years ago by the fact that at so many crucial points in her career, Jane is confronted by two hostile sisters and their mother. I knew that Charlotte Brontë's mother and her two older sisters had died during Charlotte's childhood, and the more I thought about the problem, the more I became convinced that these deaths lay at the root of the adult novelist's need to use the Cinderella motif. Having written an essay on the patterns of confrontation in *Jane Eyre*, I decided to test out my ideas on the juvenilia. I had not read any of her early writings, but I conjectured that I would find a series of tales in which a basic pattern of jealousy, murder, and remorse was worked out. What I discovered there confirmed my working hypothesis so strikingly and so completely that I decided to write a full-length study of Charlotte Brontë's life and art.

It is my contention that the single most important event in Charlotte Brontë's life was the death of her mother. This trauma, followed a few years later by the loss of her two older sisters, Maria and Elizabeth, became the prime determinant of the novelist's way of looking at reality. Since both her mother and her father were amateur writers, she quite possibly would have tried her hand at writing in any case, but I have attempted to show that it was the deprivations she experienced during her childhood which enabled her to become a major novelist.

In a general sense, the importance of death in the development of Charlotte Brontë's personality has been recognized for well over a century. Every biographer has stressed her recurrent bereavement as the cause of the novelist's shyness and her loneliness. By the time the novel-reading public became aware of her identity, she had lost her mother, her four sisters, and her brother. With the publication in 1857 of Elizabeth Gaskell's *Life of Charlotte Brontë*, the story of those losses became one of the most fascinating tales in all of English literature, as engrossing a narrative as any of the Brontë novels.

What has been consistently left out of the picture of Brontë's reaction to death is, in the first place, the centrality of her mother's death for the construction of the girl's personality, and, secondly, the importance of guilt in that personality. Brontë's early biographers made the mistake of assuming that, since Emily and Anne were the most famous of Charlotte's loved ones, and Branwell the most infamous, their deaths must have been the most important. They overlooked the fact that Charlotte's personality was already formed by the time that round of deaths occurred. It would make much more sense to see Charlotte's reaction to the loss of Branwell, Emily, and Anne as a continuation of a psychological response she had learned earlier, when she suffered bereavement as a child.

The death of her two older sisters, Maria and Elizabeth, was traumatic for Charlotte. We know that she talked of Elizabeth, and especially of Maria, obsessively throughout her adolescence, and that she structured a major portion of *Jane Eyre* around Maria's character and death. Human beings do not normally rank their affections according to the fame of their loved ones. Charlotte admired and loved Emily, but she adored Maria. Maria's death, then, had a formative influence on Charlotte's psyche which outweighed the effects of later losses.

But it was an even earlier trauma, the death of her mother, which called forth the pattern of psychological response which would control Brontë's life and her art. All the other deaths, Maria's, Elizabeth's, Branwell's, Emily's, Anne's—even, as we shall see, Charlotte's own— became repetitions of the first trauma, the loss of maternal love.

Marjorie Editha Mitchell, in *The Child's Attitude to Death*, writes: "All research workers are agreed that in the early years the most severe type of bereavement is mother loss, and unless dealt with by adequate mother substitution, it may lead to pathological changes in personality development."[1] When she was five years old, Charlotte lost her prime nurturer, her earliest contact with the external world. It was a trauma which would eventually turn her into a major writer. A decade later the girl told her best friend that she had begun to analyze character when she was five years old. It can be no coincidence that the stance of the future novelist was taken up in the year in which her mother died. Her reaction to that death formed in her psyche a complex web of feelings, a tangled knot of sorrow, loneliness, anguish, rage, and, most importantly, guilt, which she carried with her until she died. And those feelings colored all of her novels.

We do not have to seek a specific action on Charlotte's part which might have caused her to feel guilty about her mother's death. She may well have imagined a wrongdoing or a fault of hers that, in her own mind, confirmed her guilt. Perhaps she remembered and then repressed a moment of exasperation when she had wished that her invalid mother would go away. But even if that were true, such a memory would have been merely the rationalization for the presence of guilt, not its cause. The fact is that, for a young child whose mother dies, the formation of guilt feelings is nearly inevitable. And the future effect of that formation is often devastating.

In a seminal article on the subject of childhood mourning, John Bowlby writes: "In the young child the experience of separation from [the] mother figure is especially apt to evoke psychological processes of a kind that are as crucial for psychopathology as are inflammation and its resulting scar tissue to physiopathology. This does not mean that a crippling of personality is the inevitable result; but it does mean that, as in the case, say, of rheumatic fever, scar tissue is all too often formed which in later life leads to more or less severe dysfunction."[2] The Nazi death camps of World War II have taught us just how prevalent guilt feelings are among mature men and women who have outlived their loved ones. A child is even more susceptible to those feelings. As Arnold Gesell and Frances L. Ilg point out in *The Child from Five to Ten*, children do not develop the vital concept of death as a natural and inevitable process until they reach the age of eight or nine.[3] Before that, they see death in a more primitive light, as the result of a specific act of aggression, one might almost say as a murder. If a mother dies, then someone must have killed her, someone must bear the responsibility for causing her death. In the first manifestation of that sense of responsibility which nineteenth-century readers so admired in her, Brontë seems to have decided that the guilt belonged to her.

One of the mechanisms which probably helps to create, and certainly helps to reinforce, this sense of guilt in a survivor is the need to deny the fact that we are enraged with the loved one who has left us. Death is a particularly cruel form of abandonment; yet we do not like to admit that we are angered by such a wanton act of desertion. It has often been noted that Charlotte Brontë seldom mentioned her mother. This could be brought forward as evidence that her mother's death was relatively unimportant to her. But in all probability the case was just the opposite. Bowlby writes:

> Examination of the evidence suggests that one of the main characteristics of pathological mourning is nothing less than an inability to express overtly these urges to recover and scold the lost object, with all the yearning for and anger with the deserting object that they entail. Instead of its overt expression, which though stormy and fruitless leads on to a healthy outcome, the urges to recover and reproach with all their ambivalence of feeling have become split off and repressed. Thenceforward, they have continued as active systems within the personality but, unable to find overt and direct expression, have come to influence feeling and behaviour in strange and distorted ways.[4]

There is ample evidence that Brontë was unable to express even to herself her anger at her mother's departure. In her third novel, *Shirley*, a woman abandons her daughter for reasons which are patently absurd. On her return more than a decade later, she tells the girl: "I let you go as a babe, because you were pretty, and I feared your loveliness."[5] Her daughter manifests absolutely no sign of healthy resentment at such shabby treatment: "Caroline no more showed [any] wounding sagacity or reproachful sensitiveness now, than she had done when a suckling of three months old."[6] Not even in her fiction could Brontë grow angry at desertion.

Its normal course thus blocked, her anger turned inward to become guilt and self-hatred. Perhaps the most striking evidence of this displaced rage is the series of letters which she wrote in her adolescence to her friend Ellen Nussey, letters filled with cries such as this: "I abhor myself—I despise myself . . . don't desert me—don't be horrified at me, you know what I am."[7] Here the potential deserter is thoroughly innocent, while the one who would be left behind is despicable. Charlotte fantasizes that Ellen would leave her because she has become disgusted at the hidden sinfulness of her friend. Very probably the mechanism at work in this letter is one which Charlotte had learned as she watched her mother die. The one who should be scolded and punished is not the woman who is leaving, but the girl who is left behind.

Abandonment was both Brontë's greatest personal fear and the central motif of all her fiction. Her four novels are all in one way or another about forms of exile.[8] Underlying her work is a painful sense of separation. Her characters have moved away from a place where they were once contented, or someone important has left them for reasons which are either unknown or insufficient. Even in her consciously provincial novel *Shirley*, two of the four main characters are foreigners who cannot feel at home in their adopted land. By the time she wrote *Villette*, exile had become her primary metaphor for life.

The increasing complexity of this metaphor in her fiction provides us with one way of demonstrating Brontë's deepening gloom. Her first two novels, written while her younger sisters were still alive, concern the successful attempts of their protagonists to find their way home. Thus, after a lucrative career on the Continent, *The Professor*'s William Crimsworth returns to England to live out the rest of his life in Daisy Lane. And in the next novel, Jane Eyre takes her blinded lover by the hand and, like the fairy-tale heroine she is, wends her way homeward through the woods.

But soon after the completion of *Jane Eyre*, the novelist's brother and two younger sisters died, and her fiction darkened. In her last two novels, home cannot really be found. The heroine of *Shirley* and her husband live on her property, it is true, but they have altered it beyond recognition. For in the once green, wild Hollow, they have constructed an enormous factory, with a chimney "as ambitious as the tower of Babel."⁹ The industrial world has covered Old England with bricks and ashes; home is in the process of being destroyed. And in the final novel, *Villette*, home cannot even be remembered. Existence itself is a form of exile, and only death can put an end to banishment.

Both Brontë's art and her life can be seen as struggles against her will to die. Margot Peters, in *Charlotte Brontë: Style in the Novel*, points out that her fiction bears a strong linguistic resemblance to the language of suicide notes.¹⁰ That same suicidal undercurrent runs throughout her life, with ultimately tragic consequences. In the first chapter of this book I have tried to indicate the range of conscious and unconscious strategies which Charlotte Brontë used to deal with the problem of death and the anguish of survival. Writing was at bottom the healthiest of these strategies, the activity which, along with Christian faith, imparted meaning to her existence. Like all of us, she constructed a wide range of unconscious defenses against the pain of her life, and many of them were not so healthy. These strategies for survival and the deaths which made them so necessary provide the focus of Chapter 1.

The biographical essay is not intended to replace a full-length biography of Charlotte Brontë. A biography succeeds in large part by recreating something of the full flavor of a human life. For intellectual reasons as well as problems of space, this book follows a different route. Random details have been cut away in order to concentrate on what seems to be the central core of significance. The temptation to paint scenes and sketch in intellectual backgrounds has been resisted. There are no long descriptions of her family and friends. I hope that the obvious disadvantages of this technique are compensated for by the brighter light it sheds on her mind itself.

The most important aspect of that mind was its ability to create art. By the time Charlotte began to write the juvenile cycle of romances which are examined in the second chapter of this book, she had been forced to watch helplessly as three members of her family grew fatally ill. I have tried to show that she became a writer because fiction allowed her to construct a world which she could control. In fiction she could become the master of fate. The game which she and the other Brontë children played centered around death, around the experience which formed the most important part of their reality. The setting was exotic, but what happened in that setting is what had occurred in the Brontë household. Like her adult novels, Brontë's early romances served the primary purpose of all literature; they explained life for her, gave it shape and meaning.

Of course that meaning became more complex as the author matured. Charlotte Brontë is one of the few writers in whom we can trace the evolution of adolescent fantasy into adult imagination. Her childhood writings are informed by the need to deny death's finality, to reverse the process of dissolution. But the girl was blessed and cursed with a ferocious honesty, a family trait which would ultimately save her and her sisters (though not her brother) from the mawkish sentimentality which trivializes death in so much Victorian fiction. And that honesty quickly began to leave its mark on her writing. The self-pity which would fill her poetry throughout her life disappeared from her prose early on, shouldered aside by a compelling need to probe and test reality, no matter how much it hurt. Her fiction would never attain a mystic serenity, never manage to integrate life and death. The two principles would remain for her utterly opposed, irreconcilable—and her art at its finest would register their dissonant clash.

The last four chapters of the book are devoted to an analysis of the four novels which constitute Charlotte Brontë's claim to lasting recognition. If I have succeeded at all in those chapters, the reader will discern the broad and crucial relevance of the patterns of Charlotte Brontë's life to her art. Not all of the novels are equally concerned with the patterns I have traced in the first two chapters of this book. Critics are generally agreed that *Jane Eyre* and *Villette* are much finer novels than *The Professor* and *Shirley*. There is a basic psychological reason behind this difference in quality, I think. In her two masterpieces, Brontë confronted the primary issues of her mental life and tried to gain psychological mastery over them. *Jane Eyre* and *Villette* are about death and survival, or, if you prefer, death and love, and they never turn for long from those basic concerns. Moreover, for all her personal timidity, Brontë at her best was a strikingly innovative technician. The two novels probe the human psyche with a broader range of surrealistic devices than any English novelist before her had ever used.

In *The Professor* and *Shirley*, on the other hand, she was trying for realism, both of subject and of technique. But unfortunately, she saw realism as an escape from the complex of ideas which occupied so much of her thought and her dreams. As recent biographers, most notably Winifred Gérin, have pointed out, she mistrusted her own genius. She seems to have felt that artistic and emotional maturity should involve forsaking the paranoid concerns of her juvenilia and concentrating instead on the "real" world in which she lived, the world of capitalist Europe.

She tried to focus on that external reality in her first novel. *The Professor* deals with the search for financial and psychological security in the world of affairs. There, more than in any other novel, Charlotte avoids the gloomy shadows of the mind. The hero tells himself: "Look at the sooty smoke in that hollow, and know that there is your post! There you cannot dream, you cannot speculate and theorise—there you shall out and work!"[11] Like her protagonist, Brontë tried very hard not to dream in her first novel. She could never limit her vision like that for long, however; the surrealistic underside of everyday life could not fully be locked out of even that resolutely realistic book. The novel is an unmistakable product of the mind which created the juvenilia and *Jane Eyre*; the tensions are the same, the patterns of human interaction are the same. It is simply that survival has shrunk to security.

In *Jane Eyre*, Brontë opened the door to her dreams again. Jane inhabits a universe of ghouls and ogres and fairies. The early critical complaint that the author was ignorant of the manners of society seems today hilariously irrelevant. For the novel is closer in spirit to the works of Poe and Baudelaire than to the productions of Austen and Trollope. It succeeds precisely because Brontë allowed herself to surrender to her intuition that the familiar surface of existence is a thin film covering the more frightening truths of the unconscious.

In *The Professor*, Brontë had tried to narrow her vision too severely; in *Shirley* she tried to take in too much. Without sacrificing the private world she had captured in *Jane Eyre*, she returned to the industrial reality she had touched on in *The Professor*. The resulting mixture of realism and romance is an interesting failure. The author nearly succeeded in unifying the private and public worlds of *Shirley*. Caroline Helstone's psychological hunger and the industrial workers' physical starvation have both been caused by parental abandonment. Caroline's mother has left her, and the workers' employers have abdicated their paternalistic responsibilities. But the two forms of hunger never fully coalesce to form an artistic whole.

In *Villette*, the novel which I consider her finest achievement, the author returned to the deepest concerns of her unconscious. In so doing, she created a psychological study which was unsurpassed in her era. *Villette* is a hauntingly modern book. More than any other novel of its time, it is characterized by those Arnoldian hallmarks of modernity: emotion which finds no release in action, and a mind in constant dialogue with itself. Moreover, Lucy Snowe's mind does not even understand the full significance of what it is trying to tell itself. She wanders through a foreign city projecting her alienation onto everything she observes. Without fully realizing it, she is an inhabitant of hell.

Brontë's fiction moves from the bustling activity of *The Professor* to the numbing stasis of *Villette*. Yet the mundane metropolis of her first novel and the hell of her last are the same city; the change lies in the perceiving mind. In my chapter titles I have tried to indicate the progression in her view of reality: Possession, Innocence, Emptiness, Exile. The chapters thus trace the darkening of the novelist's vision from timid optimism to bleak pessimism.

The novels she wrote could not make up for the losses she had suffered, and she was too forthright an artist to disguise the depth of her steadily deepening depression. Yet her creative achievement was substantial. For she managed to fashion an art which brought the English novel to a new level of psychological and technical sophistication. Despite the brevity of her professional career—only five years elapsed between the publication of her first novel and the appearance of her last—she helped to bring about a lasting change in British fiction.

One further note. Since I finished this manuscript, a book has been published with which my own will inevitably be compared: Helene Moglen's *Charlotte Brontë: The Self Conceived* (New York: Norton, 1976), a work that treats the connection between Brontë's life and art with a sophistication that has too often been absent in previous criticism. Moglen shares many of my concerns and anticipates some of my remarks, and I have gone over my manuscript once more to take her work into account. Moglen is primarily interested in the evolution of Brontë's feminism and concentrates on the relationships between the novelist and the men in her life. I have underplayed that aspect of my subject, not because I found it unimportant, but because I was struck more by the influence of the women who are absent from Brontë's life than the men who are present. The portrait of Charlotte Brontë which emerges from my work is much darker, less logical, less militant, and less easily triumphant, I think.

That the dark tones should dominate my portrayal of Charlotte Brontë is only fitting. For in a very real sense, her life was spent in mourning.

It remains for me to express my gratitude to those people who have helped in the production of this book: to my colleagues, Lee Edwards, Morris Golden, Edward Mike

Jayne, William Mailler, Jr., David Paroissien, Meredith Raymond, Arnold Silver, and Cynthia Griffin Wolff, who read all or part of the original manuscript and made invaluable suggestions for changes; to David R. Jones, Albert D. Hutter, Jr., and Helene Moglen, whose perceptive critiques I took into consideration in completing the final draft; to the Graduate Research Council of the University of Massachusetts, for a small grant to help in the preparation of the manuscript; to Alison Heinemann, who edited the book; and to my wife, Janice A. Keefe, who read and critiqued the manuscript at every stage of its composition.

Charlotte Brontë's
World of Death

Chapter One
Silence and Language:
A Meditation on Charlotte Brontë

WHEN CHARLOTTE BRONTË was five years old her mother died, and less than four years later her two older sisters succumbed to tuberculosis. By the time she was nine, death had become the central phenomenon of her life, its pall a filter through which she saw all of existence. One of her friends reported a peculiar incident to Charlotte's biographer, Elizabeth Gaskell: "I have seen her turn pale and feel faint when, in Hartshead church, some one accidentally remarked that we were walking over graves."[1] Indeed in a broader sense Brontë can be said to have feared throughout her life that she was walking over graves, and the resultant anxiety goes far toward explaining the strange power which resides in her art.

It must be stressed at the outset that her experience of death was far from unique; the mortality rate of her era was too high for that.[2] What made her unique was the tenacity with which she forced herself to create art from her bereavement. Thus, what is ultimately important in her character is not the stoic silence which Gaskell so admired, it is the need to break that silence, to cry out, to communicate. Above all it is the drive to create artistic structures as the primary defense against the inchoate pain of existence. In becoming a writer, Charlotte chose language over silence. To examine her life is above all to study the nature of that choice.

The first years of her life seem to have been uneventful enough. Her father, Patrick Brontë, had managed to obtain a degree from Cambridge despite his Irish peasant origins and had entered the ministry. In 1812, at the age of thirty-five, he had married Maria Branwell. Their family grew rapidly. Maria was born sometime during 1813, Elizabeth on February 8, 1815, and Charlotte on April 21, 1816. Charlotte was followed by her only brother, Branwell, on June 26, 1817, and then came Emily, on July 30, 1818. The last child, Anne, was born on January 17, 1820, a month before the family moved to Haworth, the Yorkshire village where they would spend the rest of their lives. Then, on September 15, 1821, Mrs. Brontë died. She was thirty-eight years old.

Her death followed seven months of severe illness. Dr. Philip Rhodes, a leading authority on obstetrics and gynecology, concludes that she died of cardiac failure due to anemia, which had in turn been caused either by a chronic pelvic sepsis or a chronic inversion of the uterus.[3] The years of childbirth had taken their toll. Month after month Maria Brontë lay doubled over with pain, estranged from her surroundings, ignoring the children she had formerly nurtured. Mr. Brontë described his wife's agony: "She was cold and silent and seemed hardly to notice what was passing around her. . . . Death pursued her unrelentingly. Her constitution was enfeebled, and her frame wasted daily; and after above seven months of more agonizing pain than I ever saw anyone endure she fell asleep in Jesus, and her soul took its flight to the mansions of glory. During many years she had walked with God, but the great enemy, envying her life of holiness, often disturbed her mind in the last conflict."[4]

Charlotte was five years old when her mother died, and the event seems to have colored her conception of reality from that day forward, much more than she herself could have realized.[5] Her later life demonstrates that she could still love—she retained throughout her life the need to idolize and adore other people—but the loss of her mother must have destroyed much of her confidence that her feelings could ever be returned. She was thus apparently forced into the classic pose of the novelist—voyeurism. Her letters show that for the rest of her life she thought of herself as an onlooker of life, an outsider who could watch others give and receive affection, but who was not worthy of love herself. Even her memory of her mother was voyeuristic:

"Charlotte tried hard, in after years, to recall the remembrance of her mother, and could bring back two or three pictures of her. One was when, sometime in the evening light, she had been playing with her little boy, Patrick Branwell, in the parlour" (Gaskell, p. 33). Like the protagonists of *Jane Eyre* and Emily's *Wuthering Heights*, watching from exile the happiness of others on the warm side of the window, Charlotte remembers her mother showering attention on another child.

Their mother's illness deprived all of the Brontë children of the adult attention and affection they needed. During that illness Mrs. Brontë's sister, Elizabeth Branwell, came from Penzance to attend the invalid and care for the children. But Aunt Branwell, though she remained with the Brontës for the rest of her life, does not seem to have succeeded in replacing the parent they had lost.[6] She wore out her life pining for home and, without doubt, reminding the children of the sacrifices she was making for their welfare.

Nor was Patrick Brontë a warm parent. The available evidence indicates that the death of his wife turned him into a moody, silent recluse. His infrequent attempts to mingle with his children must have been looked on by his offspring with as much awe as joy.[7]

But by the standards of his day he was certainly a kind father, solicitous of his children's welfare. His income was about £200 a year, and he had six children to educate. He could tutor Branwell himself, but he would have to send his daughters to school. And he could not even afford the dismal intellectual fodder of a normal Yorkshire institution. Three years after his wife's death, he thought he had found a solution to the problem when he heard of the Clergy Daughters' School, newly established by the Rev. Carus Wilson at Cowan Bridge, in Lancashire. The school was run as a charity; the annual fee was only £14. It looked like a precious opportunity. Maria and Elizabeth made the fifty-five mile journey to the school first, arriving with their father on July 21, 1824. Charlotte followed them several weeks later and was enrolled on August 10; Emily joined her sisters on November 25.

In taking what seemed to him a prudent step toward his

daughters' well-being, Mr. Brontë had made the most disastrous mistake of his life. On his short visits to the school he had not seen anything wrong. But the physical conditions of the school, its bad and insufficient food, unhealthy location, and inadequate sanitation, were fatal. Several months after Emily's arrival, a typhoid epidemic decimated the student body. The Brontës escaped infection, but Maria and Elizabeth were struck down by tuberculosis. They had gone through a series of severe illnesses the previous spring, attacks of scarlet fever, whooping cough, and measles, and had not recovered sufficiently before being sent to the school; its ethics of asceticism soon did the rest. In February, 1825, the authorities notified Mr. Brontë that Maria was dangerously ill, and he took her home immediately. She died on May 6. Mr. Brontë wrote back to the school that she "exhibited during her illness many symptoms of a heart under Divine influence."[8] Three weeks later he made the journey to the school to bring back Elizabeth. She died on June 15, two weeks after Charlotte and Emily had left the school for good. Mr. Brontë's money was refunded.

Charlotte seems hardly ever to have talked about her mother. She did, however, talk about her older sisters, and what she had to say was revelatory. Years later, her closest friend, Ellen Nussey, reported:

> In these early days, whenever she was certain of being quite alone with [me], she would talk much of . . . Maria and Elizabeth . . . a kind of adoration dwelt in her feelings. . . .
>
> She described Maria as a little mother among the rest, superhuman in goodness and cleverness. But the most touching of all were the revelations of her sufferings—how she suffered with the sensibility of a grown-up person, and endured with a patience and fortitude that were Christ-like. Charlotte would . . . weep and suffer when thinking of her. She talked of Elizabeth also, but never with the anguish of expression which accompanied her recollections of Maria. When surprise was expressed that she should know so much about her sisters when they were so young,

and she herself still younger, she said she began to analyze character when she was five years old.[9]

Her image of Maria's character had taken shape when Charlotte was five, that is, when she was forced to ask herself why such an apparently kind woman as her mother had committed the hostile, cruel act of dying, of leaving her alone. The art of analysis requires mental distance from the object analyzed, and her mother's long illness and death must have given Charlotte that distance; that is, it must have begun the process of alienation which gradually forced Charlotte to view the human mind analytically. Nearly four years later her sister Maria suffered and died like a "grown-up person"; very likely that adult whom Maria resembled was her mother, whose name she bore. Elizabeth's death, too, was painful for Charlotte, but it was Maria whom the Brontë children, abetted by their father, had "analyzed" into the role of surrogate mother.[10] In repeating and amplifying the first death, that of the mother, Maria's departure seems to have left Charlotte's mind fixated on an unchanging image of the death of the beloved which was to control the future novelist's view of life and of art.

Charlotte later recognized that some part of her development had been arrested in the spring of 1825. Years later she told Elizabeth Gaskell that she had not grown an inch since her ten-month stay at Cowan Bridge. Her statement was inaccurate but nevertheless important. She was only nine when she came home to Haworth, and small for her age; had she not grown thereafter she would have been a dwarf. But the statement is not entirely wrong. For the evidence indicates that the growth of one portion of Charlotte's mind was impeded by its obsessive concentration on those painful deaths. She never talked about her sisters or their deaths, Ellen informs us, unless she was sure she was quite alone with her listener. The tale was apparently too frightening and too precious to be divulged to a group. The agony of separation must have been a possession to be hoarded, to be shared only with her dearest friends. Moreover, it would seem that the earlier separation, the exclusion from the warmth of her dead mother's love, was a heritage even more jealously guarded, portioned out to her own conscious mind only in disguised form for the most part. Her consciousness very possibly received from that source, for example, her lifelong fascination with ghosts. Ellen reports: "The tradition of a lady ghost who moved about in rustling silk in the upper stories [of the school which Ellen and Charlotte attended] had a great charm for Charlotte. She was a ready listener to any girl who could relate stories of others having seen her."[11] The idea of a lady returned from the dead, terrifying to her schoolmates, held a charm for Charlotte which she herself could not understand. Her later fictional attraction to the supernatural can be explained in part through recourse to the gothic fad of her era,[12] but more important, the gothic trappings of her novels might well have established contact between her unconscious and the lost object it longed for and could not through any realistic means recapture. If that is true, then supernatural fiction allowed the girl to catch glimpses of her mother which were disturbing, but which at the same time satisfied a profound need.

Patrick Brontë kept his children at home for the next six years. Their later correspondence shows that for the rest of their lives his daughters could hardly stand to leave Haworth Parsonage for any extended period. Only there did they feel safe; the external world had apparently become for them a menacing enemy to be warded off through retreat to the defensive family circle. It was during this six-year period that the outer world was repudiated by each of the four Brontës in his or her own manner. Charlotte and the others began to construct a counter reality, a universe which, as I shall try to demonstrate in the next chapter, satisfied their inner needs better than the world which had already killed off three members of their family. The literary cycle which the children began when Charlotte was ten was to hold a narcotic fascination for all four of them until their deaths. The most appealing aspect of their fictional world must have been the fact that, as opposed to the tragic reality in which the children were imbedded, the direction of their literary chronicles could be controlled.

Gaskell seems not to have understood the significance of the juvenilia, but she included in her biography a randomly chosen passage written by Charlotte in her early teens. In it, Charlotte exults in and condemns her power to control life and death. She and the other children could destroy their world if they wanted to, but they will not do it. The passage is a letter, dated July 14, 1829, to the editor of one of the magazines which the children wrote. The genii the letter complains about are the children themselves, in one of their favorite early fictional disguises. Charlotte is thus both one of the genii, and, at the same time, the moralistic observer of their barbaric activities, both aggressive impulse and the censor of that impulse:

> Sir,—It is well known that the Genii have declared that unless they perform certain arduous duties every year, of a mysterious nature, all the worlds in the firmament will be burnt up, and gathered together in one mighty globe, which will roll in solitary grandeur through the vast wilderness of space, inhabited only by the four high princes of the Genii, till time shall be succeeded by Eternity; and the impudence of this is only to be paralleled by another of their assertions, namely, that by their magic might they can reduce the world to a desert, the purest waters to streams of livid poison, and the clearest lakes to stagnant waters, the pestilential vapours of which shall slay all living creatures, except the blood-thirsty beast of the forest, and the ravenous bird of the rock. But that in the midst of this desolation the palace of the Chief Geni shall rise sparkling in the wilderness, and the horrible howl of their war-cry shall spread over the land at morning, at noontide and night; but that they shall have their annual feast over the bones of the dead, and shall yearly rejoice with the joy of the victors. I think, sir, that the horrible wickedness of this needs no remark, and therefore I haste to subscribe myself, etc. (Gaskell, *Life*, pp. 57–58)

The most striking assertion of the genii is their optimistic belief that there are certain duties which, if performed, will ward off death. It would seem that their most important duty was the creation of literature, the incessant building up of structures which could not be torn down by death. In August, 1830, Charlotte, while she was catching her breath from more creative writing, compiled a list of the works she had composed since April, 1829; the list thus covers a period of a bit more than fifteen months. The sad, earnest index of her compulsive endeavor to ward off destruction is too long to reproduce here, but her last line sums it up: "Making in the whole twenty-two volumes" (Gaskell, *Life*, p. 53). Each volume contains from sixty to a hundred pages. Throughout their adolescence, Charlotte and the others bent over their pens, fearing that if they stopped to rest the world might tumble down. Branwell tired of his effort after ten years or so, and began supplementing literature with opium and alcohol. But his sisters wrote on until they died.

The children must have felt that they themselves had in some mysterious way caused the deaths of their mother and sisters, that the deaths had been a punishment for some unknown, perhaps pervasive wickedness of the four survivors. Modern psychology recognizes that a child is the center of its own universe in a degree matched by only the most troubled adult; a child's thoughts turn the world toward good or evil, fruition or decline. Without the utmost care and tireless effort, the children must have imagined that they would one day be alone on a barren globe hurtling through a universe emptied of life. In their frightened bravado they could well claim to exult in their power, but the "horrible howl of their war-cry" was, one suspects, only the sad utterance of four lonely children in a world from which their loved ones were exiting one by one in a stately, grim procession which they tried desperately and in vain to halt. It was a nightmare from which they never awoke.

Charlotte remained at home with her family until she was fifteen, when she was sent once more to school. This time she went to Roe Head, a tiny institution run by Margaret Wooler and her sisters in their home. It was at Roe Head in 1831 that Charlotte met her two lifelong friends, Ellen Nussey and Mary Taylor, whose correspondence with Charlotte and later reminiscences comprise most of our knowledge of the author's early life.

Years later Mary told Elizabeth Gaskell of an incident which, although it has been largely ignored until recently, is central to an understanding of Charlotte's mind: "She told me, early one morning, that she had just been dreaming; she had been told that she was wanted in the drawing-room, and it was Maria and Elizabeth. I was eager for her to go on, and when she said there was no more, I said, 'But go on! *Make it out!* I know you can.' She said she would not; she wished she had not dreamed, for it did not go on nicely; they were changed; they had forgotten what they used to care for. They were very fashionably dressed, and began criticizing the room, etc." (Gaskell, *Life*, p. 68).[13] Charlotte's nightmare of rejection would recur in varying forms throughout her life. She had been told in the dream that she was wanted, but on her arrival in the drawing-room she found her sisters changed utterly; they did not seem to want her at all. They had presumably come from a wonderful place where they had been allowed to dress in finery which was never permitted, could never be afforded, at Haworth Parsonage, and they turned up their noses at the drab surroundings in which they found their little sister. They had forgotten what they used to care for. But she had not forgotten them; she carried their memory with her throughout her life. In her consciousness, her sisters were always wonders of talent and kindness. In her dreamlife, however, they could be bitingly cruel.

By the end of a year and a half at Roe Head, Charlotte had received an education which was considered quite sufficient for a female, and she returned to Haworth in May, 1832. For the next three years she remained at home, tutoring her younger sisters and writing for hours on end in her compulsive effort to come to terms with death. This period of relative contentment ended when Miss Wooler wrote to Haworth offering her old pupil a position as a teacher at Roe Head. It was a particularly tempting offer; part of the remuneration was the opportunity to bring along a younger sister as a pupil without tuition. And it came at a good time. Mr. Brontë's expenses were due to increase: Branwell hoped to journey soon to London to enroll himself at the Royal Academy in order to prepare for a career as a painter.

As it turned out, Charlotte's brother was unable, during his short and dismal sojourn in the city, to marshal his courage enough to approach the Academy. Quite clearly, Branwell had long before made the unconscious decision to become a pariah, and he never wavered for more than a short time from his plan.

But Charlotte could not foresee her brother's grim future. She seems to have gone to Roe Head in the summer of 1835 in full certainty that she was making a fruitful sacrifice of her own happiness. She would trudge through a drab career as a teacher while Branwell went off to attain greatness.

She quickly grew to hate her life at Roe Head. Within a few months Emily, who had accompanied her older sister, had become so homesick that she had to be sent back to Haworth. Anne took her place, but the young girl could be no real companion. At bottom Charlotte was surely as homesick as Emily had been, but Charlotte had appointed herself the mother of the family, the one who would give away her life for the others, and she had learned to make compromises with reality of which Emily was incapable.

Yet the resigned depression which those around her at Roe Head noticed was in part the mask for a seething indignation at her self-imposed banishment from her vocation as an author. Written with her characteristic, breathless lack of punctuation, an entry in a private journal dated August 11, 1836, captures her desperate frustration acutely:

> All this day I have been in a dream half miserable and half ecstatic miserable because I could not follow it out uninterruptedly, and ecstatic because it showed almost in the vivid light of reality the ongoings of the infernal world. I had been toiling for nearly an hour with Miss Lister, Miss Marriott and Ellen Cook striving to teach them the distinction between an article and a substantive. The parsing lesson was completed, a dead silence had succeeded it in the schoolroom and I sat sinking from irritation and weariness into a kind of lethargy. The thought came over me am I to spend all the best part of my life in this wretched

bondage forcibly suppressing my rage at the idleness
the apathy and the hyperbolical and most asinine
stupidity of those fat-headed oafs and on compulsion
assuming an air of kindness patience and assiduity? . . .
Stung to the heart with this reflection I started up and
mechanically walked to the window—a sweet August
morning was smiling without. . . . I shut the window
and went back to my seat. Then came on me rushing
impetuously all the mighty phantasm that we had con-
jured from nothing to a system strong as some religious creed. I felt as if I could have written gloriously—
I longed to write . . . if I had had time to indulge it
I felt that the vague sensations of that moment would
have settled down into some narrative better at least
than anything I ever produced before. But just then
a Dolt came up with a lesson. I thought I should have
vomited.[14]

The creative urge was welling up in the twenty-year-old
girl, threatening to burst the bonds of her self-control. Her
journal entries for the year return again and again to moments of vision which attain for Charlotte a reality denied
to the drab surroundings of her schoolroom existence.

The stay at Roe Head was crucial to her development as
an artist. At Haworth Charlotte had been relatively free
to indulge her imagination, with only the household routine
to serve as an external restraint. Her sisters and brother
had been accomplices, not hindrances, to her surreptitious
dreams. But at Roe Head the "natural" bent of her need
for expression was walled up. Except during the infrequent
vacations, and for short bursts of a few minutes stolen from
her duties as a teacher, she could not write about her beloved fictional kingdom, could not carry out the task of
composition so necessary to her sense of self. She did write
during the Roe Head years, but for the girl who had composed twenty-two volumes during fifteen months, the
scribbling of a dozen or so compositions a year was like
abstinence. The need for expression was as strong as ever,
and the secret world of her imagination which had satisfied
that need had been taken from her. The twenty miles which

separated Charlotte from Haworth and her imaginative source stretched like a continent before her mind, leaving her alone in a drab reality.

It was probably this creative restlessness which triggered the religious anxiety which she expressed in a remarkable series of letters to Ellen Nussey. The letters, most of them undated but probably written in 1836, tell of a sinner who craves but does not deserve communion with a saintly sister: "I abhor myself—I despise myself—if the Doctrine of Calvin be true I am already an outcast . . . don't desert me— don't be horrified at me, you know what I am."[15] The letters to Ellen contain strong indications that Charlotte was attempting unconsciously to express the still unutterable sense of loss which had burdened her since her childhood. She had indulged in melodrama in her secret writings and would continue to do so. But she had never before dared express to another person the depth of her feelings of deprivation, isolation, and guilt. Now she was taking the most frightening step of her life without turning back; she was allowing another human being to see just how passionate she could be. Rather than assigning her passion to one of her fictional characters, she was speaking in her own voice, daring rejection: "I have lavished the warmest affections of a very hot, tenacious heart upon you—if you grow cold—it's over."[16]

The situation which haunted Charlotte all her life was to be forcibly separated from someone she loved. In February, 1837, Ellen regretfully declined an invitation to visit her friend, and Charlotte reacted as if Ellen were dead. Her expression of desperation is one which will reappear in *Jane Eyre*: "Why are we so to be denied each other's society? It is an inscrutable fatality. . . . I cannot keep you by my side, I must proceed sorrowfully alone. Why are we to be divided? Surely, Ellen, it must be because we are in danger of loving each other too well—of losing sight of the *Creator* in idolatry of the *creature*."[17] Charlotte's jealous God will strike down His creatures so that He may be better seen.

Having developed the desperate audacity to entrust her sensibility to another human being, Charlotte used her new-found courage to further her literary ambition. The possibility of an unconscious psychological connection between Charlotte's confessional letters to Ellen and her attempts during the same period to gain literary recognition has been completely overlooked by her biographers, but that connection seems to me important for an understanding of the woman. Twice in her life a series of painfully revealing letters—the nearly hysterical notes to Ellen and the later correspondence with Constantin Heger—was followed by an attempt to become a professional writer. The letters seem either themselves to have released Charlotte's emotional power or at least to have been the first sign of a new, profound surge in her need to communicate. At any rate, in December, 1836, while she was home for the Christmas holidays, the obscure provincial schoolteacher sent several verses to Robert Southey, the Poet Laureate, asking for his opinion of her work. The suspense of her three-month wait for the verdict of the official arbiter of poetry in England must have been extreme.

Southey was a kind but an entirely orthodox man who took a dim view of women moving out of their proper sphere to write Byronic verse, and his answer drove Charlotte back into the painful haven of silence for another five years. Without knowing it, his advice must have echoed the warnings of Charlotte's own mind: "The day dreams in which you habitually indulge are likely to induce a distempered state of mind. . . . Literature cannot be the business of a woman's life, and it ought not to be. The more she is engaged in her proper duties, the less leisure will she have for it, even as an accomplishment and a recreation."[18]

Charlotte's low self-esteem would not allow her to see the insult inherent in Southey's answer. She accepted the advice gratefully, though with a touch of irony; it was cold, uncomfortable, and therefore bracing: "You kindly allow me to write poetry for its own sake, provided I leave undone nothing which I ought to do, in order to pursue that single, absorbing, exquisite gratification. . . . I find enough to occupy my thoughts all day long, and my head and my hands too, without having a moment's time for one dream of the imagination. In the evenings, I confess, I do think, but I never trouble any one else with my thoughts."[19] With this effusive apology for thinking and the mitigating plea that she normally kept her mental life to herself, Charlotte reentered the burrow of the isolated self. She would remain in its cold safety for six more years, until a Belgian school-teacher, not looking where he stepped, unwittingly sent its roof crashing down on her head. Southey's criticism had dashed Charlotte's hopes, and done a lasting service to English literature. For Charlotte was not yet mature. Had she become a professional writer at twenty, she would in all probability have been a bad one, simply one of the increasing horde of scribblers who purveyed trite love stories to a public hungry for emotional cant. Bereavement and sensibility were common enough commodities.

The next few years were a time of indecision. Charlotte left Roe Head for good in May, 1838, and spent the next year at home. She received two proposals of marriage. One, a stodgy business offer, was from Ellen's brother, Henry Nussey, who sought a wife who was qualified to help him run a school. The other was quite the opposite, an ardent letter begging for her hand from a young Irish curate, a Mr. Bryce, who had met her only once. Charlotte laughed in describing Bryce's passion to her friend, but added: "I'm certainly doomed to be an old maid Ellen—I can't expect another chance—never mind I made up my mind to that fate ever since I was twelve years old."[20] Several months later Charlotte heard that Bryce had died of a ruptured blood vessel. The incident was minor but disturbing. A man had told her he loved her, and died not long after. Death had not forgotten Charlotte.

In the spring of 1839, Charlotte made her first attempt to become a governess. She left Haworth in May to take a position with a family named Sidgwick. Within two months she had resigned her post and returned home. It was nearly two years before she tried again, and then, in March, 1841, she sallied forth once more into the world to teach the children of a Mr. White, a Bradford merchant.

Winifred Gérin has pointed out that a pattern emerged as Charlotte took up posts as governess or, later, pupil-teacher: in each new household she disliked the woman intensely, but felt that the man was rather pleasant.[21] Gérin attributes this to Charlotte's craving for intellectual conversation, but that explanation of her attitude seems inadequate; Charlotte could, after all, sit delighted for hours listening to the idle prattle of Ellen Nussey. It is much more likely that the situation at the Sidgwicks', the Whites', and, later, the Hegers' reflects Charlotte's Oedipal complex. Her mother had died over a decade and a half before Charlotte tried to become a governess. For more than fifteen years she had lived without a maternal rival for her father's affections. But now she would live as an alien in a cohesive family three times within four years. In each case she would align herself mentally with the male, seeing his wife as a suspicious adversary envious of the attainments of the intruder. She had told Ellen Nussey: "[Mrs. Sidgwick] does not know my character, and she does not wish to know it."[22]

But there seems to have been more to her attitude than simple jealousy of the matron. Charlotte, I would argue, could not live in a family without watching with unconscious jealousy the attention which the mother lavished on her children. In each household she worked in, the Sidgwicks', the Whites', and the Hegers', she seems to have taken up, without realizing it, the position of voyeur, watching with an anguish covered by disdain the way a fortunate child could be petted by its mother.[23] Thus, for example, her letter to Ellen Nussey describing her relationship with the Whites' infant can be read as an unconscious admission of the mental drama she was playing out at this time: "By dint of nursing the fat baby it has got to know me and be fond of me—occasionally I suspect myself of growing rather fond of it—but this suspicion clears away the moment its mamma takes it and makes a fool of it—from a bonny, rosy little morsel it sinks in my estimation into a small, petted nuisance—Ditto with regard to the other children."[24] Looking on with pained contempt as they manifested a mutual affection from which she was excluded, Charlotte remained with the Whites until December, 1841.

In her last months there, she constructed a plan which would free her and her sisters of the need to live in other people's houses. They had all tried working as governesses, and all three hated it. But now they would combine their teaching skills in a manner which would enable them to live together. They would open a school of their own.

The Brontë sisters lacked the educational acquirements necessary for such an undertaking, but that was part of the charm of the plan. Charlotte would go to the Continent and take Emily with her; there they would perfect their French and study German. For probably the first time in her life, Charlotte saw a realistic opportunity to travel away from home without suffering tortures from her tyrannical conscience.

Charlotte and her sister arrived in Brussels in February, 1842, and enrolled in Mme. Claire Zoë Heger-Parent's *Maison d'Education*. It was a large school for its time, with about a dozen teachers, including Mme. Heger's young husband, Constantin, a professor at the Athénée who served as the school's instructor in rhetoric and French literature. M. Heger was an intelligent, charming man, and Charlotte was fascinated with him. She wrote to Ellen: "He is . . . a man of power as to mind, but very choleric and irritable as to temperament; a little black ugly being. . . . When he is very ferocious with me I cry; that sets all things straight."[25] Heger was thirty-two years old at the time of Charlotte's arrival in Brussels; Mme. Heger, his second wife, was five years his senior.

Charlotte and Emily weathered their first months in Brussels surprisingly well. Their French was inadequate and they suffered agonies of shyness, but they had come with a sense of mission, and they worked at their studies vigorously. They tried to ignore the Catholic pupils with whom they lived, but there was a substantial English colony in the city and the sisters made several friends. Most important, Charlotte's friend Mary Taylor and her younger sister Martha were studying in Brussels. Between hard work, occasional treasured compliments from M. Heger, timid visits around the English colony, and earnest evening marches in the garden with their arms locked together in defensive alliance, they seem to have derived a quiet satisfaction from their Brussels life.

But in less than a year their career in Brussels was interrupted. Mr. Brontë's curate, William Weightman, died of cholera on September 6. On October 13, Martha Taylor died of the same disease. On October 29, their Aunt Branwell died, and Charlotte and Emily were forced to return home. In a letter to Ellen written two days after reaching Haworth, there are indications that Charlotte is placing the new series of deaths in a significant pattern, tracing similarities so that she can see the outline of the fate which seems to haunt her: "Aunt, Martha Taylor, and Mr. Weightman are now all gone; how dreary and void everything seems. Mr. Weightman's illness was exactly what Martha's was— he was ill the same length of time and died in the same manner. Aunt's disease was internal obstruction; she also was ill a fortnight."[26]

There were consolations inherent in Charlotte and Emily's return to Haworth, however. They had been away for nearly a year, and it was good to see the parsonage again. Emily would never leave there again. Anne had returned from her post as governess with the Robinson family and was allowed to remain at home through the holidays. Branwell, too, was there. He had tried his hand at portrait painting and failed. Later, he had obtained employment as a railroad clerk and been dismissed in disgrace because of his carelessness. But Anne had gotten him the post of tutor with the Robinsons. The family spent the Christmas season quietly at home before Anne and Branwell returned to Thorp Green.

Near the end of January, 1843, Charlotte set out once more for Brussels, this time alone. The death of Aunt Branwell meant that one of the daughters would have to remain home as her father's housekeeper and companion. Emily's inordinate attachment to Haworth made her the natural choice, and Charlotte was left to spend a morbidly lonely year by herself in the foreign city, a year whose aftermath was to turn her from a sensitive amateur writer into a novelist.

The Hegers were not only excellent educators, they were a highly intelligent, friendly couple, and they welcomed the lonely foreigner into their midst. In letters to England, Charlotte expressed her embarrassment at their friendliness. Alone with a family whose completeness contrasted with her own bereavement, Charlotte for the third time in four years fell into the familiar pattern of alienation. The letters show that within weeks she saw herself as an outsider, a mistrusted interloper on the territory of Mme. Heger. Constantin Heger was, according to Charlotte, the only person with whom she had the opportunity or the desire to talk. Aside from him, she had only the world of her imagination to keep her company. And her imagination was running rampant. She told Branwell: "It is a curious metaphysical fact that always in the evening when I am in the great dormitory alone, having no other company than a number of beds with white curtains, I always recur as fanatically as ever to the old ideas, the old faces, and the old scenes in the world below."[27]

By the late spring, things were clearly going wrong. The astute Mme. Heger must have been able to tell that her young boarder was becoming infatuated with her husband. Charlotte was a hypersensitive woman, and, noticing the change in Mme. Heger's attitude toward her, she began to imagine a plot to isolate her, to keep her away from Constantin Heger, her only friend in Brussels. The shape of the forces aligned against her is visible in a letter to Emily dated May 29: "I find [that Mlle. Blanche, one of the teachers] is the regular spy of Mme. Heger, to whom she reports everything. . . . Of late days, M. and Mme. Heger rarely speak to me, and I really don't pretend to care a fig for anybody else in the establishment. . . . I get on from day to day in a Robinson-Crusoe–like condition—very lonely."[28]

Throughout the late spring and summer the atmosphere at the Heger establishment remained coldly polite. And then, in September, Charlotte's internal melodrama came to a head. The school had let out for its long vacation. The pupils and the faculty dispersed to their homes, and Charlotte was left alone—with the exception of the "spy," Mlle. Blanche, and the cook—to wander through the empty halls of the school; her greatest fear, of total separation and absolute rejection, had been temporarily realized. The motherly, jealous Mme. Heger had gone from Charlotte's world and taken everyone with her.

Finally her anxiety drove her to an act of desperation which has puzzled her biographers perhaps more than any other detail of her life. She described it in a letter to Emily, dated September 2. The incident had occurred the day before, and had begun in a setting which provides the key to what came afterward: "Yesterday I went on a pilgrimage to the cemetery."[29] The grave she had visited was Martha Taylor's, but Martha must have been merely the representative of all those others, all Charlotte's loved ones whom her love had been insufficient to hold back from death. She returned to the city in the evening and stood opposite the Church of St. Gudule, listening to the single bell calling the faithful to repentence. And then something she did not understand compelled her to overcome her lifelong hatred of Catholicism, to walk into the church and down the dimly lit aisle to the area where six or seven women were waiting to confess. Flanked by the shadows of the unforgiving dead, Charlotte knelt, a penitent seeking absolution for a crime she could not fathom: "The priest asked if I was a Protestant. . . . I somehow could not tell a lie, and said 'yes.' He replied that in that case I could not '*jouir du bonheur de la confesse*' [enjoy the benefit of confession]; but I was determined to confess, and at last he said he would allow me. . . . I actually did confess—a real confession."[30] "[When] people are by themselves they have singular fancies," Charlotte explained to her sister.[31] And Charlotte was alone, caught in a magic circle of loneliness throughout almost her entire life. Her fancies were singular, powerful, and dark. For the priest was correct; no formula of contrition could absolve her of so many deaths, no penance her guilt could devise would ever give satisfaction to the implacable shadows from beyond the grave.

When Mme. Heger, her family, her teachers, and her pupils returned on October 2, Charlotte could feel the silent struggle between her persecutor and herself begin once again. The atmosphere was tense, and Charlotte clearly felt isolated, nearly as lonely as during the long vacation. At one point she expressed her alienation in a margin of her geography book: "Brussels, Saturday morning, Oct. 14th 1843. First Class. I am very cold—there is no

Fire—I wish I were at home with Papa—Branwell—Emily —Anne & Tabby—I am tired of being among foreigners— it is a dreary life.''[32] By December it was finished. She wrote to Emily informing her that she would arrive in Haworth on January 2. The Hegers did not attempt to deter her; she had been a heavy strain on the entire family's nerves.

There are disasters which seem necessary for the formation of some artists, and the Belgian fiasco was Charlotte's. She had not been all that unpopular at the Pensionnat Heger, but it was necessary for her to see herself as exiled, wandering through an alien landscape alone and unwanted.[33] She had, after all, felt that way since the fifth year of her life; the year in Brussels seems to have given immediacy and drama to inchoate emotions which had controlled her existence for twenty-one years. Her parting from Constantin Heger must have capped the experience and clarified her emotion. Her later letters show the extent of her adoration for him. He had been kind to her, talked to her of intellectual matters, trained her to write an elegant French, even allowed her to teach him English. Her severely bruised ego must have snuggled into the warmth of the knowledge that the older man liked her and seemed to appreciate the quality of her mind.

It has often been pointed out that M. Heger served Charlotte Brontë as a father figure whom she could worship, and that Mme. Heger mirrored her Oedipal fear of maternal jealousy.[34] That description seems to be accurate as far as it goes. But it is ultimately too simplistic to explain the nature and importance of the Heger experience for Charlotte. The orthodox conception of the Oedipal triangle is useful, but inadequate. Like plane geometry it attains its undeniable effectiveness by simplifying its object, ignoring the sinuous undulations of the surface it describes.

As long as Charlotte remained in Brussels she seems to have viewed Constantin Heger through the lens of her need for paternal approval. But I would contend that from the time she left him, a different pattern, a deeper and more significant one, began to take shape in her mind. She began unconsciously to align the Belgian schoolteacher from whom she was separated, with the shadowy figure of the mother who had left her years before. In Constantin Charlotte found a figure in the world of the present who, like her mother, was separated from her, and she gradually realized that this separation, like the first, would be forever. But she could write to him; after a lifetime of silence she was slowly building up the audacity to communicate her nearly inexpressible sorrow to the one who was gone, the one whose going had caused all the pain.

It is important to keep in mind that communication was always exquisitely difficult for Charlotte. Her brother was the only garrulous member of the family; Branwell was known to his friends as a master of the anecdote, without peer in the slightly blurred repartee thrown back and forth across the table of a pub. He was always ready to talk, though not of the central concern of his unconscious; he dissipated the energy of his sorrow in barroom chat as he drank his way toward an early grave. But his sisters were misers of words. Pouring their anger, their frustration, their hunger into the rhodomontade of their private writings in a desperate attempt to ward off the void of their existence, they were left with little energy for idle conversation. Elizabeth Gaskell interviewed the wife of the chaplain to the British Embassy in Brussels who had entertained Charlotte and Emily during their first months at school, and received striking evidence of their aversion to conversation: "Mrs. Jenkins told me that she used to ask them to spend Sundays and holidays with her, until she found that they felt more pain than pleasure from such visits. Emily hardly ever uttered more than a monosyllable. Charlotte was sometimes excited sufficiently to speak eloquently and well—on certain subjects; but before her tongue was thus loosened, she had a habit of gradually wheeling round on her chair, so as almost to conceal her face from the person to whom she was speaking" (Gaskell, *Life*, p. 147).

The sisters did, indeed, express themselves in their secret writings, but that was not communication: they never allowed anyone to read their juvenile productions. Yet somewhere in the vast expanse of their shyness, the Brontës had to discover a kernel of exhibitionism in order to become professional writers. They had to allow their thoughts to be examined by a potentially hostile outsider.

Charlotte was the first to break the spell of her silence, and she did it out of desperation at her distance from M. Heger. Heger allowed her to write to him once every six months; the letters which survive are crucial to an understanding of the writer's dilemma. For the letters, I would assert, are unconsciously addressed as much to Charlotte's mother as to the shocked Belgian who received them.

The earliest of the four surviving letters is dated July 24, [1844]:

> I greatly fear that I shall forget French, for I am fully persuaded that I shall see you again one day— I don't know how or when—but it must be, since I desire it so much, and then I would not wish to remain dumb before you—it would be too sad to see you and not be able to speak to you[;] to avoid this misfortune—I learn every day a half page of French by heart in a book written in conversational style. . . .
>
> . . . at present my sight is too weak to write—if I were to write much I would go blind. . . . the career of letters is closed to me—only that of teaching is open to me—it does not offer the same attractions— that's all right. . . . You too Monsieur—you wanted to be a lawyer—fate or Providence made you a teacher —you are happy despite that. . . .
>
> I have not prayed you to write to me soon, for I fear to importune you—but you are too kind to forget that I want it just the same—yes—I want it very much. . . .
>
> . . . once more adieu monsieur it hurts to say adieu even in a letter—Oh I shall certainly see you again one day—it surely must be—for as soon as I have earned enough money to go to Brussels I shall go—and shall see you if only for an instant.[35]

French was for Charlotte the language of direct emotional communication. If she were to express herself in English it would be in the form of a novel. Yet until she despaired of her ability to communicate with Heger, Charlotte wrote no novel. The weakness of her sight was very real, the result of her early attempts to copy etchings line by line for hours at a stretch. But at the same time her fear

of blindness was surely a terror of the punishment attend-
ant on realizing her greatest ambition. Self-assertion would
have been a defiance of the gods who controlled her life.
Heger had been happy with his second choice of a profession, perhaps she need not become a novelist, she tells him
plaintively. But there was still that need to communicate.
The greatest tragedy of life would be to see the figure one
had been longing after for so long, and not be able to
speak. If she could gather enough money to free her some
day for a vacation, and if she could journey to the land
where that figure lived, and if she could meet that figure,
and if she could only learn the right words to convince it
of her love, and if the figure listened, and if it understood
and responded, then her wound would be healed. The problem of language was crucial for Charlotte Brontë, but
French would not suffice for her needs. To communicate in
a manner that can be understood by the dead, one needs to
develop an instrument of the utmost precision, and Charlotte could ultimately do that only in her mother tongue,
in the language of her novels.

She had returned to England with the hope of setting up
a school, but the obstacles to her plan were in the end in-
surmountable. Their father's precarious health chained the
sisters to Haworth, and the village was far too isolated to
attract pupils. No young ladies ever enrolled at the Misses
Brontë's Establishment. "Haworth seems such a lonely,
quiet spot, buried away from the world," Charlotte admitted to Ellen, using a metaphor for her home which would
appear with ominous frequency in the years to come.[36]

Moreover, in the course of 1844 it slowly became plain
to Charlotte that Heger had no desire to correspond with
her any more. In October she used Mary Taylor's brother as
a courier for a letter in which she pleaded with Heger to
break his six months' silence. By January, she had still not
received an answer. Heger's continued silence must have
reproduced the silence of her mother. At any rate, Charlotte's next letter reveals her full desolation:

> I [have] tried hard to keep from crying, from com-
> plaining—But when one does not complain and when
> one would dominate oneself like a tyrant—the facul-

ties revolt—and one pays for outward calm with an almost unbearable inner struggle.

Day and night I find neither rest nor peace—if I sleep I suffer tormenting dreams in which I see you always severe, always somber, always angry with me. . . .

If my master withdraws his friendship from me entirely I shall be altogether without hope—if he gives me a little—very little—I shall be satisfied—happy, I shall have a reason for living, for working.

Monsieur, the poor do not need much to live—they ask only for the crumbs of bread that fall from the table of the wealthy—but if they are refused the crumbs—they die of hunger—Nor do I, either, need much affection from those I love I would not know what to do with an entire and complete friendship—I am not used to it—but you showed me, formerly, *a little* interest when I was your pupil at Brussels—and . . . I hold on to it as I would hold on to life.

You will perhaps say to me—I have not the slightest interest in you anymore Mademoiselle Charlotte—you are no longer of my Family—I have forgotten you.

Well then Monsieur tell me that frankly—that will be a shock for me—no matter it will still be less hideous than incertitude.

. . . One suffers in silence as long as one has enough strength and when this strength fails one speaks out without too much weighing one's words.[37]

Silence and impassioned communication with the self had been Charlotte's defenses against her sense of separation for nearly twenty-five years. But now a new version of the familiar pattern of abandonment had occurred which had turned her chronic alienation into an acute convulsion painful enough to make her finally speak out.

The most compelling portion of the letter is the seemingly innocuous statement "if I sleep I suffer tormenting dreams in which I see you always severe, always somber, always angry with me." Her description of what seems to be a long series of nightmares recalls her narration to Mary

Taylor of the dream of her sisters a decade and a half earlier. In that dream her sisters had changed: the two girls who had formerly loved and accepted her now hurt her with cutting remarks on her surroundings. That dream in itself was probably in part a screen for Charlotte's painful sense of her mother's disapproval. Now in her late twenties, Charlotte is dreaming of another rebuff. The Heger series of dreams is thus at bottom only another variation on the earlier nightmare; Heger has stepped into the image of the rejector, for the time being obscuring the earlier inhabitants of that image, Elizabeth, Maria, and, behind them all, Charlotte's mother. If this is true, then in one sense, and a profound one, Heger is simply another screen thrown up to reproduce and yet block the memory of the loss of Charlotte's mother. But the important point is that, quite possibly for the first time, the figure in the foreground is a man, a potential lover, and Charlotte's reaction to his rejection is a mature one comprised of articulate speech, not silence or an inarticulate moan. She has made the breakthrough into the realization that language can be used to communicate and thus lessen pain. Heger is therefore important for Charlotte not simply because he hurt her, or even because she adored him, as most biographers have asserted, but precisely because she dared to write to him. She expressed her need to an important and seemingly cold figure, was rejected, and was left with a painful yet vigorous ability to communicate. She had finally entered into the community of her fellow human beings.

Only one more letter from Charlotte to Heger is extant. Dated November 18, 1845, it is probably not the last one she wrote to him, but there is a note of finality to it which indicates that she knew that the communication was for all real purposes over. Moreover, she was struggling to free herself from what she clearly recognized was a galling dependence which limited her psychological freedom. The correspondence had outlived its usefulness and had become pernicious rather than liberating:

> [My] six months of silence have run their course.
> . . . The summer and autumn seemed very long . . . it
> took a painful effort to sustain up to now the priva-

tion I have imposed on myself; you yourself cannot conceive it, but imagine for an instant that one of your children is separated from you by a distance of 160 leagues and that you must go six months without writing to him, without hearing from him, without listening to him speak, without knowing how he is, then you will easily understand how hard such an obligation is. I will tell you frankly, that I have meanwhile tried to forget you . . . but I have been able to conquer neither my regrets nor my impatience—it is humiliating—not to know how to master one's own thoughts.[38]

The French portion of the letter is followed by a postscript in English:

Truly I find it difficult to be cheerful so long as I think I shall never see you more. You will perceive by the defects in this letter that I am forgetting the French language—yet I read all the French books I can get, and learn a portion by heart . . . I love French for your sake with all my heart and soul.

Farewell my dear Master—may God protect you with special care and crown you with peculiar blessings.[39]

Heger used the margin to jot down the name and address of his shoemaker and other small items which interested him before he tore up the letter and threw it away.[40]

In one sense the danger which Charlotte imagines in both this letter and that of January, 1845, is that Heger will banish her, or indeed has already banished her, from his family. "You will perhaps say to me . . . you are no longer of my Family [*de ma Maison*]," she had told Heger in the earlier letter.[41] Her fear is even clearer in the second letter: "Imagine for an instant that one of your children is separated from you." Charlotte seems to be that separated child, attempting without success to forget the parent she has lost.

But she seems also to be the parent, prohibited from contacting her separated child for six months at a time.[42] Imagine what it would be like if you were in my position, she challenges Heger, if you had a child to whom you could not write. The child in this sense seems to be Charlotte's banished imagination. She fears her own genius; if she were to become a novelist she would be struck blind. But her imagination strains to be born. Quite often in Charlotte's fiction, the need for imaginative expression is seen in terms which verge on the language of pregnancy: "Could this be, she demanded . . . when something within her stirred disquieted, and restlessly asserted a God-given strength, for which it insisted she should find exercise?"[43] This small but mighty being is felt as a stirring, or a gnawing hunger, or a burning sensation.

But it is not always a fetus; at times it is an infant. Jane Eyre's dreams of a baby constitute a case in point. Bessie tells Jane that "to dream of children [is] a sure sign of trouble, either to one's self or one's kin."[44] When Bessie dreams of a child, her sister dies. When Jane first dreams of a baby, her stepmother, Sarah Reed, dies. Apparently the mind's children can kill sisters and mothers. Elsewhere they can be a burden which allows a lover to escape. Jane dreams twice that she is carrying a child which impedes her attempt to catch up to Rochester.

It is clear from the evidence of her letters and her Roe Head journal that, like the dreaming Jane Eyre, Charlotte would like very much at times to be rid of her insistent child. Significantly, throughout her adult fiction the woman carrying the fetus or the infant is lonely. Charlotte's imagination must have seemed to her at times an unwanted child, a baby so powerful and so ugly that it would drive other people away from its mother. Nevertheless, she loved her ungainly infant, and evidently had to talk to it even if she had temporarily banished it to another country. Under the guise of letters to a Belgian teacher, her unconscious could contact that child, consoling it with the thought that it would never be entirely abandoned.

Thus the correspondence with Heger, for all its painfulness, allowed Charlotte to express desires which were very real and ultimately healthy. Moreover, it allowed her to come into meaningful contact with portions of her own psyche, with her sense of loss and her will to create. But she was frustrated at her dependence on her distant correspondent.

Luckily, about the time of the last extant letter to Heger, she found a key which would release her: "One day, in the autumn of 1845, I accidentally lighted on a MS. volume of verse in my sister Emily's handwriting . . . I thought them condensed and terse, vigorous and genuine. To my ear, they had also a peculiar music—wild, melancholy, and elevating."[45] For years, perhaps since their withdrawal from collaboration with Branwell and Charlotte, Emily and Anne had kept their writings to themselves. At first Emily was angry at Charlotte's intrusion into her privacy. But Anne and Charlotte brought their own poems out of their hiding places and allowed them to be read. For the first time since their childhood, all three sisters dared to communicate fully with each other. Charlotte suggested that they publish their best work pseudonymously, at their own expense, and her sisters eventually agreed, Emily with great reluctance. A volume was published in May, 1846, its authors listed as Currer (Charlotte), Ellis (Emily), and Acton (Anne) Bell.

Charlotte later claimed that the pseudonyms were a device to ward off the public prejudice against female writers, and her statement seems true as far as it goes. But I would submit that Charlotte's persona indicated her ambivalence about her own gender as well. Her self-hatred and alienation must have made it difficult to relate either to men or to women. But certainly men had most of the emotional advantages on their side. Her letters to Ellen indicate that men were strange creatures, to be envied, mistrusted, and feared. The same letters indicate that by the time she grew up, she had internalized her society's oppression of women, deciding that the main faculty of women was self-control, while the primary masculine characteristic was self-assertion.

Given a male-dominated society and the fact that the Brontë family's hopes had always centered on Branwell, it was natural that Charlotte should be rather envious of masculinity. From about the time of late adolescence, she had shortened her signature to the ambiguous "C. Brontë, or, more curtly, "C. B." And throughout her career, from the juvenilia to Currer Bell's last novel, she normally signed her works with one or another masculine pseudonym. The need to write under a man's name began long before she had to anticipate a sexually biased audience.

But Charlotte seems to have been troubled with the problem of gender to an extent that cannot be explained by envy of her brother. The need for a form of sexual equality was certainly profound enough. But there was probably another, profounder need which the masculine pen names satisfied. Throughout most of her life, Charlotte had longed for and loved three females who had died. As she grew up, she found it difficult to talk of her older sisters, and nearly impossible to mention her mother. The burden of sorrow and guilt, the sense of loss were too heavy to be put into words —or at any rate into Charlotte Brontë's words. Only in her formal writings, her juvenilia and later her novels, could she approach the complex feelings centered on those early deaths. And they were written by a "man," by Charles Wellesley, or Captain Tree, or Currer Bell, not by Charlotte.

It is entirely possible, in other words, that the very use of a masculine pen name allowed Charlotte to overcome her repression somewhat, permitting her to talk about emotional hunger, about losses which must be replaced. She had talked of these matters in her letters to Heger, but that was in French, a notoriously permissive language. Only as Currer Bell or one of the Angrian men of letters could she sustain that intensity of expression in English. For men, after all, were not repressed. If they lacked for the most part the faculty of self-control, they could not be expected to maintain silence concerning their wounds. As her fiction reached maturity, the strategy would become more elaborate and more supple: Charlotte Brontë would become Currer Bell writing as if he were a woman named Jane Eyre. And Jane Eyre would speak with shocking frankness.

The Bells' book of poetry received very little critical and no public notice, but by the time the Brontës learned of its failure, they had each, in their new burst of creative enthusiasm, written a novel. Anne's *Agnes Grey*, Emily's *Wuth-*

ering Heights, and Charlotte's *The Professor* were circu-
lated to a series of publishers for a year until, in the summer
of 1847, Anne's and Emily's novels were accepted by
Thomas Newby. Charlotte continued to mail out her work,
but it was not published until after her death. She wrote a
second book, however, which found quick acceptance at the
prestigious firm of Smith, Elder and Co. It was published
on October 16, 1847, and became an instantaneous popular
success. Only then did Newby deign to publish *Agnes Grey*
and *Wuthering Heights*, letting it be known in the trade
that they were early works by Currer Bell, the author of
Jane Eyre.

In the early part of the summer of 1848 Newby published Anne's second novel, *The Tenant of Wildfell Hall*,
and informed an American publisher that Currer Bell had
written it. The sisters were finally forced to disclose their
identity to Charlotte's publishers. Charlotte and Anne made
a hurried trip to London, were enthusiastically received by
George Smith and his associates, and returned to Haworth
four days later. They brought back a parcel of books given
them by Mr. Smith. And in all probability they carried
home with them the tuberculosis bacilli which would
shortly decimate the Brontë family in yet another round of
deaths.[46]

Branwell was the first to die, on September 24, 1848. He
had been trying to die for a long time.[47] He had been dismissed in disgrace from his employment with the Robinsons in July, 1845. Since that time he had remained at home
in an alcoholic haze. Soon after his sisters' return from
London he began to develop symptoms of the disease which
killed him in a matter of weeks. The man who had wanted
so badly to become an artist or a writer died without
ever finding out that his sisters had become professional
novelists.

The death of her brother prostrated Charlotte. She was
unable to attend the funeral and became herself the object
of the family's frightened attention. In a letter dated a bit
more than a week after Branwell's death, Charlotte reveals
more of her attitude toward her brother than she realized:
"My poor father naturally thought more of his *only* son

than of his daughters, and . . . he cried out for his loss like David for that of Absolom—my son! my son!—and refused at first to be comforted. And then when I ought to have been able to collect my strength and be at hand to support him, I fell ill."[48]

Charlotte's memory of her mother was a picture of the woman playing with Branwell. Now she saw her father's relationship to his dead son as an analogue of injured and bereaved Biblical kinship. Charlotte, a mere woman though a talented one, must have felt that she would never be able to take Absolom's place, no matter how much she tried. She wanted to be able to show her father that she too was strong, that she could be a prop to the old man as he had hoped his son would be. Instead she fell ill. More and more in recent years she had competed successfully against her brother, and now her brother had died.[49] Throughout her life self-assertion brought with it an increase in guilt. It is one of the tragic aspects of her life that the success of *Jane Eyre* was followed so quickly by the death of so many around her. Her own transient illness must have served as a punishment for Branwell's death, as a hysterical gesture toward the restoration of what her unconscious saw as the moral balance of her world. There would be many more such gestures in the years to come.

At the same time, there can be no doubt that the illness had the effect of diverting attention from her brother to herself. For months Branwell's debilitation had taken up much more of her father's attention than her own success as an author. Even after achieving her greatest ambition, Charlotte had thus in a sense been cheated out of her father's regard by his concern for her brother's weakness, a weakness for which she had expressed her disgust in letter after letter to Ellen. Now, Branwell gone, Charlotte was sick and her father had to worry about her. As she indicates in the letter quoted above, she hated her own lack of strength, but for several days she could not will herself back to health.

Charlotte's sisters, too, had grown ill at their brother's death. Emily, in particular, who seemed to have caught cold at Branwell's funeral, was a source of anxiety to Charlotte.

By the end of October the anxiety had turned into fear, and within another month the family had to face the certainty of the strange, lonely woman's death. She had always been both the strongest and the most isolated member of the family. She refused to see a doctor until the last hours of her life, refused to take to her bed, insisted on carrying out all of her household duties until the day before her death. She died on December 19, 1848.

Had Emily's death occurred during a period of relative calm, Charlotte would in all probability have broken down. But Anne, too, was developing pains in her side. Charlotte nursed her remaining sister throughout the winter and spring of 1849. Anne believed that the sea air would give her a chance to recover, and she pleaded throughout the early spring to be taken to Scarborough, a resort she had visited with the Robinsons. On May 25, Charlotte and Ellen Nussey accompanied her on her pilgrimage, but it was too late. Anne died in Scarborough on May 28, 1849, and was buried there.

Ellen returned home, but Charlotte remained away from Haworth for nearly a month, stunned by so many losses, trying to put her feelings into perspective. A week after Anne's death, she wrote to W. S. Williams, her publisher's reader: "They are . . . gone . . . and Papa has now me only—the weakest, puniest, least promising of his six children."[50] A few days later she added: "Branwell—Emily—Anne are gone like dreams—gone as Maria and Elizabeth went twenty years ago. One by one I have watched them fall asleep on my arm—and closed their glazed eyes—I have seen them buried one by one—and—thus far—God has upheld me."[51] They had entered the pattern which seemed to constitute her fate. Maria, Elizabeth, Branwell, Emily, Anne—one after another they had fallen into step with the solemn cortege which moved silently and inevitably away from Charlotte, leaving her behind. At night, though, in her dreams, they returned; and there too they became part of a crucial pattern of Charlotte's mental life: "As to the night—could I do without bed—I would never seek it—waking I think—sleeping I dream of them—and I cannot recall them as they were in health—still they appear to me in sickness and suffering—Still my nights were worse after the first shock of Branwell's death—They were terrible then—and the impressions experienced on waking were at that time such as we do not put into language."[52] By the end of June, Branwell, Emily, and Anne had already taken their places beside Maria, Elizabeth, Constantin Heger—and quite possibly Mrs. Brontë herself—in Charlotte's dreams. Like those earlier ones, they had changed; their faces had perhaps hardened into masks of suffering and disapproval of the woman they had left behind.

The characters of Charlotte's novels frequently become metaphorical statues, and statues are quite possibly connected with the slow freezing into death which the author had seen occur so many times. Her sisters and her brother dead, Charlotte's world was as if peopled with statues, rigid, unchanging figures among which the desolate woman moved. For the next three and a half years she would walk through a frozen, nearly motionless, soundless world, marking the slow cadence of the seasons through the pressure on her nerves, hiding from life.

At first she managed to fight off her depression enough to write. In the summer following her youngest sister's death, Charlotte returned to the novel she had broken off the previous autumn. The composition of the remainder of *Shirley* became a successful if temporary weapon against the worst effects of the repeated hammer blows she had received in the past year. Looking back on her struggle a month after she had completed the novel, Charlotte told Williams: "The faculty of imagination lifted me when I was sinking, three months ago; its active exercise has kept my head above water since . . . it is for me a part of my religion to defend this gift and to profit by its possession."[53] *Shirley* was published on October 26, 1849, and became an immediate success. There could be no doubt that Currer Bell was an established novelist.

Yet success did not change Charlotte's life radically. She had always longed to visit the capitals of Europe, and her new status gave her that power, but she made sparing use of it. Mary Taylor had pointed out to her friend that her will, not her poverty, held her in Haworth, and the years of fame made the point abundantly clear. Once or twice a year she would make the journey to London, and there were several short trips elsewhere, to Edinburgh, to the Lake country, to Manchester, but nearly all of her time was spent in the Haworth parsonage tending to the needs of her father. In the first months of her isolation she told Williams: "For society—long seclusion has in a great measure unfitted me. . . . The prisoner in solitary confinement—the toad in the block of marble—all in time shape themselves to their lot."[54]

Even when she did manage to tear herself away from the parsonage, she remained caught up in a reverie of the past. Although she was able to fulfill her lifelong ambition of actually seeing the great men and women of her day, she fit them where possible into images of her private dream:

> In Mrs. Gaskell's nature it mournfully pleases me to fancy a remote affinity to my sister Emily—In Miss Martineau's mind I have always felt the same.[55]

> I have seen [G. H.] Lewes . . . the aspect of Lewes' face almost moves me to tears—it is so wonderfully like Emily—her eyes, her features—the very nose, the somewhat prominent mouth, the forehead.[56]

Moreover, Charlotte's frequently morbid taste as a sightseer could be rather disconcerting to her hosts: "I selected rather the *real* than the *decorative* side of Life—I have been over two prisons ancient and modern—Newgate and Pentonville—also the Bank, the Exchange, the Foundling Hospital,—and to-day if all be well—I go . . . to see Bethlehem Hospital."[57] Reality lurks in the paranoid haunts of the unconscious, the underside of the decorative vanity which makes up everyday, conscious existence. Prisons, orphanages, insane asylums—institutional projections of the fears she had lived with for more than thirty years. Like Dickens, Charlotte Brontë scoured London in search of images of the self.

It would seem that the new round of deaths increased Charlotte's already heavy burden of guilt to the point where composition became nearly impossible for a long time. She had written her way through the final volume of *Shirley* by the end of August, 1849. For the next two years she did no creative writing at all; it was probably the longest period of creative inactivity she had endured in over two decades.

Certainly her only literary labor during this long hiatus fits the hypothesis of survivor's guilt; she undertook in the fall of 1850 to edit a reprint of her sisters' literary *Remains* and write a preface to it. Throughout the fall she went over the papers left behind by her sisters, choosing a poem here and there, editing *Wuthering Heights* in a manner which weakened its power, suppressing *The Tenant of Wildfell Hall* entirely. She wanted very much for the public and the critics to see her sisters in the best light, and she did not recognize how different their talents were from hers. The work was torture for her, but a torture for which she felt grateful. In September, 1850, she wrote Ellen: "I found the task at first exquisitely painful and depressing—but regarding it in the light of *a sacred duty*—I went on—and now can bear it better—It is work however that I cannot do in the evening—for if I did, I should have no sleep at night."[58] The revision was finished and the *Remains* published in December, 1850. After a short vacation in Westmoreland, Charlotte returned to Haworth ready to work on a novel.

Yet she could not write. She had discharged her debt to Anne and Emily superficially, and she felt that now she should be able to create. Yet the obligation must have been deeper than she realized. For behind her two sisters were all those others, and they would not accept Charlotte's propitiatory gifts. Thus she was left in an unconscious dilemma, torn between her need to please her publishers and her compulsion to placate the dead. Her humorous suggestion to George Smith, in a letter of February, 1851, was more serious than either she or her biographers were willing to admit: "I don't deserve to go to London: nobody merits a change or a treat less. I secretly think, on the contrary, I ought to be put in prison, and kept on bread and water in solitary confinement—without even a letter from [you]—till I have written a book."[59] If the joke seems rather morbid, it is well to remember that Charlotte was in a sense already in prison—she had thought of her life in the parsonage as a form of solitary confinement since the death of Anne—and that her hypochondria would soon provide the excuse for carrying out the rest of her sentence.

A year later, still having written no book, she could tell Ellen: "I am to live on the *very plainest* fare—to take *no butter*—at present I do not take tea—only milk and water with a little sugar and dry bread—this with an occasional mutton chop is my diet—and I like it better than anything else."[60] The diet must have been the continuing price for creativity. She had finally begun *Villette* in the fall of 1851. Yet she could make no real progress with the book, even on her prisoner's fare. Moreover, the guilt of her survival tumbled her into nightmare after nightmare when she could sleep at all. Later, she described the experience of the winter of 1851–52 to Mrs. Gaskell: "Sleep almost forsook me, or would never come except accompanied by ghastly dreams; appetite vanished, and slow fever was my continual companion. I thought my lungs were affected . . . , and could feel no confidence in the power of medicine."[61]

She had, in other words, developed the symptoms she had observed in her dying sisters. When she finally consulted a doctor he pronounced her lungs sound; there were no organic indications of tuberculosis. But a part of her unconscious mind must have remained convinced that it would be a fitting punishment for her survival, and more particularly for her success as a novelist, if she were struck down by the same disease which had carried off her sisters and brother. The realization of her greatest terror, tuberculosis would at the same time mean that she was not different from the others, and thus not isolated. At any rate no mere doctor's advice could end her fixation on consumption; she continued to suffer from the same symptoms. And she was still unable to write. From November through March she could not write a word in the novel, though she brought herself repeatedly through sheer force of will to the brink of composition.

This creative impotence was ended in all probability through a strange excursion whose symbolic nature has been overlooked by her biographers. She decided to undertake a pilgrimage to Scarborough to Anne's grave, and demonstrate her sisterly devotion to the dead in her attention to the gravestone. The ritual nature of the trip is demonstrated in her secretiveness. She said nothing to Ellen of her plan until she arrived at the boardinghouse outside the town where she and Ellen had stayed on a vacation years before. Then she wrote to her: "I am at Filey utterly alone. Do not be angry. The step is right. I considered it and resolved on it with due deliberation. Change of air was necessary; there were reasons . . . why I should come here. On Friday I went to Scarboro', visited the church-yard and stone—it must be refaced and re-lettered—there are 5 errors. I gave the necessary directions—*that* duty then is done—long has it lain heavy on my mind—and that was a pilgrimage I felt I could only make alone."[62] She returned to Haworth and began to write. She worked rapidly now, finishing the first two volumes of *Villette* in about three months, and sent the completed book to London on November 20, 1852. Her pilgrimage to her sister's grave had enabled her to placate the dead long enough to write one final novel.

Within a month of the completion of *Villette*, an event occurred which would ultimately change Charlotte's life: Arthur Bell Nicholls proposed to her. Nicholls, a year and a half younger than Charlotte, had been Patrick Brontë's curate since 1845. Like Mr. Brontë, he was an Irishman born and bred. Charlotte described to Ellen the manner of his proposal: "Shaking from head to foot, looking deadly pale, speaking low, vehemently yet with difficulty—he made me for the first time feel what it costs a man to declare affection where he doubts response. The spectacle of one ordinarily so statue-like, thus trembling, stirred, and overcome, gave me a kind of strange shock."[63] A statue had moved, had trembled in its love for her. She had dreamt of faces frozen into gloom, and suddenly a gloomy man, part of the furniture of her life for nearly a decade, had burst into her room and his face had crumbled into love. Though she had no intention of marrying Nicholls, she was disturbed and flattered.

When Patrick Brontë heard of Nicholls' proposal, he

was furious. He immediately banished the curate from his home and his sight. Charlotte watched the struggle between the two men with a mixture of indignation and excitement. On December 18, she was able to tell Ellen that "the poor man is horrifying his landlady . . . by entirely rejecting his meals."[64] Two weeks later she informed her friend: "Mr. N[icholls] is one of those who attach themselves to very few, whose sensations are close and deep—like an underground stream, running strong but in a narrow channel."[65] Her admiration for the depth of Nicholl's love for her was apparently beginning to cloud the fact that she did not love him.

Villette was published on January 28, 1853, and became an immediate popular and critical success. But Charlotte was more interested in the struggle going on around her than she was in her public career. In May, Nicholls, under pressure from Mr. Brontë and from his own realization that he was Charlotte's social and intellectual inferior, took another curacy in Yorkshire and left Haworth. His departure seems to have been seen unconsciously by Charlotte in the light of all those who had left her before him, all those whose departure she had somehow caused. She told Ellen: "He is gone—gone—and there's an end of it. I see no chance of hearing a word about him in future. . . . In all this it is not I who am to be pitied at all, and of course nobody pities me. They all think, in Haworth, that I have disdainfully refused him, etc. . . . They may abuse me if they will; whether they do or not I can't tell."[66]

Nicholls left, but he did not, like the others in Charlotte's life, remain silent. He was in love and he wrote to her often. She was shocked at first, though rather pleased at the persistence of her suitor. Gradually she began to answer the letters, and a correspondence was carried on for a while without the knowledge of her father. Charlotte had never been deceitful; at last she told her father about the exchange of letters and received his grudging permission to write to Nicholls and even to see him on his occasional visits to Haworth. In January, 1854, Nicholls spent ten days in the neighborhood. During that period Charlotte saw him daily. She accepted his love.

By April, Brontë had consented to their marriage.

Nicholls would again become his curate at a salary of
£90. Charlotte stipulated that she would never leave her
father, and her suitor agreed to this condition. She told
Ellen: "I trust to love my husband—I am grateful for his
tender love to me. I believe him to be an affectionate, a con-
scientious, a high-principled man; and if, with all this, I
should yield to regrets, that fine talents, congenial tastes
and thoughts are not added, it seems to me I should be
most presumptuous and thankless. Providence offers me
this destiny. Doubtless then it is the best for me."[67] The
marriage, for all its disadvantages, must have satisfied one
of the deepest needs of Charlotte's psyche. After a lifetime
of rejection, she had found someone who accepted her
absolutely, who had even endured banishment for her sake.

She was married on June 29, 1854. After a month's
honeymoon with Nicholls' family in Ireland, the couple
returned to Haworth Parsonage to begin their new life.
It was quite different from anything she had known before.
For one thing, her new duties left no time for brooding
on the past. In August she told Ellen: "Since I came home
I have not had an unemployed moment; my life is changed
indeed—to be wanted continually—to be constantly called
for and occupied seems so strange. . . . As far as my experience of matrimony goes—I think it tends to draw you out
of, and away from yourself."[68]

There was a more solemn side to marriage, however.
Charlotte in all probability added a personal neurotic fear
of her own sexuality to the sexual neurosis of her age, and
she hinted darkly to her friend in the same letter of the
connubial mysteries into which a new wife must be initi-
ated: "Dear Nell—during the last 6 weeks—the colour of
my thoughts is a good deal changed: I know more of the
realities of life than I once did. I think many false ideas are
propagated perhaps unintentionally. I think those married
women who indiscriminately urge their acquaintance to
marry—much to blame. . . . Indeed—indeed Nell—it is a
solemn and strange and perilous thing for a woman to become a wife."[69] Her father had warned Charlotte that marriage was a dangerous business for a woman of her frail
constitution, that—based on his own bitter knowledge—
motherhood could be fatal. And indeed Charlotte died

within her first year of marriage, soon after she found out that she was pregnant.

Her biographers, searching for a reason for this last tragic irony of Charlotte's life, have stressed the accidents and mishaps of the last year of her life, the fact that she took a nasty fall from a horse during her honeymoon, the cold she caught during a walk in the rain, the extreme dampness of the last winter. They have ignored the almost ritualistic correctness of the death, the strangely artistic suitability of such a death for such a life.[70] The death fit the life as if it had been arranged by a fine artist. And I would contend that it was. For it seems to me that Charlotte willed her own death as effectually as if she had consciously thought it out.

During January she began suffering from nausea. She assumed that it was a sign of pregnancy, and a doctor confirmed her diagnosis. But her symptoms seemed much worse than the stories of other women had led her to expect. In order to explain the severity of these symptoms it is necessary to look at what can be pieced together of her attitude toward motherhood. She had watched her own mother's agony, and had in all probability known that the pain was in some way connected with excessive childbirth.[71] She had probably feared becoming a mother all her life. She had no real model for maternity; mothers were creatures to be looked on with unconscious suspicion and mistrust. Her attitude toward maternity can be glimpsed in her reaction to a trip to Scotland she had made in August, 1854, with Mary Taylor's brother and his family. The trip was cut short because of the baby's illness, and Charlotte described to Margaret Wooler the behavior of the parents with undisguised contempt: "The world does not revolve round the Sun—that is a mistake; certain babies I plainly perceive—are the important centre of all things. . . . Tenderness to offspring is a virtue, yet I think I have seen Mothers—the late Mrs. Allbutt for instance—who were most tender and thoughtful—yet in very love for their children—would not permit them to become tyrants either over themselves or others."[72]

The relationship between mothers and children was one which Charlotte never fathomed. She tells Miss Wooler that she has known a mother—one who is dead—who did not spoil her children, who refused to let them tyrannize over her attention. As she had done in her posts as private governess, Charlotte watched the antics of the Taylor infant with an almost conscious jealousy as its mother cuddled and preened it. And now in the winter of 1855 she was pregnant, carrying a child who was to receive the love and attention which she herself could never remember. There must have been a burden of unconscious jealousy of the child, and of anger toward the role of motherhood in which she found herself.

Her disease has recently been diagnosed by Dr. Philip Rhodes as *hyperemesis gravidarum*, a term which describes excessive nausea in early pregnancy: "The disorder only seems to become excessive in those who display neuroticism, and they require firm treatment. . . . Some doctors have suggested that hyperemesis gravidarum is an unconscious rejection of the baby on the part of the woman, and this might have been so in Charlotte's case."[73] She had always described the need for affection in terms of hunger. We recall that she had told Constantin Heger: "Monsieur, the poor do not need much to live—they ask only for the crumbs of bread that fall from the table of the wealthy— but if they are refused the crumbs—they die of hunger— Nor do I, either, need much affection from those I love." In her novels, hunger is a recurrent metaphor for loneliness or rejection, expanding at times into symbolic action such as Jane Eyre's begging journey toward Marsh End.

This linguistic concentration on the analogy between physical and psychological undernourishment does not seem surprising in a woman who had lost her mother, her prime nurturer, at an early age. What is striking is that at the end of her life Charlotte acted out the ultimate implications of her insistent metaphor. She must have been unconsciously showing herself just how terrible it can be when a child is "starved" for affection. Pregnancy allowed Charlotte for once in her life to play both roles in the strange drama of abandonment which had colored her mental life for three decades: both mother and child were part of her body. On the one hand her persistent vomiting can be seen as an unconscious attempt to rid her body of the fetus, to reject this child as she herself had been rejected. But at the same time the nausea gave the pregnant woman a new rationale for refusing food. Thus both child and mother could be punished for an ancient crime which had never been properly avenged.

Time and again throughout her life Charlotte had gone on strenuous diets. The adolescent vegetarianism whose origins have puzzled her biographers, the prisoner's fare of bread and water during the composition of *Villette*— recurrently throughout her life she had placed arbitrary limits on what she would eat. And now, in a last, fatal demonstration of what it is like to be rejected and unloved, she would eat almost nothing at all. The chilling implications of a statement made by a member of the household to Elizabeth Gaskell have gone unnoticed: "A wren would have starved on what she ate during those last six weeks" (Gaskell, *Life*, p. 399).

Charlotte was repaying her final, mortal debt to the dead, punishing herself and rejecting her child as she herself had been rejected. Her neurosis had run its devious course and returned to its starting point. Near the end of March a change took place. She became delirious and begged constantly for food. A part of her mind was apparently trying to ward off the death which another part willed. But it was too late. She died during the night of March 31, 1855. Gaskell describes her final moment of consciousness: "Wakening for an instant from this stupor of intelligence, she saw her husband's woe-worn face, and caught the sound of some murmured words that God would spare her. 'Oh!' she whispered forth, 'I am not going to die, am I? He will not separate us, we have been so happy'" (Gaskell, *Life*, p. 400). Her final sacrifice was acceptable. The cause of her death was listed as tuberculosis, and she was buried next to her sisters, her brother, and her mother. She had chosen a fitting time to die. She was thirty-eight, the age of her mother at the death which had haunted Charlotte Brontë all her life and finally struck her down.[74]

Chapter Two
Death and Art: Juvenilia

IT WOULD BE a mistake to see the fictional world which the Brontë children built up out of the shards of their existence as an escape from their death-filled surroundings. Nobody escapes. Charlotte Brontë's early fiction does not run from death; it concentrates obsessively on the act of dying. From her earliest scribblings to the final chapter of *Villette*, Brontë's imagination is fascinated with death, approaches it with affection and fear, examines it tentatively but persistently, backs away from it only to creep up again, to grapple with it and overcome it temporarily without gaining any real respite from the compulsion to struggle with it again and again, in work after work after work. But it is in her juvenilia, where no one was listening but her sisters and brother, that her struggle and her strategies for temporary victory are clearest.

The Brontë children began to create their imaginative world in June, 1826, when Patrick Brontë returned from a trip to Leeds with a new set of twelve painted wooden soldiers for Branwell. The date is crucial, though its full significance has escaped Brontë scholars: exactly a year had elapsed since the death of Elizabeth, following closely on that of Maria, had rocked the Brontë household. Thus the shiny toys which Branwell received after the period of formal mourning must have represented his father's attempt to lead his children back along the first tentative steps to the land of the living. The effect of the gift was to be astounding, although Patrick Brontë would learn nothing of it until after the last of his children had died.

Branwell's toys were not the only new playthings which the children discovered as they awoke on the morning of June 6; their father had left a present beside the bed of each sleeping child. He had bought a set of ninepins, a toy village, and a dancing doll for the girls. But it was the soldiers which captured the children's fancy. They did not begin to play house with the toy village, as their father had hoped. Rather, they took the toy soldiers and played at life and death. They gave the individual riflemen names. Charlotte christened the largest and handsomest figure after the Duke of Wellington, who had beaten Napoleon at Waterloo a year before her birth. Branwell, characteristically, named one of the soldiers Napoleon. Emily and Anne named their favorites in honor of Edward Parry and William Ross, the Arctic explorers. The children began a game which would soon channel and control their imaginations. The twelve wooden soldiers gave up their military careers to become explorer-adventurers, leaving England for a life of excitement and eventual wealth on the Ivory Coast. The children followed the escapades of their toys avidly and soon began to write them down. The resultant literary game went through many permutations during the next twenty years or so. At first all of the children played it together. Later, after Charlotte had left home to become a pupil at Roe Head, Emily and Anne rebelled against Branwell's rule and founded their own game and their own kingdom, Gondal, which they kept up till their deaths. Charlotte and Branwell went on chronicling their mythical realm for at least another decade. As late as her second year in Belgium, Charlotte, then in her late twenties, could be caught in the mental web of her childhood game.

Charlotte and her brother composed over one hundred booklets, printing their stories laboriously in a tiny hand in order to fit hundreds of words onto pages as small as one by two inches. Their secret books and magazines chronicled the events of the world they had created. At first the children founded Glass Town, located somewhere on the Ivory Coast. Later, as Branwell's knowledge of Greek and Latin increased, it seemed more dignified to them to translate Glass Town into Verreopolis. That name quickly blurred into Verdopolis, as the children shifted their attention from the city's miraculous buildings to its lush setting. At a still later date Charlotte and Branwell created Angria, an adjacent and rival kingdom. For the sake of simplicity, the entire body of magazines, novellas, poems, political pamphlets, and miscellanies can be called the Angrian cycle.

Almost from the beginning, two characters dominated the game. On the one hand there was Northangerland, the successor to Napoleon in Branwell's affections. Early in the cycle he had been a pirate with the functional name of Rogue, but on land Branwell's personal toy soldier aspired to greatness again and took the name of Alexander Percy. He attained through marriage the title Lord Ellrington, and ended the cycle as the Earl of Northangerland. For the reader's sake I shall refer to him anachronistically as Northangerland throughout this chapter.

Northangerland's antagonist, the hero of the cycle, is Zamorna, the son of the Duke of Wellington. Whether Charlotte calls him Arthur Wellesley, Marquis of Douro, or gives him his later, more ornate identity, Arthur Augustus Adrian, Duke of Zamorna and King of Angria, her favorite character remains an unconscious parody of the Byronic hero.[1] And there is ample evidence that Charlotte worshipped him.[2] Her brother exorcised his anguish by pushing his malicious toy into battle against the fathers of Glass Town; Charlotte assuaged her loneliness by adoring a wooden soldier who could never leave her because he did not exist.

Zamorna is surrounded by admiring women and married in turn to two young girls whose only functions are to love, to pine, and to die. Marian Hume and, later, Maria Henrietta Percy, whose first names bear a suspicious resemblance to Charlotte's sister and mother, are innocent young girls who have the misfortune to be the first and second wives of a rake. They suffer continually, and their suffering only increases the cruelty of Zamorna. We will watch them die repeatedly in this chapter.

Much of their pain comes from the machinations of an evil older woman who cannot stand to see them happy. Lady Zenobia Ellrington is old enough to be their mother—she is in fact the step-mother of Maria Percy—and carries out her role of Oedipal rival with malignant flair. She is the second wife of Northangerland, Maria Percy's father, and takes an occasional turn as Zamorna's mistress. A precursor of *Jane Eyre*'s Bertha Mason, Zenobia is highly intelligent, but brutalized by years of vaguely suggested debaucheries into a nervous if brilliant wreck. She is large, stout, and powerful enough to throw Zamorna's younger brother down the stairs from time to time. She would kill Marian Hume or, later, Maria Percy if she could.

These main figures and the dozens of other characters of the cycle populated a world which did more for the still mourning children than merely supplement an existence grown suddenly and irrevocably thin. For well over a decade their obsessive dream—"the infernal world," or "the world below," as Charlotte termed it—was the focal point of their lives. Fannie Ratchford claims that it was a world "where sin was shorn of its consequences."[3] Certainly sin's outcome was softened, and that was important to the children. For in their unconscious patterning of the world, the most crucial of sin's consequences was death. And the game of the toy soldiers, which Mr. Brontë hoped would set a period to the year of mourning, became for Charlotte and the others a mediatory device, a stage on which they could examine and tinker with death, over and over, as they obsessively set into motion the event they most feared.

In *Beyond the Pleasure Principle*, Freud describes a game played by a one-and-a-half-year-old child. The boy (Freud's grandchild) would take small objects and throw them as far as he could, making a sound which his parents decided represented the German word *fort* ("gone"), followed by gurgles of pleasure and interest. One day Freud observed a more complicated game. Sitting on the floor, the little boy held a reel by its string and tossed it up over the edge of his crib so that it disappeared from his sight. He then pulled the string so that the reel fell back out of his crib. As he did so he squealed *da* ("there"). "This, then, was the complete game—disappearance and return," Freud comments.[4] By throwing the reel away and then pulling it back, the child was training himself to undergo with fortitude the temporary loss of a beloved object by demonstrating to himself that a thing which has gone can return when one needs it.

But what of the simpler game, the disappearance without return of a toy? Why would the child play this game, and play it with obvious pleasure? Freud's answer is both simple and profound. The child never cried when his mother left him for a few hours, although he was greatly attached to her. The complete game, the rejection and retrieval of the toy, lessened his fears by assuring him that beloved objects do return. The starker, more frightening game of disappearance strengthened his resolve to do without that which had gone away, whether it came back or not. In the first place, it was an act of defiance, a demonstration that he could do without the presence of a favorite toy or even a mother. And, more profoundly, the child could derive a bitter pleasure from his ability to initiate and thus in a sense control a painful occurrence: "At the outset he was in a *passive* situation—he was overpowered by the experience; but, by repeating it, unpleasurable though it was, as a game, he took on an *active* part. These efforts might be put down to an instinct for mastery."[5]

The Angrian cycle provided Charlotte with both the game of disappearance and the game of disappearance and return. We will look at both games. Working thematically rather than chronologically, we will examine a small group of representative tales from the period 1829–1834, written by Charlotte between the ages of thirteen and eighteen. These will be followed by a later group. Charlotte's artistic strategies for dealing with death changed considerably during this period. But her basic feelings toward death seem to have remained relatively static and fixed, since the spring of 1825 when her sisters sickened and died. Charlotte's image of her sister Maria's death seems never to have softened, never to have changed; it remained a timeless abrasive which tortured her for the rest of her life. And that is understandable, for the death was traumatic in and of itself, and seems to have served as an emblem for the other deaths—for Elizabeth's, and years later for Branwell's, and Emily's, and Anne's; above all, it must have functioned as a screen for the first loss, the death of Charlotte's mother. But what follows will for the time being concentrate on Charlotte's sister Maria herself as the figure of the lost beloved.

"Albion and Marina" (1830), like so many of Charlotte's contributions to the game, centers on the death of a young girl. As in *Jane Eyre*, the plot depends on a mysterious communication between widely separated lovers. But the message here is from the dead to the living.

Albion, the nineteen-year-old son of a nobleman from the south of England, falls in love with Marina, the daughter of his family physician. His father reluctantly accepts the idea of eventual marriage to a commoner, but insists on first taking his son to Glass Town for a visit which lasts four years. Albion wiles away his African years by writing great epics, the most famous of which, fittingly enough for an Angrian poem, is a Byronic extravaganza entitled "Necropolis, or the City of the Dead," which features a heroine patterned after Marina. At a dance in Glass Town the young poet meets Lady Zelzia Ellrington, who fascinates him momentarily. Walking home later that night, he is confronted by a vision of Marina, who tells him: "Do not forget me; I shall be happy when you return."[6] Albion rushes back to his English estates to find total desolation. On his arrival at Marina's house he sees his beloved playing the harp and singing of her loneliness, but the apparition vanishes leaving him staring at her ruined home. A small boy comes out of the bushes and leads him to Marina's grave; she had died, the victim of Albion's neglect, at precisely the moment her spirit appeared to him in Glass Town. The forlorn lover leaves the south of England and is never heard from again.

The story could be taken simply as one piece of evidence that Charlotte quite naturally hates to see girls with names like Maria die. But more lies under the surface. The narrative purports to be written by Charles Wellesley. It is prefaced by a confused and guilt-ridden statement in which Charles tries to explain to the reader and to himself why he wrote the story: "I have written this tale out of malignity for the injuries that have lately been offered to me. Many parts, especially the former, were composed under a mysterious influence that I cannot account for" (I, 24). Charles explains that Albion represents his older brother, Zamorna, that Marina is Zamorna's wife, Marian Hume, and that Lady Zelzia is modelled on Lady Zenobia Ellrington,

Zamorna's mistress. In effect, then, Charles, as the author of the piece, has killed off his sister-in-law and driven his older brother from the country. Seen in this light the tale is an act of outright aggression. But Charles negates the results of his aggression with this denial: "The conclusion [of the story] is wholly destitute of any foundation in truth, and I did it out of revenge. Albion and Marina are both alive and well for aught I know" (1, 25). The narrator of the tale seems both fascinated and horrified by the possibility of creating a fictional homicide. As creator he can kill, but he regrets his godlike power.

Charles is a complex man, and one of Charlotte's intimates; she uses him constantly as the narrator of her stories in the early years of the Angrian cycle. In "The Foundling" an innkeeper describes him to a foreign visitor as a rather nasty man:

> "Has the [Duke of Zamorna] any sisters?"
> "No, but he has a small imp of a brother."
> "Any likeness in their dispositions and persons?"
> "Not the least. Lord Charles is a little vile, ugly, lying, meddling, messing, despicable dirty ape, who delights in slandering all good and great men and in consorting with all wicked and mean ones." (1: 241)

Charles is a favorite of both Branwell and Charlotte, but they handle him in crucially different ways. Branwell tolerates him as an impertinent clown, a tiny imp who intrudes farce into tragic scenes. Charlotte, too, likes the clever little man. But frequently her humorous affection turns to screaming rage or bitter sarcasm; she will turn from her proper narrative pursuits to growl out a gratuitous insult at her hapless friend. Poor Charles has no role to play in "The Foundling"; he never even appears in the story. Thus the innkeeper's slander leads the plot nowhere.

A casual digressive reference like this need imply nothing more than the author's imperfect control over the material. But digressions piled high enough take on a central meaning of their own. Charlotte seems to treat Charles as a masculine projection of herself. The similarity of her name to that of her creature is obvious but in itself proves nothing. The frequency with which her stories are filtered through Charles is a further step toward identification. However, the most important indication of the face behind the mask is the similarity between his features and Charlotte's image of herself. She felt she looked horrid. "I notice," she told Mrs. Gaskell, "that after a stranger has once looked at my face, he is careful not to let his eyes wander to that part of the room again!" (Gaskell, *Life*, p. 380). In her early writing she could slough off her ugliness onto Charles and poke fun at it. Charles does not mind; he is a man and feels no need of beauty.

But that "little vile, ugly . . . despicable dirty ape" is not always able to laugh off his lack of beauty; for his homeliness is in Charlotte's hands often the mirror of his vile soul. Charles' occasional anguish over his looks arises at least in part from his fear that ugliness might not be merely skin-deep.

The impulse behind "Albion and Marina" goes beyond Charles' usual malice; his misery has turned homicidal. Why does he kill Marina? "Out of malignity, . . . out of revenge," he claims in the Preface. But his revenge is sadly displaced. Charles refers in the Preface to Marina's "incomparable superiority" over her rival, Lady Zelzia. He bears no animus toward Marian Hume, the Angrian counterpart of Marina; his hatred is reserved for his older brother, who treats him like dirt throughout the cycle. In fact one of Charles' main characteristics is his impotent hatred for this older sibling who is the adored favorite of the Verdopolitan aristocracy. If one is not permitted to kill one's sibling in reality, one may at least punish him in a short story. But even there, released aggression causes extreme anxiety: "Many parts . . . were composed under a mysterious influence that I cannot account for." And aggression's consequences are unpredictable: Charles discovers that his malice has produced, not the death of the hated sibling, but the destruction of a girl whom he loves as a sister.

Marina is Marian Hume; is she also Maria Brontë? If so, then Charlotte has produced a tale which must indeed have troubled her, as well as her persona. But Charles' malediction can be cancelled: "The conclusion is wholly destitute of any foundation in truth . . . Albion and Marina are both alive and well." Thus one can kill and not kill. In fiction one can release the most aggressive tendencies of one's nature and yet know beforehand that they will have no "real" effect. Charles tells the reader at the outset that Marina isn't dead, that the report of her death is a strange little lie, a make-believe. Death may obsess the imagination, but in "real" life, the life of Glass Town which provides the setting in which Charles Wellesley writes his aggressive tale, it shall have no dominion. Both Charles and the young girl writing furiously behind the mask of Charles can breathe freely again, having committed no crime. In this limited sense the Angrian writings constitute a literature of escape. But neither literature nor any other form of activity provides a true escape from the dilemmas of existence. Fiction can bring a temporary release of mental pressure, but there is no real exit from the prison of the mind.

Thus throughout the Angrian cycle Charlotte Brontë finds herself repeatedly confronted with variations of the same situation, a dilemma which she has herself constructed out of her unconscious need to track her agony back to its traumatic source, to confront and conquer the causal event: the beloved has died—how can one explain it, who is to blame for it, how can death's echo be muted once and for all? The Angrian cycle, like Albion's poem, is a Necropolis, lingering with tenderness and horror and remorse over the figure of a corpse.

In the early years of the cycle the children developed a filter through which they could continually gaze without pain on death. Their solution to their problem resembles an unwitting parody of the novelistic practice of their era. The young artists took on the attributes of gods. They appear in their early stories as genii: Chief Genius [sic] Brannii [Branwell], Chief Genius Talii [Charlotte], Chief Genius Emii [Emily], and Chief Genius Annii [Anne]. Their playthings, the fictional characters, retain their autonomy only so long as the genii are willing to hide from them. But the authors step into their fictive world at moments of crisis to make certain that the story goes well. Their physical appearance and the exotic names they give themselves are reflections of *The Arabian Nights*, but their function is at bottom a childish variation of the role of the nineteenth-century narrator: out of the chaos of the essential vision they create the artificial order of novelistic form and authorial intervention. Their most frequent intrusion into the "natural" order of events is the resuscitation of the dead.[7] Blatant resurrection would of course be objected to by an adult reading public. But the children themselves were their only audience, and the return to life of the dead was without doubt a fulfillment of one of their deepest wishes. Out of grief and resentment they kill off character after character in their writings, but they need carry no heavy burden of guilt for their actions, since they can cancel the death of their victims. The subplot of "The Foundling" (1833) provides a good example of the pattern.

The main plot of the tale concerns the adventures of Edward Sydney, one of the dozens of orphans who appear in Charlotte Brontë's fiction. Abandoned as an infant on the doorstep of a Derbyshire peasant, he travels in his adulthood to Glass Town, where he finds out that he is the grandson of England's George III. Jane Eyre's discovery that she has inherited a few thousand pounds is dwarfed by comparison with Edward's good fortune. Orphans do not simply find their relatives in Charlotte's juvenilia; they find them in hilariously high positions. Edward Sydney is only momentarily discomposed by the revelation that his father is the Duke of York, for he knows through experience that Glass Town is a land where loss is offset by miraculous gain. He has already seen Zamorna reborn.

Zamorna had been poisoned. Northangerland and a friend, Montmorency, while sipping a casual one hundred and thirty glasses of rum, had plotted his death. Northangerland had heard of the perfect weapon, a potion compounded by Manfred, the sage of Philosopher's Island. A bit later the reader meets this sage, and hears Manfred explain to his disciples what happened when he discovered an elixir of life: "I at last succeeded in compounding a fluid, so pure, so refined, so ethereal that one drop of it distilled on our mortal clay penetrated to the soul, freed it from all grosser particles, raised it far above world troubles, rendered it capable of enjoying the calm of heaven amid the turmoil of earth, and, as with a shield of adamant, forever warded off the darts of death" (1: 276). But the Genii, enraged at Manfred's presumption, have transformed his discovery into an elixir of death. (They had presumably not noticed that the state of euphoria produced by the original fluid was itself suspiciously deathlike.) The conclusion to be drawn from their action is obvious, though neither they nor Manfred draw it: the Genii have made themselves accomplices to any murder committed with the new weapon.

The sage announces that someone has poisoned Zamorna. And then a scene occurs which will be staged in slightly varying form repeatedly throughout the Angrian cycle: "He paused again and made a mystic sign with his sceptre. An iron door immediately unfolded, and six dark figures, bearing a bier covered with a white sheet, entered" (1: 277). Zamorna's corpse is followed by two men in chains, Northangerland and Montmorency. They confess to the murder and must themselves drink the elixir.

By the time Edward Sydney and the Duke of Wellesley arrive at Philosopher's Island, the Duke's son and his murderers have been buried, and Manfred is crooning a dirge:

> Damp lies his corpse in the folds of the shroud;
> Low to the dust his bright forehead is bowed.
>
> .   .   .   .
>
> And why was that fair form, all fettered and shrouded,
> So early laid down in its long dreamless sleep?
> What hand can dispel that dense, shadowy gloom
> Which hides from our vision the volume of doom?
> (1: 286)

In Haworth, Manfred's question would be rhetorical and futile. But Glass Town is a kingdom where death has lost its finality: "On looking up they perceived the four chief Genii, who rule the destinies of our world, appearing through an opening in the sky. 'Mortals,' they cried, in a voice louder than . . . thunder, 'We, in our abundant mercy, have been moved to compassion by your oft-repeated and grievous lamentations. The cold corpse in the grave shall breathe again the breath of life, provided you here pledge a solemn oath that neither he nor his relatives shall ever take revenge on those who slew him'" (1: 288). And they resurrect both the victim and his murderers.

In the context of the story, the men whom the Genii are shielding from revenge are Northangerland and Montmorency. But on a deeper level Charlotte, the author as Genie, is protecting herself. For she is an accomplice to the crime in two crucial senses. In the first place she is one of the demi-gods who changed the nature of the potion from benevolent to malign; her jealousy of her creatures' potential immortality fashioned the weapon which killed Zamorna. Secondly, she is the author of the tale: her imagination plotted the murder, guided the poison to the victim's lips, and destroyed him. Yet the narrative insists that death is not the immutable end of life, that destructive impulses can be blunted in the mind's arena, that victims of those impulses can even be called back to life in an act of generosity—under the condition that the risen victims bear no animosity toward their killers. The reign of death is provisional, even whimsical.

Not all Glass Town corpses rise from the grave, however. In one strange fragment included in "My Angria and the Angrians" (1834), Charlotte imagines Northangerland dead. His widow, Lady Zenobia Ellrington, is troubled, but cannot fathom the cause: "Detached fragments of the past, the long-past, the never to return, have since morning been gliding through my memory like that cloud. And still as they vanished one haunting fancy remained behind and what is it? A foolish one but I cannot think it unfounded—that I had something to do before midnight, some important and solemn duty to perform. I know not its nature. I only feel the impression, and that at times is so strong that I have started from my seat in urgent horror" (2: 36). Her anxiety is soon focused; a courtier arrives to remind her of a promise they had made to her husband. The three of them years before had argued about the nature of death. Northangerland had ended the discussion by making his wife and his friend swear that they would open his coffin and examine his corpse on the twentieth anniversary of his death. Lady Zenobia thus seems to resemble her creator, Charlotte Brontë: they are both compelled to stare at death. Moreover, both have repressed that need, banished it from consciousness. Neither the character nor the author analyzes the nature of the compulsion; but each of them apparently feels and is disturbed by an amorphous "haunting fancy," which Zenobia will act out while Charlotte stares down on her surrogate and pulls its strings.

Now throughout the Angrian cycle Zenobia normally despises her husband. In one typical conjugal chat she calls him a "base villain" and a "wretch," and scorns his "bloodstained . . . crime-blackened hand" as he threatens to kill her (1: 260). But in this fragment, thinking of a vision she had while gazing on his portrait, she can talk of her love for him:

> [The face] vivified, as it often does when I am alone and thoughtful, into Life, flesh and existence. Though dead he yet lived. The eye looked at me so strangely. A melancholy, a warning, a commanding light, filled it and inspired it, till I trembled with the marvellous reality of the likeness. Then a recollection rushed on, of what I had said, what I had promised. . . . I tried to keep and unfold it. I gasped with eagerness. I gazed again and again on the picture that it might enlighten me, but vainly, all died off. Alexander's form was no longer the one I had known and loved." (2: 36–37)

Death changes hatred into desperate love. As we saw in Chapter 1, Charlotte too had looked on the faces of the dead in her dreams; they, like Northangerland, had gazed at her in solemn and mournful admonition, perhaps commanded services which she could not understand. Perhaps they commanded her to resurrect them. Zenobia Ellrington does not notice it, but in gazing on the picture of her dead husband she had attempted to resuscitate him. The portrait "vivified . . . into Life . . . Though dead he yet lived." The miracle could not be sustained; "All died off." Now she must visit his crypt, lift the coffin's lid despite her repulsion, and gaze on his face. Perhaps her unconscious mind hopes to resurrect him. Or, just as plausibly, perhaps it is the need to prove that her husband is still in the coffin, still dead, which impels her toward his tomb. Securely locked in their coffins, the dead cannot carry out schemes of revenge on the living. The Genii had been forced to proscribe vengeance before they called Zamorna back to life. The desire for revenge would be natural for one who had lain motionless in a grave for years while the luckier ones romped in the free air over one's body. Surely then the corpse, its mind slowly decomposing into sheer malice, would wish to elicit obscure promises from the living, to circumscribe and gradually compress their freedom till they too were locked as in a coffin.

Northangerland has forced the living to come and do homage to the dead. Probably Zenobia, like her creator, wonders with a mixture of hope and fear whether she will find the corpse inside the coffin. The courtier urges Zenobia:

> Bride of his living breast draw near,
> Bend Lady o'er thy husband's bier;
> For ere the night lamps farther wane
> We'll look on Percy's face again! (2: 41)

And then the fragment breaks off, ending with an anti-climactic stage direction: "*Lifts the coffin lid, curtain drops*" (2: 41). Charlotte has not been able to carry out her resolve to see the corpse.

But for a few moments she has identified herself with a character she usually hates. Zenobia's normal role in the cycle is that of Oedipal rival to a series of young girls. When Charlotte sends the older woman into a tomb, however, Zenobia seems to become Charlotte's surrogate; she takes on a new personality in order to act out her creator's own compulsion.

The fragment is one of the few tales in the Angrian cycle in which the reader does not get even a glimpse of a corpse. More normally the body lies like a gruesome centerpiece, profoundly disturbing but inescapable, in the middle of the tale. This is the case, for example, in "The Fairy Gift" (1830). Captain Bud, who tells Charles Wellesley the story, is an Angrian politician who comes from humble origins. In the days when he was still a farmhand, he was approached by a fairy who offered him three wishes. The first was the crucial one: the ugly young man wished for beauty. He immediately became handsome: "There I stood, tall, slender, and graceful as a young poplar tree, all my limbs moulded in the most perfect and elegant symmetry, my complexion of the purest red and white, my eyes blue and brilliant, swimming in liquid radiance under the narrow dark arches of two exquisitely-formed eyebrows, my mouth of winning sweetness, and lastly, my hair clustering in rich black curls over a forehead smooth as ivory" (1: 53). The description of the rough laborer's transformation is feminine to the point of being unintentionally comic. Surely the rugged Captain Bud would never want to look like that. But Charlotte Brontë might.

Armed with new beauty, Bud meets and marries a rich hag, Lady Beatrice Ducie. He tires of the marriage almost immediately; the neighbors snub him, the servants insult him, his wife is insanely jealous. His misery comes to a climax when, having met young Lady Cecilia Standon, he is foolish enough to praise her beauty in front of his wife, who he soon discovers is a witch. That night Bud secretly follows Beatrice to the dungeon, where his wife's magic calls forth this scene: "At length the dead silence that had hitherto reigned unbroken was dissipated by a tremendous cry which shook the house to its centre, and I saw six black, indefinable figures gliding through the darkness bearing a funeral bier on which lay arrayed . . . in robes of white satin and tall snowy ostrich plumes, the form of Cecilia Standon. Her black eyes were closed, and their lashes lay motionless on a cheek pale as marble. She was quite stiff and dead" (1: 56).

The understandable desire of the young man to overcome his physical ugliness by supernatural means has resulted in the death of a young girl he was beginning to love. He had wished for beauty, for the power to be loved, and his hatred of his inadequacy caused the death of an innocent girl; he repudiates the gift of beauty when he sees its victim's corpse. In other words, "The Fairy Gift" represents yet another variation of the pattern of self-assertion, death, and remorse which we have seen in "Albion and Marina" and "The Foundling."

But there is more to the problem than that. Throughout the Angrian cycle the corpse is a constant obsession. The point is not simply that Charlotte is fascinated with death, though that fact should be obvious by now. More particularly, she seems obsessed with visions of the grave, the crypt, the corpse itself. In their most developed state, her compulsive visions take the form of a coldly beautiful corpse in white surrounded by six pallbearers dressed in black.

The corpse which would seem to be the immediate object of Charlotte's obsession is that of her oldest sister, Maria. Not that Charlotte didn't love her sister; she clearly adored her. She thought of Maria as a saint. But this very adoration, which the other Brontës shared, must have helped to reinforce and disguise an unacknowledged resentment of the model held up before her. The underlying pattern of destruction, observation, and regret which controls much of the Angrian cycle can best be understood as the mirror of the little girl's quite understandable ambivalence toward her sister, an ambivalence which was accompanied by the wish to replace her rival in her elders' affections. That wish received a horrifying fulfillment: Maria died, Elizabeth followed her to the grave, and Charlotte became the oldest child.

In reality there was no way of repudiating the abhorrent fairy gift of preferment. In Charlotte's adult writings, aimed at a public audience, death is an absolute. Charlotte was to portray Maria as Helen Burns, who dies in *Jane Eyre*. Jane describes her burial site: "Her grave is in Brockleridge churchyard: for fifteen years after her death it was only covered by a grassy mound; but now a grey marble tablet marks the spot, inscribed with her name, and the word 'Resurgam.'"[8] In adult fiction only the pious hope of resurrection remains: "I shall arise." In the imaginative world of the adolescent, however, unrestrained by the thought that adults are watching, the wish can be given more concrete form. The dead really do awake—not in an insubstantial afterlife, but now, in the body, in Glass Town.

The provisional hypothesis of sibling rivalry is useful but ultimately inadequate as an explanation of the myth of disappearance and return which structures the Angrian cycle. Most significantly, the victim in many of the tales is totally innocent of any offense against the murderer. If we were dealing only with sibling rivalry, it would seem that the victim would normally have somehow insulted the sensibilities of the murderer. But in many cases there had been no prior tension between them. Instead, the aggressor rushes blindly at the thing he hates only to discover that he has killed the thing he loves.

A sequence of tales later than the one we have so far examined sheds light on this drama of displaced revenge which seems to have haunted Charlotte's psyche. In 1834, Charlotte and Branwell decided to reward Zamorna by giving him a kingdom, Angria, just east of Glass Town. Perversely, they chose Northangerland as his prime minister. It was a strange alliance, and quickly broke down. In January, 1836, Branwell decided to let Northangerland begin a full-scale civil war, gathering together the Ashantee army, the dissident democrats of Angria, and the conservative aristocracy of Glass Town to form a coalition which quickly overwhelmed Zamorna.

The Zamorna-Northangerland alliance and feud were further complicated by the fact that they had for several years been related by marriage. In "Politics in Verdopolis" (1833), Branwell had introduced a new character to the cycle, Maria Henrietta Percy (known also as Mary Percy), Northangerland's daughter by his first wife. Maria had been reared in absolute retirement in the countryside and only now, on the verge of adulthood, entered the aristocratic world of Glass Town. She quickly became engaged to an aristocratic nonentity, but then met Zamorna. They fell in love, Zamorna told his wife Marian of the affair, and Marian obligingly dropped dead.

It must have been painful for Charlotte to let Branwell kill Marian Hume. Fanny Ratchford indicates one of the mechanisms which made it psychologically possible for Charlotte to get rid of the original heroine of the Angrian cycle: "Charlotte did not give her up any more than she had given up the wooden soldiers who fell in battle; she merely resorted to a new form of resuscitation, and continued to write about her in retrospect, adding new traits of character from time to time and new incidents to her life, until Marian Hume dead grows into a vastly different person from Marian Hume living, gradually merging into Mary Percy, and through her into Paulina Mary Home of *Villette*."[9]

In her late adolescence Charlotte was devising more sophisticated mechanisms for overcoming death. The blatant intervention of the author into the processes of life and death had disappeared; instead there was now the manipulation of the past tense and the merging of the characters of one work into their literary descendants in the next. In replacing the discarded Marian with her double, Maria, Charlotte had rediscovered a mature novelistic defense against death; she had taken a step closer to becoming an adult artist, resolving her psychological dilemmas with the standard tools of her trade.

By the time the Angrian Civil War began, Charlotte was teaching at Roe Head, separated from Branwell by twenty long miles. She was unable, except during vacations, to read her brother's manuscripts. Thus when Branwell wrote to her that he was going to kill Maria Henrietta Percy, Charlotte was thrown into an agony of suspense. For nearly a year Charlotte tried desperately to come to terms with this new tragedy, the death of yet another girl named Maria. And this time she was able to stave off the hated event.

Maria Percy was to be a victim of the feud between her husband and her father. Charlotte's long poem, "And, when you left me," dated July 19, 1836, describes the family situation. The poem, patterned after Byron's "Childe Harold's Pilgrimage," is a monologue spoken by Zamorna. He has been captured by his father-in-law and sent off to exile on a ship wandering around the Mediterranean. The poem is an imagined confession to the absent Northangerland. Zamorna describes the mutually sadistic relationship

between Northangerland and himself, in which each part-
ner was able to inflict exquisite psychological wounds on
the other. Moreover, both were masochists; each willingly
offered the other the opportunity to return the wound:

> if one
> Had in his treasures some all priceless thing,
> Some jewel that he deeply doated on
> Dearer to him than life, the fool would fling
> That rich gem to his friend. (2: 241)

And the friend would immediately destroy it.

Zamorna's analysis of the relationship is followed by the
charged statement: "Percy, your daughter was a lovely
being" (2: 241). In Charlotte's eyes the Angrian Civil
War was simply the mechanism which triggered the compulsion of two people to kill the thing they loved.

In a manuscript dated April 29, 1836 (its modern title
is "History of Angria III"), Charlotte had discussed the
relationship between Northangerland, Zamorna, and Maria
in more political terms than in Zamorna's poetic monologue, but even that work had stressed the taut emotional
quality of the situation. Zamorna had told his aide-de-camp:
"I swore that if he broke those bonds and so turned to
vanity and scattered in the air sacrifices that I had made
and words that I had spoken; if he made as dust and nothingness causes for which I have endured jealousies and
burning strife and emulations amongst those I loved; if he
froze feelings that in me are like living fire, I would have
revenge" (2: 156). The language here is vivid but vague.
It is possible to read the passage in entirely political terms.
But the vocabulary bears a striking resemblance to that of
love, described, as in *Jane Eyre*, in terms of fire and ice.

If there is any doubt that Zamorna views his father-in-
law with outraged love, Zamorna makes the point perfectly
clear a bit later on: "You know what accursed way I tend
after my Mother, and you know how I loved Percy, and
what it is costing me to send him to the D . . . l!" (2: 158).
The older man had taken the younger as his son-in-law.
But the relationship is closer to that of parent and child.
In substituting Maria Henrietta Percy for Marian Hume,

Charlotte and Branwell had made explicit a relationship which had become more and more strongly implied in the earlier years of the cycle. The compact of mutual torture understood so fully by both the older man and his son-in-law thus becomes intelligible: it is a romantic reflection of the paradigmatic stance of parent and child. They are allies, they present for a time a common front to the world, they love and admire one another, but they are also the victims of a compulsive need to inflict pain on each other. Maria Henrietta Percy is a pawn in this libidinal game, beloved and used by both men in their struggle with one another.

In the poem we have been examining, "And, when you left me," Maria is still alive, but Zamorna already speaks of her as if she were dead. He envisions a way in which a woman might die. His companion, a courtier named Robert King, who, quite appropriately for Charlotte's juvenilia, is known by the nickname "Sdeath," had suggested that they should have taken Maria along on the voyage and drowned her while she was asleep. Zamorna contemplates the thought:

> It would look well, says Sdeath, to see her sinking,
> All in white raiment, through the placid deep,
> From the pure limpid water never shrinking,
> Calmly subsiding to eternal sleep,
> Dreaming of him that's drowning her, not thinking
> She's soon to be where sharks and sword-fish leap;
> And, if she rose again a few days hence
> Looking like death, it would but stand to sense.
>
> To common sense, a corpse laid in the water
> Must putrefy whosever corpse it be,
> And neither [Zamorna's] wife nor
>   [Northangerland's] daughter
> Can be left out in Nature's great decree. (2: 244–245)

Charlotte is now twenty years old and her vision of death has apparently lost its connection with the childish hope for immediate resurrection in the flesh. The compulsive pattern is still there: a murder occurs, the aggressor stares at the corpse, and the dead girl rises. But she bobs to the surface in bitter parody of the earlier myth. The bloated resurrection takes Charlotte a long step in her adolescent journey to an acceptance of reality. The genii have been left behind with the other toys of childhood. Still, Charlotte insists on holding a buffer between herself and death. Maria's drowning was merely a suggestion, and Zamorna can luxuriate in the vision while refusing to take his counsellor's advice.

Meanwhile Branwell was forging implacably ahead in his neurotic need to kill once again the saintly ghost who tormented him. Maria must die no matter how much Charlotte complained. By the end of the summer Charlotte was undergoing the remorseful agonies of an accomplice:

> I wonder if Branwell has really killed [Maria]. Is she dead? Is she buried is she alone in the cold earth on this dreary night with the ponderous coffin plate on her breast under the black pavement of a church in a vault closed up, with lime and mortar. No body near where she lies—she who was watched through months of suffering—as she lay on her bed of state. Now quite forsaken because her eyes are closed, her lips sealed and her limbs cold and rigid. . . . A set of wretched thoughts are rising in my mind, I hope she's alive still partly because I can't abide to think how hopelessly and cheerlessly she must have died, and partly because her removal if it has taken place, must have been to Northangerland like the quenching of the last spark that avoided utter darkness.[10]

Charlotte was apparently able to dissuade her brother from killing the duchess. For although in a manuscript dated September 19, 1836, Branwell had written that she could last "not more than an hour or two" (2: 216), Maria still lingers on in Charlotte's "The Return of Zamorna," written in the winter of 1836–1837. The language of that story mirrors its author's need to compromise her dream of resurrection with reality. Maria is still sick, but is now at least ambulatory. Charlotte writes: "Wasted and blanched as she looked, her attendants wondered often how she could bear to walk so long, but her uncomplaining melancholy awed them too much for expostulation. They never dared advise her to seek more repose, and there all day long the light rustle of her dress might be heard as she traversed the measured walk with noiseless and languid tread, *more like a flitting shade* than a living woman."[11]

Though in Branwell's imagination Maria had been scheduled to die on the night of September 19, for Charlotte her death had become metaphorical. The device of the simile, which allows her to state a proposition and cancel it at the moment of its expression, will continue to function throughout Charlotte's career as a mediator between dream and reality. In the long progression from the wild romances of her childhood game to the somber close of *Villette*, the simile becomes one of Charlotte's most successful tools for balancing her private vision with the need for a myth which is acceptable both to her own sense of reality and to a public audience. In the description of Maria Percy she continues her metaphoric play with death. She writes: "The remembrance of the thousand characters who had moved and shone around her was grown dim and vague. . . . Their appearance in her presence would have startled her as though one had returned from the dead" (2: 286). Other devices used in the story also approximate and cancel death. For example, a servant tells the narrator: "I have thought it would not be long before we should have to dress her corpse in its shroud and to lay her out, young as she was and divinely beautiful, stiff and icy in her coffin" (2: 287–288). The subjunctive here has much the same function as the similes above. And Maria herself asks: "How is it that I am kept here in such solitude, such deadliness of Life?" (2: 288). Again, an approximation of death is followed by life.

The attempted murder of Maria Henrietta Percy contains the necessary material for moving a step beyond the provisional hypothesis of sibling rivalry developed in the first part of this chapter. Maria was to die because her father had deserted Zamorna. If we schematize the triangular relationship between the three characters, the implications of this statement become clearer. Zamorna loves Maria. But he is willing to let her die because her father has turned against him. Zamorna's indignation is not simply the result of rational political considerations. Rather, he sees himself as a man whose offer of love has been rejected. How will he take revenge on this father-figure whom he loved (and hated) and who repudiated him? He will wound Northangerland in his only vulnerable spot, his love for his daughter Maria.

The stance of rejected love is common to Charlotte Brontë's works from "Albion and Marina" to *Villette*. But the poem "And, when you left me" seems to me the clearest statement of the paradigm which the later fiction echoes and distorts. The speaker has been cast off by an older man; therefore he will destroy that man's daughter, the only creature the older man really loves. The pattern bears a striking resemblance to the emotional constellation of the Brontë household, in which Patrick Brontë's loved ones were taken from him one by one until he was left face to face with his only remaining child.

Charlotte's unconscious identification with the mighty Zamorna which this pattern of rejection and revenge implies may at first sight seem strange. But although her worship of Zamorna had made her identify with his forlorn mistresses, she had at the same time almost certainly viewed him as a projection of the self-assurance and aggressiveness she longed for and lacked. Like all idols, Zamorna had always served his worshipper in part as compensation for her own inferiority complex. Zamorna had been repeatedly attracted to the daughters of rough or evil men: Marian Hume, Maria Percy, Maria Sneaky and Caroline Vernon are all daughters of less than admirable fathers, and all are loved and mistreated by Zamorna.

A parent-figure is punished and a young girl mistreated in "The Green Dwarf" (1833). And the perpetrator of the crimes bears a strong resemblance to Charlotte Brontë. The tale, an imitation of *Ivanhoe*, centers on a triangle consisting of the Count of St. Clair, Northangerland, and the woman they both love, Lady Emily Charlesworth. The fourth major figure of the story is Northangerland's spy in the service of St. Clair, Andrew, known as the Green Dwarf because of his costume and his height. After Andrew has nearly managed to get his master executed as a traitor, St. Clair complains: "I know not what demon has possessed my vassal's breast, what hell-born eloquence has persuaded the orphan, who, since his birth, has existed only on my bounty, to aid in the destruction of his lord and bene-factor."[12] The demons which possess Andrew are those which possessed Charlotte Brontë: bereavement and self-hatred. He has lost his parents, and he is painfully aware of his ugliness. At one point he is said to have "withered, unnatural features" (p. 94), and elsewhere Charlotte refers to his "keen eyes and shrivelled, ill-favoured" looks (p. 82). In punishment for betraying his master Andrew is sentenced to a term as a galley slave. On his release he takes up an occupation which will exploit his alienation and channel his aggression away from crime: "He . . . took to the trade of author, published drivelling rhymes which he called Poetry, and snivelling tales, which went under the denomination of novels" (p. 102). Andrew, then, seems to serve as a projection of Charlotte's self-hatred and re-pressed aggression. But though he gives the story its title, he is not the main character nor does Charlotte seem par-ticularly fascinated with him. Her interest seems focused more on the heroine, Lady Emily Charlesworth. Lady Emily can be seen as a composite character: to the qualities associated in the Angrian cycle with the Maria-figure, she adds the names of Emily and Charlotte. She does not die, but she faces the danger of starvation, and her peril is a crucial point in the psychological pattern of Angria.

Andrew helps Northangerland abduct her. (The dwarf has learned that the most effective way to punish his fatherly benefactor is to take the older man's most prized possession away from him.) Northangerland imprisons Lady Emily in a tower which is guarded by a woman named Bertha, whom Charlotte describes as a malevolent shrew: "The portal [of the tower] slowly unfolded and revealed . . . an old woman bent double with the weight of years. Her countenance, all wrinkled and shrivelled, wore a settled expression of discontent, while her small red eyes gleamed with fiend-like malignity" (p. 59). But Bertha's supposed malice breaks forth in nothing worse than brusque speech. Most of the time she merely ignores her captive: "During a period of four weeks Lady Emily had pined in her lonely prison under the surveillance of the wretched Bertha, who regularly visited her three times a day to supply her with food, but at all other times remained in a distant part of the castle" (p. 99). And then Bertha drops dead, leaving Emily to starve. The young poacher who saves the heroine tells her that "in his perambulations through the desolate halls he had, to his horror, stumbled upon the corpse of an old hideous woman, who, to his mind, looked for all the world like a witch" (p. 100). He had buried the corpse under a heap of stones.

Thus in "The Green Dwarf" Charlotte as author does not gaze for a long time at a beautiful corpse, but takes only a timid peek at a dead old crone and passes on. Moreover, the body is removed from direct view by a series of narrators. The story is told by Charles Wellesley. It has been recounted to him by Captain Bud, whom Emily had presumably told of her adventures in the tower. She in turn had been informed by the poacher of his discovery of Bertha's corpse. The compulsive view of the body, in other words, is separated from Charlotte's eyes by four protective layers of narrative. This filtering device seems to me to indicate that something about Bertha's death disturbs Charlotte profoundly.

Normally the author succeeds in satisfying her need to stare at dead Angrians. The dead are not coy: Zamorna's corpse in "The Foundling" and Lady Cecilia's in "The Fairy Gift" had thrust themselves into the viewer's gaze with festive shamelessness; at the first hint of incantation they had been carried in sad triumph onto the stage to take up their role in the gloomy ritual. But when the corpse is of someone older, a parent-figure, then the voyeuristic desire of the author remains unsated. Thus the curtain closes when Zenobia lifts the lid of her husband's coffin in the fragment from "My Angria and the Angrians." And here, in "The Green Dwarf," the poacher hauls the hag's carcass into the yard with unceremonious haste and piles stones on it before Charlotte can get her fill of staring. Charlotte seems to have exercised unconscious censorship and placed a barrier before the eyes of the curious.

The cause of this taboo can be seen if, ignoring the surface plot, we concentrate on the abstract pattern of Lady Emily's agony. The young heroine is abducted from her friends and taken to a lonely building where she is neglected; the man who has kidnapped her never reappears, and the woman who feeds and cares for her spends most of her time in another part of the tower. The wrinkled, grumpy, red-eyed woman, bent double with age and pain, caps her malign neglect by dying, leaving the heroine totally alone with no one to care what happens to her. The story seems like a distortion of Charlotte Brontë's childhood. In all probability Bertha's corpse cannot be seen because she represents Charlotte's mother, and the sight of her remains would send the whole traumatic year flooding back into her daughter's consciousness, overwhelming it with pain and remorse. It must remain walled up, blocked from Charlotte's view by the long line of younger, more beautiful corpses on which the Angrian narratives dwell.

Fanny Ratchford finds Bertha the most interesting character in the story. She writes: "Bertha is a direct adaptation of the Saxon Ulrica of Front de Bœuf's castle in *Ivanhoe.* Commonplace and childish as the plagiarism seems in itself, it fixed in Charlotte's mind an image which under the heat of her imagination fused in the course of years with Lady Zenobia Ellrington to become Bertha Mason, the mad wife of *Jane Eyre.*"[13] True. But we must try to go beyond the mere recognition of similarity to ask what it was that heated Charlotte's imagination to the point where it could fuse a slattern like Bertha with the voluptuous, brilliant Zenobia, wife of Northangerland and mistress of Zamorna. I would suggest that the catalyst lies in the fact that both women are projections of Charlotte's complex infantile image of her mother. And one more character should be added to the mix: Lady Beatrice Ducie, the witch in "The Fairy Gift."

Lady Beatrice is as rich and powerful as Lady Zenobia. Unfortunately she is as hideous as Bertha. But ugly mothers

are better than none at all, and Bertha's considerable draw-
backs do not stop Bud from hoping that his new-found
beauty will attract her attention and love: "Though her
ladyship had passed the meridian of life, was besides fat
and ugly, and into the bargain had the reputation of being
a witch, I cherished hopes that she might take a liking for
me, seeing I was so very handsome" (1: 54). Lady Beatrice does love Bud in her insanely possessive way, to the
point of murdering Cecilia Standon out of jealousy. And
then she turns on Bud:

> At this appalling sight I could restrain myself no
> longer, but uttering a loud shriek I sprang from be-
> hind the pillar. My wife saw me. She started from her
> kneeling position, and rushed furiously towards where
> I stood, exclaiming in tones rendered tremulous by
> excessive fury: "Wretch, wretch, what demon has
> lured thee hither to thy fate?" With these words she
> seized me by the throat and attempted to strangle me.
>
> I screamed and struggled in vain. Life was ebbing
> apace when suddenly she loosened her grasp, tottered,
> and fell dead.
>
> When I was sufficiently recovered from the effects
> of her infernal grip to look around I saw by the light
> of the candle a little man in a green coat striding over
> her and flourishing a bloody dagger in the air. (1: 56)

It is the fairy whose gift to Bud was beauty. Like the Green
Dwarf this little man in green has struck down a parent-
figure.

The maternal figures of Angria hate young girls. Lady
Zenobia is prettier than her two ugly doubles, but no nicer:
"Who would think that that grand form of feminine maj-
esty could launch out into the unbridled excesses of passion
in which her ladyship not infrequently indulges? . . . it
would seem as if neither fire nor pride nor imperiousness
could awaken the towering fits of ungoverned and frantic
rage that often deform her beauty. . . . is it natural that such
hands should inflict the blows that sometimes tingle from
them?"[14]

In the early stages of the Angrian cycle, the object of

Zenobia's fits is often Marian Hume. "The Rivals" (1830) dramatizes the contest between the woman and the girl for Zamorna's love. Marian (who, like the Green Dwarf and Lady Beatrice's murderer, is dressed in green) cannot understand Zenobia's accusation that she loves the Duke: "'Tis to me a problem,/ An unsolved riddle, an enigma dark" (1: 48). She has no conscious need of Zamorna's love, since she receives enough affection at home: "I've a father" (1: 47). The statement enrages Zenobia. Screaming "Wretch, I could kill thee!" (1: 48), she seizes Marian and tries to decide whether or not to throttle this presumptuous girl who brags of her father's love. When Zamorna calls from the woods and Marian tries to run to him, Zenobia restrains her, saying: "Nay! I will hold thee firmly as grim death!" (1: 49). In Angria the deathlike grasp of the older woman who restrains the young girl from the enjoyment of love is often quite powerful. Zamorna comes out of the woods with a rose for Marian. When he gives in to Zenobia's cajolery and presents her the rose instead, Marian falls down as if dead. Zenobia has won the round.

"The Rivals" presents in relatively straightforward fashion the Oedipal triangle of an older woman, a young girl, and the man they both love. Often the constellation is more complex, but in one form or another it runs throughout the cycle. One of the constants in Charlotte's juvenilia is Zenobia's hatred for whatever young girl happens to fall in love with Zamorna. When Marian Hume dies and Zamorna marries Maria Henrietta Percy, the daughter of Northangerland's first wife, the picture comes into even sharper focus. For Northangerland's second wife is Zenobia. Thus Zenobia is both Maria's stepmother and her rival.

Maria Percy was named after her mother, a gentle, quiet woman who died when Maria was an infant. It is apparent that Charlotte has split off the two aspects of motherhood which fascinate and torment her: separation and jealousy. The good mother, who if she were only alive would love and understand her daughter, is dead. The one who is there is an evil stepmother who stands between the young girl and sexual love.

Despite the maternal barrier, however, girls do fall in

love in Angria—usually with Zamorna—but they quickly find themselves caught in a trap as restrictive as the lonely existence they sought to escape. Two emotions, anguish and love, dominate Angria, and each of them is a psychological prison. Anguish turns to aggression: the sufferers hurl themselves like weapons at an imagined persecutor, unmindful of the consequences to themselves. Love too results, not in the expansion of the lover's sense of self, but in dehumanization: the lover becomes an object. Charlotte describes one of her lovesick young girls: "Miss Laury belonged to the Duke of Zamorna. She was indisputably his property, as much as the Lodge of Rivaulx or the stately wood of Hawkscliffe, and in that light she considered herself."[15]

Mina Laury is the most interesting character in the late years of the Angrian cycle. In a sense she is a transitional figure between Charlotte's juvenilia and her adult novels. She does not suffer the anguish of bereavement. Her problem is not how to scramble back to a hiding place in the mind where she can stare at a beautiful corpse, her gaze forming the last tenuous bond between the living and the dead. Rather, like the characters of Charlotte's novels she is concerned with the dilemma of psychological survival in an empty, alien world. She has found a simplistic and excruciating solution—love—and she grips it with the ardor of a woman dangling from a cliff: "You know Sir, my mind is of that limited and tenacious order, it can but contain one idea, and that idea whilst it lasts affords a motive for life, and when it is rent away leaves a vacancy which makes death desirable as a relief" ("The Return of Zamorna," 2: 298). Mina and the other young girls who took up more and more of Charlotte's attention in the fiction of her late adolescence are creatures who desperately need a tangible motive for their existence. Charlotte's novels will concern themselves with the quest for such a motive; the protagonists of her maturity will change and develop as they wander in search of meaning. Mina and the other Angrian heroines cannot develop, for they are chained to their premature and faulty solution of the dilemma of their loneliness.[16] Love has given them a reason for living, the love-object filling the conscious mind to the extent that it disguises existence's void. Take away the idol, and a blank would be left which the worshipper would not be strong enough to face.

In "Mina Laury" (1838), one of the last of the Angrian tales, Charlotte examines this emotional trap. Mina is kept in a location which will reappear in *Jane Eyre*. There it will be called Ferndean Manor, the gloomy haven where Jane and Rochester will spend their married life. Here it is a hunting lodge with the significant French name of *Rivaulx* ("rivals"), an out-of-the-way mansion where Zamorna hides his young mistress from the jealous wrath of his wife. Charlotte's ambivalence toward both her older sister and her mother is mirrored in the complex nature of her Oedipal fictions: Maria Percy, usually the victim of Zenobia's jealousy, is herself an older rival of Mina Laury. Maria is a tortured woman. In fact, of all the characters of the novella only Zamorna is relatively happy. But the most tormented of all is Lord Hartford, a middle-aged man who has the audacity to try to seduce Mina away from her master. The attempt fails. In his anguish the rejected suitor can only think to fight a duel with Zamorna. Not that he believes it would gain him anything; it is simply that anguish must find its outlet in aggression. Zamorna wounds Hartford mortally, and then tells Mina what he has done: "She said not a word, for now Zamorna's arms were again folded round her, and again he was soothing her to tranquillity by endearments and caresses that far away removed all thought of the world, all past pangs of shame, all cold doubts, all weariness, all heart-sickness resulting from hope long deferred. . . . She lost her identity; her very life was swallowed up in that of another."[17] Angrian love is psychic suicide. Like the sage Manfred's elixir of life in "The Foundling," it solves life's puzzle too effectively; its victims, cuddled in the possessive embrace of the man who owns them, will never search further for meaning. A piece of property defines itself through reference to its owner. With so many dying around them the young women of Angria cling to an idol who will help them forget their mortality. The protagonists of Charlotte's adult novels, however, will not be so easily trapped by the paralyzing solution to the problem of emptiness which Angria poses. Unattached, all of them orphaned, they will have to ask who they are, not simply whose they are.

By the time she wrote "Mina Laury," Charlotte was becoming more and more aware of the psychological fetters which the shape of the Angrian world placed on her mind. Angria had served its purpose; for well over a decade it had provided her with the means of working through her grief and her loneliness. But its solutions were immature and its boundaries, established by years of description, could not be stretched to cover the adult woman's soberer sense of reality. In a fragment probably written in 1839, Charlotte expressed her resolve to break out of her imaginative confinement:

> I have now written a great many books and for a
> long time have dwelt on the same characters and scenes
> and subjects. I have shown my landscapes in every
> variety of shade and light which the morning, noon,
> and evening—the rising, the meridian and the setting
> sun can bestow upon them. . . . So it is with persons.
> My readers have been habituated to one set of fea-
> tures. . . . but we must change, for the eye is tired of
> the picture so often recurring and now so familiar.
>
> Yet do not urge me too fast, reader: it is no easy
> theme to dismiss from my imagination the images
> which have filled it so long; they were my friends and
> my intimate acquaintances, and I could with little
> labour describe to you the faces, the voices, the actions,
> of those who peopled my thoughts by day, and not
> seldom stole strangely even into my dreams by night.
> When I depart from these I feel almost as if I stood
> on the threshhold of a home and were bidding fare-
> well to its inmates. When I strive to conjure up new
> inmates I feel as if I had got into a distant country
> where every face was unknown and the character of
> all the population an enigma which it would take
> much study to comprehend and much talent to ex-
> pound. Still, I long to quit for awhile that burning

clime where we have sojourned too long—its skies
flame—the glow of sunset is always upon it—the
mind would cease from excitement and turn now to
a cooler region where the dawn breaks grey and sober,
and the coming day for a time at least is subdued by
clouds. (2: 403–404)

It was to take Charlotte several more years before she
could leave the cruelly familiar homeland of her imagination. Before she could break away imaginatively, she had
to go to Belgium and act out her sense of exile. And that
would not happen until 1842. Four years later, after two
years in a foreign country and two more years of separation
from the object of her own worship, Heger, she finally left
her fictional home to become a professional novelist. For the
rest of her life she looked back on Angria with an expatriot's fondness, drawing constantly on the experiences of her
childhood game for the characters and incidents of her
novels.[18] She would never feel comfortable in the realistic
middle-class world of the Victorian novelist, but her very
discomfort would be her greatest advantage. For in her
impatience with the attenuated minutiae of the novel of
manners, she would turn to the only subject she knew
thoroughly, the soul's hunger.[19] And her work would attain a psychological depth which the English novel had not
known since Richardson.

Chapter Three
Possession: The Professor

CHARLOTTE BRONTË'S first novel represents a conscious attempt to tone down the shrill rhetoric of Angria and, at the same time, an unconscious and unsuccessful attempt to escape from the theme of death and remorse which had obsessed the author's imagination for so many years. *The Professor* tries to be a book about everyday, surface reality, about a world where people concentrate on the struggle for success, and the more profound problem of death has gone underground. The garish sunsets of Angria have been abandoned for the bracing if sooty atmosphere of the industrial revolution. Yet even in this, Brontë's most resolutely realistic and optimistic novel, there is a disturbing undertone of melancholy which cannot be fully accounted for by the incidents of the manifest plot. The tone of the novel is frequently reminiscent of Defoe, but Brontë cannot sustain the earlier writer's single-minded concentration on the struggle for economic survival. For the past keeps getting in the way of the present and future; the sense of a world irretrievably lost clouds over the world which lies before the protagonist, waiting to be gained.

For Charlotte Brontë, the very act of composition constitutes an elegiac celebration of the past, of lost worlds. Her first novel is a creative reminiscence of the Brussels experience, of a time now dead, and the imagination serves as a means of resuscitation. William Crimsworth, her narrator-protagonist, calls up images from his youth: "Belgium! I repeat the word, now as I sit alone near midnight. It stirs my world of the past like a summons to resurrection; the graves unclose, the dead are raised."[1] The passage is indicative of the distance Brontë has already travelled from Angria; it is a sign that the transition to maturity is well under way. Angria had been a magic land, but in her adult-hood, creativity is the only effective form of necromancy left. There are no genii. But the creative imagination can perform their duties, can blend the past into the present, call it from the grave and give it an objective and abiding reality by molding it into written language. Transformed into a palpable thing, a novel, the past can thus be fully possessed. And in that way death can be overcome, if only precariously.

Brontë's four novels serve essentially the same psychological function as her juvenilia: they provide her with a series of worlds she can control, an array of settings where she is free to project her deepest human needs. The precise nature of the problems she is dealing with changes as the author matures and as the external circumstances of her life develop and modify. Yet underlying all the superficial shifts, all the waves and eddies of her mind, is one unresolved, unresolvable question whose dark outline is always at least faintly visible through the surface layer of the novels: whether it is better to live or die.

Her protagonists decide that question temporarily for her; they come down on the side of life. But not without a struggle. Each novel approaches the brink of the void in Brontë's mind more closely; in each successive book the protagonist is poised more precariously and for a longer period of time over the gulf before setting off resolutely on the road back to life. By the end of her career the longing for death will cancel out the fear of dissolution.

The Professor stands at the beginning of her career, and William Crimsworth, its protagonist, is in no great or immediate danger of following the call of his mind toward darkness. Like his creator, he tries hard to concentrate on the plain and homely aspects of existence, to ignore the imaginative drift of his psyche. Yet even William can hear death's song. At the very moment when he seems to have attained success and love he hears a voice cry: "In the midst of life we are in death" (p. 202). For more than a week the goddess Hypochondria remains at his side, driving him to thoughts of suicide: "She would discourse to me of her own country—the grave—and again and again promise to conduct me there ere long; and, drawing me to the very brink of a black, sullen river, show me, on the other side, shores unequal with mound, monument, and tablet, standing up in a glimmer more hoary than moonlight. 'Necropolis!' she would whisper, pointing to the pale piles, and add, 'It contains a mansion prepared for you' " (p. 202). William resists the gentle tug toward the black river by holding fast to the things of this life. Thus, although he despises the capitalist world into which he was born, he shares that world's need to acquire. For acquisition gives shape and meaning to his existence, fills up the void; the things he obtains will form a wall which might save him from his own vague attraction toward darkness. It is this polarity, the tension between the dark formlessness of death and the comforting outlines of the world and its goods, which gives the novel its interest.[2]

William does not understand the nature of his compulsion to acquire things until, having fallen in love, he experiences a moment of revelation: " 'If ever I possess a home, it must be of my own making, and the task is yet to begin.' And, as I spoke, a pang, new to me, shot across my heart: it was a pang of mortification at the humility of my position, and the inadequacy of my means; while with that pang was born a strong desire to do more, earn more, be more, possess more" (pp. 153–154). The final subordinate clause is fascinating. What is "born" in that clause is merely a desire. The fulfillment of that desire, the finished product of existence—"be more"—is apparently the result of activity, reward, and possession. Only in that way can existence successfully, if temporarily, vanquish dissolution, nothingness. The proof of a secure identity lies in what one has done, what one has earned, and what one owns. Middle-aged William Crimsworth, the narrator, is a solid burgher, pulling up the past from his memory like old claret from a bin; he has constructed an identity whose outlines are clear. The novel is primarily about that process of construction, about a young man's struggle to put together a viable self, one which is stable enough to withstand the pressure of dissolution.

The Angrian narratives had centered around death

itself. Brontë's first novel concerns the long aftermath of early bereavement. Having lost his parental models early in life, Crimsworth arrives at the threshold of adulthood with no real idea of what it means to be an adult. He does not know how to act or even who to be. Throughout the novel he will lunge at an identity like a swimmer struggling toward a safe shore.

In Crimsworth's eyes the best proof of a secure identity seems to be masculinity. His doubts about his own manhood—doubts which reflect his creator's ambivalence about questions of gender—force him into an exaggerated rhetoric of male heartiness in the first chapter of the book, and continue to plague his language throughout the novel.[3] They can be seen most clearly in the images of armor to which he periodically reverts. Human relationships are battles to be fought, and he walks into them weighted down with the rubble of knighthood. "I thought he was trying to read my character, but I felt as secure against his scrutiny as if I had had on a casque with the visor down" (p. 15), he remarks on being introduced to a fellow clerk. And later: "I came to the counting-house prepared, and managed to receive [Edward's] blasphemous sarcasms, when next levelled at me, on a buckler of impenetrable indifference" (p. 17). The armor seems to be an indication of the brittleness of Crismsworth's psyche. The world is a threatening place; identity can only be attained and preserved through continuous warfare, so armor becomes a necessity. Like a little boy's toy sword, it gives him a feeling of masculine strength.

But the imagery of knighthood is matched and undercut by another set of images which seem at first sight very different. His Belgian employer, a perceptive man, notices something strange about William: "Any woman sinking her shaft deep enough, will at last reach a fathomless spring of sensibility in thy breast" (p. 79). Later William himself remarks: "Still [Mlle. Reuter] persevered, and at last, I am bound to confess it, her finger, essaying, proving every atom of the casket, touched its secret spring, and for a moment the lid sprung open; she laid her hand on the jewel within; whether she stole and broke it, or whether the lid shut again with a snap on her fingers, read on, and you shall know" (p. 90). Here again a delicate interior is protected by a tough exterior, but the metaphors are distinctly feminine. Though he prefers to see himself encased in masculine reserve, he is really quite feminine, guarding the jewel of his sensitivity like a maiden her virtue.[4]

Whether masculine or feminine, however, the self is a precious, fragile substance, encased for its protection against the encroachments of a threatening external world. Life for William Crimsworth is a nearly unremitting series of struggles against powerful, at times insidious enemies. Maturation thus becomes the result of accumulated victories.

Crimsworth is the first literary character whom Brontë ever allowed to develop and mature, and the route he takes to adulthood is illuminating. In order to attain psychological independence and maturity, he has to defeat first a sibling and then a mother-figure. They are precisely the two figures—albeit under different masks—who had tormented the author throughout the juvenilia.

Crimsworth's sibling combat occurs on the masculine battlefield of trade.[5] A friend tells him: "It is you, William, who are the aristocrat of your family, and you are not as fine a fellow as your plebeian brother by a long chalk" (p. 20). He must show the world and himself that he is more of a man than his brother. This is one of the primary psychological advantages of the use of a masculine protagonist for Brontë. It distances the idea of sibling rivalry, removes it from the psychologically dangerous arena of struggle with an elder sister.[6]

The threatening nature of the struggle is softened in another way as well, by placing it within the confines of a factory counting-house. William had come to Bigben Close to work as a clerk for Edward, but the older brother's tyranny had forced him to rebel. In Angria the rebellion would have entailed bloodshed. But the rivalry of the Crimsworths, befitting a novel which claims to rivet its interest on the "real" world, plays itself out in business terms: "[Edward] feared that I too should one day make a successful tradesman" (p. 24). The world of Angrian extremes has not been totally abandoned: Edward owns a whip which he likes to flourish, and William compares himself to a slave, stretching the metaphor at one point to become Israel in Egypt. But when William has finally broken the whip and freed himself from his older brother's oppression, Edward still lives. Angrian melodrama, though it still survives, has exchanged its gaudy costume for a drab suit in workaday England, where homicidal anger must be softened.

From Bigben Close William moves to Brussels and a new battleground. His Belgian antagonist, Mlle. Zoraïde Reuter, is a figure who had troubled Brontë for years. Or rather she is an avatar of two figures, one from a real past, the other from a fictive one. Mlle. Reuter's relationship to Mme. Heger, the author's Oedipal rival during her stay in Brussels, is obvious and has been amply documented. But the fact that William's friend, Yorke Hunsden, insists on calling her Zénobie, hints at an older identification: Zoraïde is a mask of Zenobia Ellrington, the maternal rival who had threatened the adolescent heroines of Angria.[7]

This double identification is representative of an aspect of Brontë's novelistic practice which needs comment. Since the publication of Fanny Ratchford's *The Brontës' Web of Childhood* more than three decades ago, there has been a sporadic argument among Brontëans as to the origin of various characters in the novels. Did they come from Angria, or were they products of Charlotte Brontë's "real" life—of her Belgian experience, for example?[8] The choice of one side or another in that debate is simplistic. Usually they came from both places, or more precisely, they *occurred* in both places. They *came* from her deepest needs, arising from the psychological dilemmas which her childhood and her mentality constructed for her. She needed certain characters to work through those dilemmas; she therefore found these characters wherever she looked, both in her everyday life and in the worlds she created. Mrs. Brontë, Zenobia Ellrington, the hag Bertha, Lady Beatrice Ducie, Mrs. Sidgwick, Mrs. White, Mme. Heger, Mlle. Reuter, Sarah Reed, Mme. Walravens—the list is long and entwines Brontë's life and imagination. The women were like land-

marks she had trained herself to recognize in any new landscape, objects she needed in order to take her bearings and
find her way.

Thus it is both significant and predictable that William
Crimsworth should be faced with Mlle. Reuter at the point
where he has just asserted his adulthood for the first time.
Moreover, this wily Belgian is seconded by an entirely
suitable ally, M. Pelet. His name derives from the French
pelé—"the bald one"—and serves as a reminder of an
important fact about the man: he is old enough to be William's father. The older man in fact likes to refer to Crimsworth as *mon fils*.

This fatherly man points out to Crimsworth that there
would be a piquant hint of incest in an alliance with Mlle.
Reuter: "*Elle est . . . plus âgée que toi peut-être, mais juste
assez pour unir la tendresse d'une petite maman à l'amour
d'une épouse dévouée*" (p. 79—"She is perhaps older than
you, but just enough to unite the tenderness of a little
mother with the love of a devoted wife"). The suggestion
disgusts Crimsworth: "No, Monsieur; I should like my
wife to be my wife, and not half my mother" (p. 79). The
arrangement, in other words, would be a classic Oedipal
trap, a dangerous obstacle in the way of Crimsworth's passage to full maturity.

William escapes from this new threat to the self through
a coincidence whose significance has been overlooked in
criticism of the novel. His bedroom at M. Pelet's is tiny,
like a child's chamber. One of its windows looks out onto
an *allée défendue*—literally, a "forbidden path"—of the
garden belonging to Mlle. Reuter's school for girls. When
he contemplates this window, which has been boarded up
to guard against voyeurism, William becomes strangely
excited: "The first thing I did was to scrutinise closely the
nailed boards, hoping to find some chink or crevice which
I might enlarge, and so get a peep at the consecrated
ground. My researches were vain, for the boards were well
joined and strongly nailed. It is astonishing how disap-
pointed I felt. . . . Not only then, but many a time after,
especially in moments of weariness and low spirits, did

I look with dissatisfied eyes on that most tantalising board, longing to tear it away and get a glimpse of the green region which I imagined to lie beyond" (pp. 54–55).

The *allée défendue* with its surrounding garden is a forbidden paradise, consecrated to the pleasure of young girls, and, more importantly, to the coy enticements of Mlle. Reuter herself. But as an Eden where Crimsworth's *petite maman* tests her sexual attractiveness, it is for him a forbidden paradise, a "consecrated ground" which he is not allowed to view. William frees himself from Mlle. Reuter's threat to his independent existence by spying on this holy and taboo area. Having managed to get the boards taken down from the window, he sits idly wondering where Zoraïde's bedroom is located and contemplating marriage. Suddenly he stops: "I ceased to think, that I might listen more intently. . . . What murmur was that which, low, and yet near and approaching nearer, frustrated the expectation of total silence?" (p. 94). The sound is the quiet love-chat of Mlle. Reuter and M. Pelet. William listens horrified while the two affirm their love for one another and laugh at the foolish amorousness of the young Englishman.

Crimsworth is liberated by becoming the unwilling witness to the intimacy of the older couple in this consecrated and forbidden ground where they meet at night. Within a few pages he expresses to the reader his sense of mastery over both M. Pelet and Mlle. Reuter.

With the conquest of the parental threat to his independence, he has succeeded in proving his maturity to himself and, apparently, to his author. It is a maturity marked by a strange hypermasculinity, a domineering brutality worthy of his brother Edward. His attitude toward his students is a good example of his hostility toward the world in general: "There was a pause, during which I regarded them all with a steady and somewhat stern gaze; a dog, if stared at hard enough and long enough, will show symptoms of embarrassment, and so at length did my bench of Belgians" (p. 53). This "masculine" hardness has successfully covered over the "feminine" vulnerability of his nature. He has used his manly ability to concentrate on the present,

on the task at hand, to struggle and fight his way to adulthood and a position of some authority. And it is at precisely
this stage of his development that his feminine alter ego,
Frances Henri, enters the novel.

With the introduction of Frances into *The Professor*,
Brontë begins to find her proper subject as a writer. For
at this point her interest begins to shift from the masculine
narrator of the story to the young woman struggling to
make her way in an alien world. At bottom, William and
Frances are best seen as masks of the same character, facets
of Charlotte's attempt to come to terms with her own painful experiences as a pupil-teacher in Brussels. They are the
same figure split off into a masculine and a feminine representative.[9] The teacher, William Crimsworth, his shy sensitivity successfully hidden behind a baleful manly stare,
confronts and conquers his enemies. His pupil, Frances
Henri, is strong, persevering, but shows very little aggression. Her very name indicates her potentially androgenous
nature—the name Frances Henri, like Currer Bell, is very
nearly masculine—but she has no need to assert masculine
aggressiveness since William is there. She is thus left, at
least at first, to concentrate on suffering.

Brontë is still too reticent to construct a full woman, with
anything like the full range of a woman's problems and
possible responses. But her tentative approaches to Frances'
psychology are crucial to her development as a novelist.
For example, there is Frances' attitude toward teaching:
"Her success as a teacher rested partly, perhaps chiefly, upon
the will of others; it cost her a most painful effort to enter
into conflict with this foreign will, to endeavour to bend
it into subjection to her own" (p. 114). Jane Eyre will
combine Frances' shyness with the quiet ferocity of William. The passage is the first full enunciation of the character profile which nearly all the later protagonists will
share and attempt to overcome. All of them except Shirley
Keeldar have been subdued by early sorrow into nearly
total passivity. If left alone they would prefer to peer out
at life from a shadowed window, soundlessly tapping their
fingers to the muffled rhythms of the world outside. But the

world impinges. Though they shrink from the roughness of human interaction, they must all, like Frances, "enter into conflict with [a] foreign will."

The introduction of Frances turns the novel away from William's single-minded concentration on present and future. Frances too knows that there is a world which must be gained, but she is much more willing than her male counterpart to dwell on worlds which have been lost. Her latent power as well as her deep melancholy come to light in a *devoir* she writes for Crimsworth. Here too she resembles the later heroines; their quiet exteriors can only be penetrated when one takes the trouble to examine their art. Frances' homework, Jane's paintings, Caroline Helstone's poetry-reading, Lucy Snowe's acting, all become—like Charlotte Brontë's writing—esthetic vehicles for the expression of the inhibited emotions which the women themselves deny. William has fortuitously chosen a homework subject which can call forth from his orphaned, exiled pupil a disguised expression of her own alienation: his students must compose a lament supposedly spoken by Alfred, the English king in lonely retreat from the conquering Danes. Mlle. Henri's Alfred complains: "I, whose inheritance was a kingdom, owe my night's harbourage to a poor serf; my throne is usurped, my crown presses the brow of an invader; I have no friends. . . . Fate! thou hast done thy worst. . . . I do not despair" (pp. 116–117). An exile's lament for a time before the Fall, Alfred's speech expresses the condition of the Brontë protagonists. Despair will be the small black void in their souls against which they will all have to struggle. Frances takes over a language and style which Charlotte Brontë had practiced before in the laments of the exiled Zamorna. In one form or another exile will remain the central theme of her art.

Interestingly enough, it is at this point, when Frances Henri has begun to show a talent for composition which is similar to Brontë's own, that William falls in love with her and Zoraïde Reuter becomes her enemy. On hearing William read another composition by Frances—this one an emigrant's letter from America to the friends he left at home—Zoraïde realizes how powerful her young rival

really is. The letter brings in the themes of Brontëan isolation: "Past days were spoken of; the grief of parting, the
regrets of absence, were touched upon; feeling, forcible and
fine, breathed eloquent in every period" (p. 132). Zoraïde
cannot, like some elderly Angrian siren, kill her young
rival. But she can and does send her into exile, banish her to
the Rue Notre Dame aux Neiges ("the Street of our Lady
of the Snows"), a location implying a cold virginity. And
at that point the nature of the novel seems to change.

In introducing Frances into the novel, Brontë has moved
closer to the complex of ideas which have troubled her
throughout most of her life. What had been buried under
truculent reserve in William's character—exile, separation,
loneliness, the fear of inadequacy—rises to the surface
in Frances' consciousness. But Brontë could not open herself up to the emotions which accompany bereavement and
still outrun the thought of death itself. As long as her creative attention had centered only on William, then death
could be held at bay through a single-minded concentration
on William's problem of getting ahead. But the entrance
of Frances opens the door to the thought of death. The
novel moves, in a seemingly random but psychologically
compelling fashion, from exile to the grave.

For the grave is where William finds his banished pupil.
After days of searching, he discovers Frances seated beside
the tombstone of her aunt in the Protestant Cemetery. In
real life it is a place which Charlotte Brontë visited time
and again, the site where her friend Martha Taylor was
buried.[10] In bringing William and Frances together in that
cemetery, she seems to be giving up, albeit perhaps only
unconsciously, her novelistic attempt to run away from the
central concerns of her psyche: "I little thought to have discovered my lost sheep straying amongst graves," William
intones (p. 149). But that is precisely where a Brontëan
lost sheep would wander.

The two of them stray among graves, but they do not
die. William leads his pupil back into life: "I drew her
arm through mine, and led her out of the cemetery" (p.
149). The faculty which holds Crimsworth back from the
grave, the quality which allows him and his alter ego to

remain safely in this life, is his embattled reason. He talks about his regrettable tendency to dream from time to time in the novel, but we are seldom allowed to glimpse into the fantasy life of this reticent man. What we do see allows us to assume that two important fantasies have to do with human intimacy and with death. Furthermore, the two thoughts seem somehow connected; for William the avoidance of human intimacy seems to be one means of staving off thoughts of death. We can see the psychological connection at work in the courtship section of the novel.

William in love is a fascinating spectacle. Throughout his courtship his mental faculties are at war; the captains of the opposing armies are reason and imagination. Imagination whispers suggestions of intimacy to him, and intimacy might prove fatal. But lifesaving reason normally prevails, and William remains unharmed. Thus he reports with smug relief his sage departure from Mlle. Henri's apartment: "I had much ado to resist a strong inward impulse, urging me to take a warmer, more expressive leave; what so natural as to fold her for a moment in a close embrace, to imprint one kiss on her cheek or forehead? . . . and Reason denied me even this; she ordered me to . . . quit her as dryly and coldly as I would have quitted old Madame Pelet" (p. 156).

If he cannot maintain that inhibited attitude, then he will not go near the woman he loves. Later he tries to decide whether it would be safe to visit Frances, and the internal battle heats up. The first to enter the lists is the enemy: "Imagination began with her low whispers, infusing into my soul the soft tale of pleasures that might be" (p. 176). But Crimsworth is strong: " 'I will *not* go,' was my answer to the sweet temptress. 'A man is master of himself to a certain point, but not beyond it. Could I seek Frances tonight, . . . and address her only in the language of Reason and Affection?' 'No,' was the brief, fervent reply of that Love which had conquered and now controlled me" (p. 177). William and reason conquer their common enemy, the insidious temptress who hints that William's terror of human contact can be overcome, that isolation is not to be equated with virtue. William fights on the side of the encapsulated self without knowing it.

When William finally gives in to his imagination, when he takes his first tentative step toward a timid intimacy, the consequences are nearly fatal. His marriage proposal to Frances is answered with a kiss. Typically, he treats kissing as a complicated business transaction in which an exact equivalency of exchange must be reached. After the "sweet delirium" of love's barter, he goes home, falls asleep, and awakes to his week-long bout with thoughts of suicide. His explanation of the severe attack is striking: "Man is ever clogged with his mortality, and it was my mortal nature which now faltered and plained; my nerves, which jarred and gave a false sound, because the soul, of late rushing headlong to an aim, had overstrained the body's comparative weakness. A horror of great darkness fell upon me" (p. 202). To give in, however slightly, to the felt needs of the body is to invite the call of death. The body, a human being's "mortal nature," is definable through its affinity to death. To align oneself with one's body is thus almost by definition to become "clogged with mortality."

Yet William wins out over his imagination's siren call toward intimacy and death. And even neurotic victories bring prizes in this novel. Within two paragraphs of William's first defeat of his imagination, his friend Yorke Hunsden arrives from England with the victor's spoils. After a bit of verbal sparring, Hunsden asks a startling question: "You know, of course, that your brother failed three months ago?" (p. 184).

Edward Crimsworth's business affairs have been forgotten for sixteen chapters. They seem to reenter the novel gratuitously at this point. But Charlotte Bronë has a much more severe sense of the logic of narrative construction than is commonly supposed. The problem is that part of that logic is unconscious.

Charlotte herself was fascinated with the partially unconscious nature of creativity. In apologizing for Emily's *Wuthering Heights*, she remarks:

> This I know; the writer who possesses the creative
> gift owns something of which he is not always mas-
> ter—something that at times strangely wills and works
> for itself. He may lay down rules and devise prin-

ciples, and to rules and principles it will perhaps for
years lie in subjection; and then . . . comes a time
when it will no longer consent . . . As for you—the
nominal artist—your share in [creation will then be]
to work passively under dictates you neither delivered
nor could question—that would not be uttered at your
prayer, nor suppressed nor changed at your caprice.[11]

Edward's problems seem to enter the novel at the behest
of this unconscious gift. In the creative dynamics of the
novel the final defeat of William's older brother comes as
no coincidence at this point. For William has just proven
himself master of his own rebellious imagination. He is
rewarded for virtue with the report of his brother's downfall. In Angria Edward would perhaps have died; in capitalist Europe it is enough that he go bankrupt.

Even in the bracingly practical world of the industrial
revolution, however, Brontë's old dream has not faded
completely, and the compulsive pattern must be carried to
its finish. If one's wish has come true and one's sibling has
failed, then one must rescind the tragic consequences of
aggression. Yorke Hunsden quickly relieves William of any
possible sense of guilt for the fulfillment of his resentment
against his brother: "Don't be alarmed; he put himself
under the protection of the court, compounded with his
creditors . . . in six weeks set up again, coaxed back his
wife, and is flourishing like a green bay-tree" (p. 184).
But Edward has at any rate fallen, if only temporarily, and
there is one crucial emblem of his ascendancy over William
which he will never recover.

He had owned the only portrait of their mother, a painting which for William had been both a shrine and an emblem of his alienation from his brother's milieu: "No fibre
of sympathy united me to any living thing in [my brother's] house; I looked for and found my mother's picture.
I took a wax-taper from a stand, and held it up. I gazed
long, earnestly; my heart grew to the image" (p. 18).
Now, nineteen chapters later, William becomes the possessor of that picture. For the portrait of his mother was
sold in auction during Edward's bankruptcy, and Yorke

Hunsden bought it. Like a fairy gift, it is left at William's door while he sleeps.

Brontë writes in the "Author's Preface" that Crimsworth was to receive nothing that he had not earned. The gift seems at first sight to break that resolve. But her protagonist really has earned the portrait of his mother; his chastity has brought him the suprarational wages he had longed for. The rules of business existence have not been broken; they have been transferred to a different plane of meaning.

On awakening the young bachelor discovers this ultimate prize of his virtue: "A listener . . . might have heard me, after ten minutes' silent gazing, utter the word 'Mother!'" (p. 186). William now owns the prime possession, the talisman which will ward off despair if anything can. His existence is no longer empty; with the image of his mother hanging safe on his wall he can stride into life a natural conquerer. The joyful shout of filial recognition, the orphan's triumphant "Mother!" marks the turning point in Crimsworth's fortunes. The dispossessed has become the possessor. Within a page the formerly shy protagonist can deal with Victor Vandenhuten, one of the richest men of Brussels, with condescension: "I had not sat five minutes alone with him in his bureau, before I became aware of a sense of ease in his presence, such as I rarely experienced with strangers . . . my mind . . . instinctively assumed and kept the predominance" (p. 187).[12] Unto every one that hath shall be given: within a few pages of the reception of his mother's portrait, Crimsworth goes from unemployment to an assured annual income of 6000 francs. Within a dozen pages he has won Frances' hand. Moreover, his full ownership of his future wife is certain; with stunning complacency, Crimsworth tells the reader that Frances is "as stirless in her happiness as a mouse in its terror" (p. 199).

It must be admitted that the portrait is a serious flaw in the novel. Brontë normally controlled and channeled her psychological concerns, in her art if not in her life. They became the source of her creative power. But there are times in her art when they become the source of weakness. It is artistically inept, though true to her own experience, that she should see a portrait of his mother as the most important of William's possessions, almost the badge of his adulthood.

At any rate, though the portrait is crucial to Crimsworth's sense of identity, it cannot give him much respite from his need to struggle with the world. Nor can any of his other possessions. Returning to England from their exile, he and his wife will end the book in snug middle age, portioning out complacency and tea in a bourgeois paradise called Daisy Lane. William will indeed have done more, earned more, owned more, and—if he is right—thus been more. But there are disturbing hints that the tiny black void will not have been outrun, that his trellised porch, his lawn furniture, his roses and his ivy, his silver and his porcelain, and even his mother's picture, will not suffice to buffer him from life's ache or from his periodic fascination with death. For his dilemma is not merely external, and he cannot litter his existence with enough trinkets to protect him from his own mind.

Ultimately Crimsworth's attempt to construct a secure identity fails for the same reason that Charlotte Brontë's attempt to restrict herself to realism fails. Neither William nor Charlotte can escape from the obsession with death that holds their imagination in thrall. There is a disturbing undertone of jealousy and resultant violence which undercuts the nominally placid ending of the novel. The final section of the book resembles a novel of manners superficially, but the surface is only a thin veil covering Angrian rage.

The problem is that William is at bottom an insecure man, and he cannot entirely overcome his impulse to struggle against an enemy, to fight off threats, whether real or imagined. He finds an enemy in the person of his son Victor. Something about the boy bothers him: "Though still, he is not unhappy—though serious, not morose; he has a susceptibility to pleasurable sensations almost too keen, for it amounts to enthusiasm" (p. 233). We do not have to search far for the radical source of Victor's susceptibility to pleasure; as William himself knows, it stems from maternal affection.

Motherly love was a subject which bothered Brontë all her life, a concern to which she returned repeatedly both in her letters and in her art. She apparently could not remember her mother showing her any affection, but she could recall the woman cuddling Branwell. *The Professor* contains a scene which seems to be psychologically analogous to this childhood reminiscence: "[Frances] bent above the pillow and hung over a child asleep; its slumber . . . was sound and calm; no tear wet its dark eyelashes; no fever heated its round cheek; no ill dream discomposed its budding features. Frances gazed, she did not smile, and yet the deepest delight filled, flushed her face" (p. 225).

But in order to visit her little boy's cradle, Frances must turn for a moment from her husband, whose reaction can be judged by his vocabulary: "Always at nine o'clock I was left—abandoned" (pp. 224–225). Crimsworth can report the bedroom scene so precisely because in his jealousy he spies on his wife: "I have followed her sometimes and watched her. . . . I followed and observed her . . . I saw . . . her heart heave, her lips were a little apart, her breathing grew somewhat hurried" (p. 225). The sibling rivalry which the novelist had tracked obsessively through the Angrian cycle, and which had controlled the opening chapters of *The Professor*, has been transformed into the struggle between William and his son.

Earlier criticism of the novel has taken due note of the probability that William's strictures against coddling a son reflect Charlotte's disapproval of her brother's education and its unfortunate consequences. But there is more to William's attitude than simple rational disagreement. His disapproval of the child's upbringing is only the surface of a thoroughgoing resentment of Victor, a resentment which in all probability mirrors Charlotte's own attitude toward the coddled male of her family.

Little Victor is after all a subtly dangerous threat to his insecure father. For one thing he is already, like his father, a collector, slowly building up around him the evidence of his existence: "For those [things] he possesses, he seems to have contracted a partiality amounting to affection; this feeling, directed towards one or two living animals of the house, strengthens almost to a passion" (p. 233).

Daisy Lane is not large, and the efforts of two collectors would produce a clutter intolerable to William's sensibilities. He demands neatness in his surroundings; he can stand neither physical nor mental untidiness. So it bothers William that his son becomes angry when he shoots Victor's dog. Hearing that his son's favorite pet might possibly be rabid, he had reacted immediately, without waiting for preliminary symptoms of disease: "I went into the yard and shot him where he lay licking his wound: he was dead in an instant" (p. 233). Although William insists that he meant well—"it was my affection for [the dog] and [Victor] which had made me act so" (p. 234)—the boy is quite troubled. His mother, caught between the needs of her two males, explains to the boy that his father is not really as cruel as he seems. William solemnly describes to the reader the outcome of the strange incident: "Some hours after, he came to me in my library, asked if I forgave him, and desired to be reconciled. I drew the lad to my side, and there I kept him a good while, and had much talk with him, in the course of which he disclosed many points of feeling and thought I approved of in my son" (p. 234). Even in Daisy Lane Brontë's old Angrian drama of jealousy, revenge, and remorse must still be played out. But Crimsworth has the advantage of adulthood over his son, and so, though he is the killer, he can be the one who forgives. "Victor learns fast," his father comments (p. 235).

Even this object lesson in the danger of becoming too attached is not enough, however. William still feels that his son is too soft. He has found a way to toughen him, though: "[Victor] must soon go to Eton, where, I suspect, his first year or two will be utter wretchedness" (p. 235). Banishment to his father's old school will have the salutary effect of turning the boy into a man just like his father: "To leave me, his mother, and his home, will give his heart an agonised wrench; then, the fagging will not suit him—but emulation, thirst after knowledge, and the glory of success, will stir and reward him in time" (p. 235). And while this boy with the threatening name of Victor grows up in exile, acquiring the social goad of alienation, his father will sit in tenuous security in Daisy Lane, sole owner of everything around him.

William Crimsworth has thus established an identity—however insecure—and defended it against all opponents. He has impressed the image of his self on the external world. Everything in his environment mirrors his personality, and when the time comes for him to leave the safe shore of his identity, to forsake his possessions and swim out into the darkness of death, Crimsworth will at least have left behind traces of himself, proof that he has lived.

Brontë seems to have been unaware of the many ironies inherent in the final section of her novel. She seems to have viewed Crimsworth as a model of firm righteousness, a paragon of fatherly concern. Instead, he is a man too insecure to be affectionate. William's impulse to kill Victor's dog is almost certainly a reflection of a deeper impulse to kill Victor. Rage is softened in this novel, and homicidal envy finds its release in a strange form of preventive medicine. The novelist has avoided, not confronted, the issue of rivalry between her protagonist and his son.

But there are greater problems than anger which are avoided in the book. Above all there is the issue of death. *The Professor* is the only one of the four novels in which death is not central. Yet it is there when one looks for it; the small circle of light on which the book concentrates is surrounded by unending darkness. And the darkness has its attractions. For life is ceaseless struggle, and death would be repose. In this first novel, Brontë tries for the most part to ignore those attractions, to keep her eyes resolutely fixed on life. In her second novel she will turn toward the darkness, confronting the impulse toward death and trying to defeat it.

Chapter Four
Innocence: Jane Eyre

Jane Eyre represents the culmination of Charlotte Brontë's esthetic victory over death. In *The Professor*, the struggle between existence and annihilation had been muted, cloaked for the most part in the language of respectability. Befitting a novel about capitalist Europe, life and death had been softened into success and failure, symbolized primarily by the acquisition and loss of goods. But in *Jane Eyre*, Brontë returns to the emotionally charged vocabulary of Angria, and, more importantly, to the central, undisguised issue of the presence of death in the midst of life.

She might have kept trying to skirt this issue if the publishers had let her. She had attempted to run from it, and if *The Professor* had been successful, she might well have continued to write quasi-realistic novels. But *The Professor* fell flat. It was turned down repeatedly by publishers who, according to Charlotte, wanted something "with a taste for pathos, with sentiments more tender, elevated, unworldly" ("Author's Preface," *The Professor*). She accordingly obliged them by writing *Jane Eyre*, presenting the British reading public with one of the most unworldly heroines of the Victorian era. Jane's private world is like the universe she sees in the mirror of the red-room: "All looked colder and darker in that visionary hollow than in reality."[1]

Yet Jane's unworldliness, her shyness and her attraction to the supernatural, do not by any means constitute an attempt to escape the dilemmas of reality. We have seen that the Angrian cycle was a continuing effort to solve the riddle of the relationship between life and death, not run from it. The same is true of *Jane Eyre*.

In the final analysis, Jane cannot afford to run from her central problems: the issues involved are too great. In Brontë's first novel, William Crimsworth could describe his experiences in temperate language, since he carried no grievous burden of personal guilt. He was weighted down only by his fair share of the fruits of original sin: "As Adam's son he should share Adam's doom, and drain throughout life a mixed and moderate cup of enjoyment."[2] The failure of *The Professor* forced Brontë to realize that moderation was not a mode of expression for which she was suited, and in her next novel she opened the gates to the full enormity of her sense of a threatening universe. Guilt-ridden herself, she created a heroine whose sense of guilt resembled her own. Jane Eyre broods on a single, frightening proposition: "All said I was wicked, and perhaps I might be so" (p. 13). It is a problem which Charlotte Brontë had spent a lifetime working out.

For more than a hundred years, critics have recognized that one portion of *Jane Eyre* is particularly relevant to the author's life. Lowood is an imaginative rendering of Cowan Bridge, the school where Charlotte's two older sisters died. Charlotte herself admitted as much, telling Elizabeth Gaskell, moreover, that Helen Burns, Jane's Lowood companion, was an "exact transcript" of her sister Maria (Gaskell, *Life*, p. 44). We have seen the complex nature of Charlotte's reaction to the death of her beloved sister. That reaction, it seems to me, provides the creative impulse behind *Jane Eyre*.

Lowood is Jane's Valley of the Shadow of Death, a charnel house where typhus strikes down forty-five out of eighty girls. But Jane wanders through it unscathed. She will later be reproached for her survival. Sarah Reed will complain: "What did they do with [Jane] at Lowood? The fever broke out there, and many of the pupils died. She, however, did not die; but I . . . wish she had died!" (p. 203). The accusation is, in all probability, an echo of an indictment which a corner of Charlotte Brontë's mind had been making for two decades. For Charlotte, like Jane, refused to die with the others, held on to life with a tenacity which at times must have seemed criminal to her. Sarah Reed gives voice to the accusation which lies at the heart of *Jane Eyre*, the complex problem of survival with which Brontë attempts to come to terms in the novel.

Helen Burns is of course the most important one of those who die at Lowood. Most critics have accepted Charlotte's idealized portrait of her sister at face value, seeing Helen's influence as beneficial to Jane's development.[3] The issue is more complicated than that, however; certainly the little girl is a saint, but that very sainthood is an insidious threat to Jane. For Helen Burns is a creature in love with death. The little admirer of Dr. Johnson's pessimistic tome, *Rasselas*, tries to demonstrate to her friend that all of life is vanity, that no satisfaction is to be found on this earth. Only death will bring fulfillment: "Debasement and sin will fall from us with this cumbrous frame of flesh, and only the spark of spirit will remain. [My creed] makes Eternity a rest—a mighty home, not a terror and an abyss" (p. 51). It is an ingenious solution to the problems of life. The believer can find a parent in God, a rest and a home in Heaven. And all one need do to attain these rewards is die. Despite her benevolence, Jane's friend is a Christian siren who would lure the young pilgrim to her death on the rocks of sanctity.

But Brontë's protagonist is tough-minded. On the day before Helen's death, Jane returns to the school after a romp in the woods. The very fact that so many are dying around them has made life easier for the survivors: "We did what we liked, went where we liked: we lived better too" (p. 67). Some die and some live, and the removal of the dead gives the survivors a spacious freedom they had not known before. It apparently gives them guilt, too, but Jane does not know that. She does realize, however, that life is preferable to death. The sight of the surgeon's pony at the door of Lowood sets off a meditation which is central to the meaning of the novel: "How sad to be lying now on a sick bed, and to be in danger of dying! This world is pleasant—it would be dreary to be called from it, and to have to go who knows where?" (p. 69). Helen knows where and is willing to die. But she would rather not die alone. That same evening, just before midnight, Jane goes to her friend's sickroom. The scene contains echoes of the Angrian fixation on corpses: "I advanced; then paused by the crib side: my hand was on the curtain, but I preferred speaking before I withdrew it. I still recoiled at the dread of seeing a corpse" (p. 70).

Helen is still alive, though barely. To Jane's naïve question—"Are you going somewhere, Helen? Are you going home?"—she gives an alluring answer: "Yes; to my long home—my last home. . . . God is my father . . . You will come to the same region of happiness: be received by the same mighty, universal Parent, no doubt, dear Jane. . . . Don't leave me, Jane: I like to have you near me" (pp. 70–71). Jane makes a promise she cannot, in the nature of things, keep: "I'll stay with you, *dear* Helen: no one shall take me away" (p. 71). But her love is not strong enough; she falls asleep and the nurse carries the child away from the now stiffening corpse. The living cannot remain truly faithful to the dead. Years later Jane will provide Helen's grave with a stone on which is written *Resurgam*— "I shall arise." Jane will remember Helen and regret her death. But she will not join her in any shadowy afterlife if she can help it.

The ambivalence of Charlotte's attitude toward her saintly sister Maria shows through the idealization of the portrait. And near the center of that ambivalence there seems to be a feeling that Maria provided her with an example which she could not, would not follow.

The demise of Helen Burns is of course not in itself the cause of Jane's terror of death. Something has happened years before that event to sharpen her natural instinct to remain alive. Jane has seen death before, and it fascinates and repels her. In the years prior to the opening of the novel, her parents had died. As narrator, Jane lingers over Helen's death, but passes quickly, almost cursorily, over that earlier loss. Her narrative strategy thus resembles Brontë's own attitude toward the death of her mother and her oldest sister: the loss of a sibling provides reinforcement and focus for feelings which originate as repressed reactions to an earlier death, one which is too painful to dwell on.

We can only conjecture, however, about the actual origins of Jane's guilt feelings: perhaps like her creator's, they derive from parental loss. But their origin is unimportant.

The crucial point is that Brontë's most famous heroine serves as a vehicle for working off her own guilt feelings, her own complex attraction for and horror of death. And we have seen where these feelings come from.

As opposed to her rather pedestrian forerunner, William Crimsworth, Jane Eyre inhabits an immense mental universe. She sees her life in apocalyptic terms, hovering precariously in this Middle Kingdom of Earth, avoiding both Hell and Heaven. In her world defeat would not be, as in *The Professor*, temporary bankruptcy; it would be eternal damnation. But victory, too, poses a threat to Jane's integrity, a threat which has been largely overlooked in criticism of the novel. Her avoidance of Helen's example is part of a larger pattern in the novel. Death holds a strong attraction for Jane, and it is this inner compulsion to die which she fights off throughout the novel, not simply external threats. Her need for exoneration from some shadowy guilt opens her up to the temptation of becoming a Christian martyr and submitting to a righteous death in order to be taken off to Heaven.

The catechism scene with Brocklehurst provides a good example of Jane's dilemma:

> "What must you do to avoid [Hell]?"
> "I must keep in good health and not die." (p. 27)

Jane's answer is a childish expression of a complex problem. In order to prove her innocence, Jane has to confront her sense of sin. At the same time, in order to live, she has to conquer her own need to die. Thus in Jane's mind, the will to avoid death and the will to believe in her innocence coalesce. To grow sick and die would simply be the logical consequence of her sense of guilt; to remain healthy is a moral struggle in the face of her need to punish herself for crimes whose nature she does not understand. Therefore she cannot give Brocklehurst the answer he wants; she cannot tell him that she will be good and go to Heaven. For Heaven, like Hell, presupposes death.

Much of what earlier criticism thought of as Jane's dreamy, romantic nature can be traced back to this fixation on death. It shows up in the books she chooses to read, the poems she remembers, the artifacts she looks at, the art she herself creates. The paintings she shows to Rochester provide a good example of the texture of her mind.

But not just *Jane*'s mind. In a seminal article on the paintings, Laurence E. Moser suggests that the pictures can be fruitfully examined with the aid of "the surrealistic tenet that art of necessity mirrors the artist's personality and mentality, in this case both Jane's and Charlotte's, and tends violently toward a complete revelation of self."[4] Moser's point is well taken. And, as he notes, what the paintings reveal about Jane and Charlotte is their attitude toward death and separation.

The second painting seems the most mysterious. Unlike the first and the third there seems to be no drive toward narrative in the second picture at all. It is, Jane tells us, a symbolic portrait of the evening star: "Rising into the sky was a woman's shape to the bust. . . . The dim forehead was crowned with a star; . . . the eyes shone dark and wild; the hair streamed shadowy, like a beamless cloud torn by storm or by electric travail" (p. 110). The seemingly threatening supernatural figure will appear in other guises throughout the novel—as the moon, as Mother Nature, as an anthropomorphic figure whom Jane calls "Mother." Throughout the novel the sky will be filled with cosmic reactions to, and portents of, Jane's adventures. Although we cannot tell what emotion the figure in the painting is experiencing—whether agony or maenadic frenzy or anger—the power of the heavenly woman is obvious. Jane's world contains God, but—like Charlotte's—it also includes a potentially hostile female presence which looks down on the attempts of a young girl to make her way through this life.

The first painting can be seen as a strange variant of a figure which Brontë had portrayed over and over again since her childhood. Like an Angrian mourner, a cormorant stares at a corpse: "The first represented . . . a swollen sea. [It contained] a half-submerged mast, on which sat a cormorant, dark and large . . . : its beak held a gold bracelet, set with gems. . . . Sinking below the bird and mast, a drowned corpse glanced through the green water;

a fair arm was the only limb clearly visible, whence the bracelet had been washed or torn" (p. 110). But two elements are missing from the older Angrian pattern. In the first place, there is no possibility of resurrection implied in Jane's painting.[5] And secondly, the survivor suffers no remorse. Because it is inhuman, the carrion creature need feel no emotion at all. In fact it has stolen the jewels of the dead.

In the plot of the novel, Jane will do her best to avoid the cormorant's crime. She will be horrified when, during their engagement, she hears that Rochester plans to give her jewelry that once belonged to his mother: "Oh, sir!—never mind jewels! I don't like to hear them spoken of. Jewels for Jane Eyre sounds unnatural and strange: I would rather not have them" (p. 227). And when she finally flees Thornfield, she will leave behind a symbol of her close brush with sinful audacity: "I encountered the beads of a pearl necklace Mr. Rochester had forced me to accept a few days ago. I left that; it was not mine" (p. 281). To wear fine jewelry, particularly Rochester's family heirlooms, passed from the dead to the living, would be to turn a symbol of guilt which the girl has kept hidden in the recesses of her mind or in cryptic art, into a public badge of shame. For Jane, as for Charlotte Brontë, survival itself is apparently a form of grave robbing, a theft of life from the dead. And thievery ought to be punished.

Punishment is implied in the third painting:

> The third showed the pinnacle of an iceberg piercing a polar winter sky: a muster of northern lights reared their dim lances, close serried, along the horizon. Throwing these into distance, rose, in the foreground, a head,—a colossal head, inclined toward the iceberg, and resting against it. Two thin hands, joined under the forehead, and supporting it, drew up before the lower features a sable veil; a brow quite bloodless, white as bone, and an eye hollow and fixed, blank of meaning but for the glassiness of despair, alone were visible. Above the temples . . . gleamed a ring of white flame, gemmed with sparkles of a more lurid

tinge. This pale crescent was "The likeness of a
Kingly Crown"; what it diademed was "the shape
which shape had none" (pp. 110–111).

The Miltonic quotations at the end of the description indicate that Jane sees the picture as an allegorical representa-
tion of death. The shapeless shape is Milton's Death, the
offspring of Sin. But the actual figure in the drawing is,
however distorted, not death but a female mourner—its
sable veil indicates both its gender and the social function
in which it is engaged. Nevertheless, it is entirely possible
that, as in so much of Brontë's art, death really is the child
of sin in this drawing—the sin of the mourner. One cannot
say with certainty that the death of a loved one has sprung
from her sin, but surely the survivor sits in Hell, her head
encased in a ring of white flame, that coalescence of heat
and cold which characterizes the nondialectic union of op-
posites in the timeless and unprogressive world of the
damned. There are perhaps guards in the prison in which
the woman exists (the northern lights have lances), but
there seems to be no danger of the mourner escaping. For
the weight of her depression has chained the woman to her
iceberg. In fact she "rests" against it; the iceberg has apparently become a haven of depressive passivity, a familiar
if painful cushion against which she leans in quiescent
agony. She would apparently not attempt to escape if she
could, since her eye, and presumably her mind, are blank
of any meaning but despair.

The paintings seem to bring not only Jane, but more importantly Charlotte, out of hiding. Yet they do not present
the complete pattern with which *Jane Eyre* is concerned.
Death in Jane's paintings is the death of someone else. The
paintings do not move forward in time to contemplate the
eventual death of the survivor. For emblems of the completed pattern, we have to return to the opening chapters
of the novel.

By comparing a book that the little girl studies and a
ballad she listens to, we can arrive at the juxtaposition of
the two faces of death—death as punishment and death as
justification. In the opening chapter of the novel, Jane sits

"shrined in double retirement," turning the pages of Bewick's *History of English Birds.* The book reminds her of the nature and the probable outcome of guilt.[6] Jane scans literature for images of the self and its dilemmas. Certainly she finds relevant images in Bewick; her selection of pictures can be seen as a drama projected from her unconscious onto the pages of the book. First she examines the "death-white realms" of northern countries. Throughout the novel she will return again and again to an awed consideration of what it must be like to be dead, to be a spirit in a frozen world. She gazes at a moonlit cemetery, then at two ships which seem like "marine phantoms." The cemetery, like the ships, seems "haunted."

This concentration on the realm of the dead is thoroughly natural for a child whose parents are dead. But Jane does not stop there. Significantly, the images of death and spirits are followed by two pictures which represent crime and punishment. In the first, Jane finds a supernatural avenger of crime, a fiend who has captured a thief by pinning down his booty sack behind him. "I passed over [that one] quickly: it was an object of terror," Jane remarks (p. 6). We might legitimately ask at this point what it is that the thief had stolen. Is the sack filled with jewels, perhaps? Jane gives no answer. We only know that there is a thief who cannot escape the vengeance of a creature from the afterlife. It is perhaps that same thief who is executed in the final picture from Bewick. Jane is terrified by that one, too, frightened by a "black, horned thing seated aloof on a rock, surveying a distant crowd surrounding a gallows" (p. 6).

Jane's taste in books resembles her creator's. The Brontës had been fascinated with Bewick's book during their childhood. The portrayal of the thief and the avenging fiend, in particular, had held their attention for years.[7] Where other children might search the book for robins and sparrows, Charlotte and her heroine find death and apparitions, arrest and execution.

Brontë will allow her protagonist to triumph over the guilt feelings which both she and Jane seem to project onto the pages of the ornithology. To offset the emblems of guilt in the novel, Brontë composes a ballad which treats survival differently. Bewick portrays guilt tracked down; Jane's servant friend Bessie teaches her a song which celebrates the triumph of a persecuted little girl.

Death without the inheritance of guilt by the survivor is assumed in the ballad beginning "My feet they are sore, and my limbs they are weary" (p. 18). The survivor is termed "the poor orphan child" and the poem concentrates on her persecution. The child wanders through the moors and rocky hills of a landscape symbolic of pain and isolation. She has been "sent" there, however; she is not fleeing in frightened culpability, like the thief in Bewick, but has been banished because of the cruelty of others. She takes comfort in the knowledge that "kind angels . . . watch o'er" her (p. 18). Where the supernatural eyes in the bird book had belonged to fiends who watched the shamefaced movements of a criminal, here the lonely child is observed by benign spirits who will take care of her. The orphan is protected by God, who will give her both parentage and an eventual home. But there is a catch: "Heaven is a home, and a rest will not fail me" (p. 18). As in Helen Burns' theology, the entrance fee for the refuge of innocence is death.

In Bewick's book and Bessie's ballad, then, Brontë holds out to her protagonist alternate, sinister explanations of the problem of orphanhood, the problem of survival when loved ones have died. On the one hand, survival might be the result of crime. In that case, death would be a fitting punishment. On the other hand, orphanhood might simply be a martyrdom imposed on an innocent child. If that were true, then perhaps martyrdom ought to be accepted with Christlike resignation to receive a divine, otherworldly reward.

These two possibilities converge during Jane's imprisonment in the red-room. The complex ambivalence of Charlotte's own attitude toward death seems to be mirrored in the questions Jane asks herself: "What thought had I been but just conceiving of starving myself to death? That certainly was a crime: and was I fit to die? Or was the vault under the chancel of Gateshead Church an inviting bourne?" (p. 13). Brontë's choice of the term "bourne" here is important. It is a word which appears frequently in her writing; she probably associated it above all with one of her favorite books, *Pilgrim's Progress*. In Bunyan's work it refers to the Heavenly City. In *Jane Eyre* it refers ultimately to the goal Jane reaches when she marries Rochester. But for our understanding of the novel, it is important to keep in mind that the first bourne the little girl considers in the novel is the grave. Mr. Reed was her mother's brother and took Jane in after her parents died. Now his ghost might come to take her away: "I thought Mr. Reed's spirit, harassed by the wrongs of his sister's child, might quit its abode—whether in the church vault, or in the unknown world of the departed—and rise before me in this chamber. I wiped my tears and hushed my sobs, fearful lest any sign of violent grief might waken a preter-natural voice to comfort me, or elicit from the gloom some haloed face, bending over me with strange pity" (p. 13). Mr. Reed would pity Jane to death. But Jane rebels against receiving comfort from beyond the grave: "I rushed to the door and shook the lock in desperate effort" (p. 14). That desperation is the beginning of wisdom for Jane. *The Professor* had opened with the stern resolve of an adult to become independent. In *Jane Eyre*, Brontë centers on that same motif of independence, but adds to it another dimension—the sometimes frenzied effort of a human being to resist the will to die. The polarity which controlled *The Professor* was success and failure; *Jane Eyre* hovers between life and death, marriage and the grave.

We have dealt so far with isolated scenes and descriptions emblematic of what I believe to be the novel's deepest concerns. But what of the actual story? Surely *Jane Eyre* did not achieve its abiding popularity through a tortured concentration on Charlotte Brontë's personal problems. The novel's striking ability to capture the imagination of its audience has moved more than a century of readers to see themselves mirrored in its heroine. Yet relatively few of those readers can have lost a major portion of their families. *Jane Eyre* is a book for those setting forth into life, not those contemplating death.

That is precisely the wonderful thing about the novel. There is very little morbidness about the story, or rather we do not *notice* much morbidness on first reading it. For the underlying gloom of the novel's psychological cast is balanced and partially veiled by a narrative which moves toward the light. And it is at least in part the resultant tension between the darkness of Brontë's underlying vision of the world and the surface optimism of the story line which has given so many generations of readers such pleasure.

The story taken in its broad strokes is very nearly a fairy tale, after all. Its movement from darkness to light, from oppression and imprisonment to autonomy and freedom provides illusory solutions to problems which are not really solvable.[8] But in so doing, the book helps to illuminate the problems. We do not ask of fiction that it solve life's riddles. At most it can show us something about the pressures under which we live, and provide us with a temporary release of our tension. It could be argued that without the naïveté of *Jane Eyre*'s story line, Brontë could not have attained the profundity of the novel's metaphoric drift. Without the existence of illusory, fictive solutions, the problems which tormented her mind would have remained unexpressed, hidden away in the psyche of a woman who, like all of us, would have preferred to avoid them.

We can begin to understand the function of the narrative in the novel by looking at Jane's adventures in the light of two popular tales which help structure the book's events and its attitude toward existence: *Pilgrim's Progress* and *Cinderella*.[9]

The episodic structure of *Jane Eyre* is a reflection of *Pilgrim's Progress*. This is not to say that the novel is in any sense a copy of Bunyan's work; the great Victorian novelists did not write Christian allegories. But from *The Old Curiosity Shop* to *Tess of the d'Urbervilles*, the vision of Christian fleeing the City of Destruction in search of the City of Salvation haunted the Victorian imagination. The action of *Jane Eyre* takes place in five localities with the appropriately symbolic names of Gateshead Hall, Lowood Institution, Thornfield Manor, Marsh End (also called Moor House), and Ferndean Manor. In each of these locations the pilgrim is forced into combat against a mighty antagonist; she emerges from each contest the victor, ready to continue her quest for independence and love.

Gateshead, as its name implies, is the beginning of Jane Eyre's spiritual journey. Here the heroine is forced to fight a double battle, against both John Reed and his mother. Although neither is as ugly as Bunyan's monster, Apollyon, John is described in a manner which is rather startling when one remembers that the boy is only fourteen: "[He was] large and stout for his age, with a dingy and unwholesome skin; thick lineaments in a spacious visage, heavy limbs and large extremities. He gorged himself habitually at table, which made him bilious, and gave him a dim and bleared eye and flabby cheeks" (p. 7). By defeating the onslaughts of this beast and his mother, Jane earns the right to a warrior's boast: "I was left there alone, winner of the field. It was the hardest battle I had fought, and the first victory I had gained" (p. 32).

But John is simply the smallest and least threatening of the male enemies who will take their places one by one in the lists opposite the tiny Christian soldier. The events at Gateshead set the pattern for the action in each of the following sections. In Lowood, Jane's second arena, her battle is fought with the weapon of silent endurance, rather than her fists, but she wins as surely as if she had wielded a sword. Brocklehurst is no mean opponent: "I looked up at—a black pillar: . . . the grim face at the top was like a carved mask . . . What a face he had, . . . what a great nose! and what a mouth! and what large prominent teeth!" (pp. 26–27). Like all of Jane's male enemies, Brocklehurst, a combination of the devil and Red Riding Hood's wolf, is a devourer. He would swallow his enemy whole if he could. On a more sophisticated moral level, he can be seen as a perversion of Christ the judge. Jane fears his arrival at Lowood as if it were the appearance of Jesus at the Second Coming. She thinks of him as "the dread judge" and "the coming Man," and shivers at the thought of his condemnation. When he finally visits Lowood he humiliates her in front of the entire school.

In terms of the pattern of confrontation we have been examining, we can say that the novel's heroine has graduated in the space of a few months from the infantile violence of scuffling with a peer, to the quieter and more deadly threat to the ego posed by a sanctimonious school authority. Moreover, the metaphysical trappings of Brocklehurst's indictment represent an enormous expansion of Jane's guilt since the child left Gateshead. There the primary charge had been "a tendency to deceit," and the punishment was expulsion from the family circle. But for Brocklehurst, both crime and punishment are theological in scope. Expulsion now is not merely a bar to acceptance by the family; it is exile from salvation: "This girl, who might be one of God's own lambs, is a little castaway: not a member of the true flock, but evidently an interloper and an alien. . . . worse than many a little heathen who says its prayers to Brahma and kneels before Juggernaut—this girl is—a liar!" (pp. 57–58). True to the essentially paranoid structure of the world Brontë is portraying, Jane is at fault not because she has done anything wrong, but because she is, by definition, guilty. The specific crime for which she has been brought forward is merely the dropping of a slate. But Brocklehurst is a judge by nature and function, and if he cannot make the crime fit the punishment, he will not let the disparity deter him.

Brocklehurst is the conscious portrayal of the Reverend Carus Wilson, the hated proprietor of the school in which Brontë's older sisters died, and she allows him no redeeming features. He is a devil quoting scripture, a beast who cloaks his action in the role of Christian ministry. But despite his power, the little pilgrim defeats him. Brocklehurst in his turn is humiliated and rendered powerless by an inquiry into his management of the school.

From Lowood Jane moves on to Thornfield, where, as the name of the manor implies, she will have to undergo the temptations of the flesh. Its upper stories remind her of Bluebeard's castle, she tells us, and the master of the house, like his predecessors in the novel, is a potential devourer: "Do you suppose I eat like an ogre, or a ghoul, that you dread being the companion of my repast?" (p. 237).

Rochester is the representative of an infinitely more appealing, and thus profounder, danger than John Reed or Brocklehurst. He offers Jane love, for the first time in her life. But love is no longer, as in Brontë's Angrian writings, a solution to the problems of life. As in the earlier confrontations in the novel, the relations between Jane and this new male antagonist are described in terms of combat: "Beyond the verge of provocation I never ventured; on the extreme brink I liked well to try my skill" (p. 138), Jane tells us, and later: "A movement of repulsion, flight, fear, would have sealed my doom" (p. 266). The aggressiveness which underlies their courtship is typified in the aftermath of Rochester's love song: "He rose and came towards me, and I saw his face all kindled, and his full falcon-eye flashing, and tenderness and passion in every lineament. I quailed momentarily—then I rallied. . . . a weapon of defense must be prepared—I whetted my tongue. . . . I laughed in my sleeve at his menaces: 'I can keep you in reasonable check now,' I reflected; 'and I don't doubt to be able to do it hereafter: if one expedient loses its virtue, another must be devised' " (pp. 240–241).[10] Rochester is clearly an offspring of the devastating Zamorna, but Charlotte's earlier worship has lost its naïveté. Throughout their engagement her young heroine fights successfully to keep her amorous lover at bay.

When she experiences the full strength of her temptation to surrender to Rochester's offer of an illicit relationship, the Christian pilgrim flees Thornfield. At a crossroads with the fitting name of Whitcross, she providentially chooses the path which leads her eventually to Marsh End, the home of the Rivers family. From its name, one would infer that this house marks the end of her troubles, and indeed she does find both family and fortune here. But Marsh End is also known as Moor House, and in one sense Jane is still out on the moors, has not yet reached safety. For Brontë forces her protagonist to enter the lists again, and this combat is perhaps the strangest and certainly the most dangerous of them all.

St. John Rivers and Jane Eyre wage polite but implacable warfare, with St. John demanding nothing less than unconditional surrender. Of all her male enemies, the young clergyman represents the ultimate threat to her existence, for he is the only character in the book who is able to understand her fully, to comprehend in its paradoxical completeness her simultaneous expectation of both damnation and divine reward. Like Jane, he suffers from the malady of restlessness, and he will use their affinity to push his young cousin toward India and death. His sister's description of him is apt: "St. John looks quiet . . . but he hides a fever in his vitals. You would think him gentle, yet in some things he is inexorable as death" (p. 314). Charlotte associates him with the Book of Revelation; his name, in one sense a sanctified version of John Reed's, derives more crucially from the author of the Apocalypse. And his vision of reality is apocalyptic, as fervent as that of Helen Burns and as fierce as Brocklehurst's. His challenge to Jane is a parody of salvation: "You shall be mine: I claim you—not for my pleasure, but for my Sovereign's service" (p. 354).

St. John's summons from Heaven seems to hold out the possibility of total redemption, of a full and satisfactory penance for whatever sinfulness resides in the soul of the heroine. But Jane will accept no mediator to recommend her to her God. Moreover, like Brocklehurst and Helen Burns, St. John demands a sanctified death as the precondition for salvation. But Jane can find no charm in death: "God did not give me my life to throw away," she tells her tormentor (p. 364).

St. John is a spiritual vampire, a greater threat to Jane than any of the previous antagonists who attempted to devour her or lure her to the grave. He dangles in front of her the bait of sanctity, waiting confidently for his victim to follow it into the maw of his insatiable lust for power. And she nearly surrenders: "I was tempted to . . . rush down . . . into the gulf of his existence, and there lose my own" (p. 368).

She is saved from destruction by the mystic voice of Rochester calling her name. The cry comes at a crucial moment in the struggle, a point when she has nearly agreed to accept the holy death which St. John holds out to her: "I stood motionless under my hierophant's touch. My refusals were forgotten—my fears overcome—my wrestlings paralysed. . . . All was changing utterly, with a sudden sweep. Religion called—Angels beckoned—God commanded—death's gates opening, showed eternity beyond: it seemed that for safety and bliss there, all here might be sacrificed in a second" (p. 368). In *The Professor*, this call from the far side of death's gates had been terrifying. William Crimsworth had not been blinded for an instant by the gruesome hag in his mind who attempted to lure him out of life. But Jane nearly allows herself to be seduced into dying. For Brontë's first protagonist, death had been silence, emptiness, rest. In the guilt-ridden mind of her second protagonist, death just might represent safety, bliss, the possible assuagement of the sense of sin which seems so inescapable a part of life. Jane is saved by the sound of her name, the supernatural reminder from her distant lover that she possesses an identity which she must guard and nurture at all cost. Reminded of this precious identity, Jane defeats her enemy easily.

Her final joust takes place at Ferndean Manor, the secluded lodge where the blinded Rochester has taken refuge from the world. But Jane herself is this time clearly the aggressor, and the combat is largely comic, a strange little episode of teasing in which she repays her former tormentor in kind. Blinded and maimed, Rochester represents only a vestigial threat: he reminds his former governess of "some wronged and fettered wild beast or bird, dangerous to approach in his sullen woe" (p. 379). But she does approach him. She torments him a little—rather cruelly, it seems—and then marries him. At Ferndean, "as still as a church on a week-day" (p. 379), the little pilgrim finally finds her bourne.

The quasi-religious odyssey here briefly summarized seems to be used quite consciously as a shaping principle of the novel. Yet it would be difficult to maintain that the book is religious.[11] Some of the novel's emotional overtones seem unconscious. G. Armour Craig has pointed out just how closely the plot approximates pure wish fulfillment on the author's part.[12] For example, the extent of Jane's triumph, the degree of innocence she manages to attain, seems thoroughly irreligious. She even addresses the reader near the end of the book in a paraphrase of the Virgin Mary's response to the adoring shepherds: "I kept these things then, and pondered them in my heart" (p. 394). But while Jane has become someone approximating the Mother of God, Rochester, in the penultimate chapter of the novel, is compared to Samson, Nebuchadnezzar, Saul, and Vulcan—all struck down for disobedience to a deity. It seems doubtful that Brontë's extreme moral exclusiveness is entirely conscious; it seems to emanate from her fantasy life, rather than from her conscious religious opinions.[13] It is in the nature of fantasy to reward favorites and punish rivals; and Rochester is both love-object and potential tyrant—a position which Jane tacitly recognizes by calling him "my master" again and again. The triumphant nature of the novel's ending can be seen in her exultant statement: "I am my own mistress" (p. 383). Rochester offers a prayer of contrition and thankfulness; then comes "he stretched his hand out to be led" (p. 395).

We can explain the peculiarity of the novel's ending somewhat more fully by examining the narrative in the light of *Cinderella*. Jane's struggles, after all, are not always against aggressive males. She also undergoes a series of combats against female antagonists. And here she is not Christian seeking a quasi-religious form of salvation, but a poor little stepdaughter seeking marriage and a distinctly secular freedom from oppression. I suspect that this pattern comes much closer to private fantasy than does the paradigm taken over from Bunyan.

The version of *Cinderella* which Brontë seems to be using is that of the Brothers Grimm.[14] The singularity of that version lies in the ending of the tale. When the prince arrives to seek the owner of the slipper, Cinderella's eldest stepsister, abetted by her mother, chops off her toes to make the slipper fit, but the prince discovers her deception. The second stepsister chops off her heels; she, too, is caught. The prince returns to the house for the third time and discovers his true love. The story ends happily, but with a grisly touch: at Cinderella's wedding, two birds, who throughout the story have been agents of the girl's dead mother, come down and peck out the eyes of both step-sisters.

If we examine *Jane Eyre* with Cinderella in mind, we notice that in each of the first three sections, there is a hostile grouping of women: two nasty, but pretty, sisters, and their equally horrid mother. At Gateshead, John is the physical aggressor, but he is aided and abetted by his sisters, Georgiana and Eliza. And of course the primary maternal enemy whom Jane must confront in the novel is her evil stepmother, Sarah Reed. The book opens with the three children "clustered round their mama in the drawing-room" and Jane separated from them both physically and spiritually. She complains to the reader that she is "employed . . . as a sort of under-nurserymaid, to tidy the room, dust the chairs, &c" (p. 25). Mrs. Reed's maid brings out an aspect of rivalry which Jane is unwilling to admit herself: "If [Jane] were a nice, pretty child, one might compassionate her forlornness; but one really cannot care for such a little toad as that. . . . I doat on Miss Georgiana! . . . Little darling!—with her long curls and her blue eyes, and such a sweet colour as she has; just as if she were painted!" (pp. 21–22). This comparison hurts Jane as much as John's overt aggression or his mother's hatred. It sets the outlines of her self-image throughout the novel.

The antagonist of the second section, Lowood, is Brocklehurst, but here too the male enemy is associated with a grouping which resembles Cinderella's persecutors—Brocklehurst's wife and daughters. As in the first section, their beauty and their expensive clothes are played off against the small, plain, almost ragged protagonist. They appear just after Brocklehurst has declared that his plan of education is to mortify in his charges the lusts of the flesh: "Mr. Brocklehurst was here interrupted: three other visitors, ladies, now entered the room. They ought to have come a little sooner to have heard his lecture on dress, for they were splendidly attired in velvet, silk, and furs. The two younger of the trio (fine girls of sixteen and seventeen) had gray beaver hats, then in fashion, shaded with ostrich plumes . . . the elder lady was enveloped in a costly velvet shawl, trimmed with ermine" (p. 56). As in the

Gateshead section, here the male is the overt aggressor, while the females are malicious witnesses; in their presence, Brocklehurst describes Jane as "not a member of the true flock, but evidently an interloper and an alien" (p. 57). One of them comments "How shocking!" and then the three women drop from the novel entirely. Their only readily apparent function is to serve as an ironic counterpoint to Brocklehurst's platitudes on humility. Actually, as we shall see, they are central to our understanding of the dynamics of the novel's creation.

The Cinderella pattern becomes more overt in the Thornfield section of the book. Rochester, the aggressive male successor to Brocklehurst and John Reed, presents Jane for the first and only time in the novel with masculine love. If we combine for a moment the Christian and folk motifs, we can say that in Rochester the frightening figure of Apollyon is merged with the sympathetic figure of Cinderella's young prince. Rochester threatens Jane with violence, not in the form of assault and battery or spiritual degradation, but seduction, and at one point something approaching rape, that merger of the actions of enemy and lover: "'Jane! will you hear reason?' (he stooped and approached his lips to my ear) 'because if you won't, I'll try violence.' His voice was hoarse; his look that of a man who is just about to burst an insufferable bond and plunge headlong into wild license" (p. 266).

The appearance of the Cinderella configuration in the Thornfield section is dwelt on at much greater length than in Lowood. This time the figures of Cinderella's enemies are represented by Lady Ingram and her daughters, Blanche and Mary. Rochester, like Cinderella's prince, is hosting an entertainment which lasts several days, and Jane is ordered to attend. Jane's humiliation this time comes in the form of the women's discussion of governesses:

> "You should hear mamma on the chapter of governesses. Mary and I have had, I should think, a dozen at least in our day; half of them detestable and the rest ridiculous, and all incubi—were they not, mamma?"

"My dearest, don't mention governesses, the word makes me nervous. I have suffered a martyrdom from their incompetency and caprice; I thank Heaven I have now done with them!" (p. 155).[15]

Throughout most of this part of the novel, Rochester pretends to be in love with Blanche. It is not until Jane has returned to Gateshead and established her moral ascendency over her childhood rivals, the Reeds, that Brontë allows Rochester to cease his cruel hoax and propose to Jane. Then the Ingrams, like the Reeds and the Brocklehursts, are banished from the novel.

If we examine the Marsh-End segment of the novel with the Cinderella pattern in mind, we find a strange variant of the situation we have been tracing up to this point. Diana and Mary Rivers step into the outline vacated by the Reeds, the Brocklehursts, and the Ingrams, but they bear no moral similarity to them. When Jane first views them, she is still an outsider—literally, this time, since she is gazing through their cottage window. She is not only drab now, but ragged and starving. This is in part what she sees: "Two young, graceful women—ladies in every point . . . ; both wore deep mourning . . . , sombre garb. . . . I had nowhere seen such faces as theirs: and yet, as I gazed on them, I seemed intimate with every lineament. I cannot call them handsome—they were too pale and grave for the word. . . . This scene was as silent as if all the figures had been shadows" (p. 292). Diana and Mary, we are informed later, are temporarily working as governesses, but are studying German in the hope of enabling themselves to teach foreign languages.

On her discovery of Jane at the door, the third figure, the older woman, rebuffs her as a vagrant. Stepmothers, it would seem, are more implacably hostile than stepsisters. But Hannah's importance has already been downgraded in the mind of the starving suppliant: "They could not be the daughters of the elderly person at the table; for she looked like a rustic" (p. 292). Diana and Mary themselves, with their brother, receive Jane with compassion and tact, calling forth this comment from Jane to the reader:

"Somehow, now that I had once crossed the threshold of this house, and once was brought face to face with its owners, I felt no longer an outcast, vagrant, and disowned by the wide world. I dared to put off the mendicant—to resume my natural manner and character. I began once more to know myself" (p. 297). The stepsisters have turned into sisters; Jane makes the miraculous discovery that she is related to her new friends, and that she has inherited a small fortune.

We can see in the text a preliminary reason for this remarkable transformation in the Cinderella pattern. For the heroine has paid a heavy sacrifice to her conscience in running away from Thornfield. But not simply to her own conscience. She had been ordered away from her suitor in a dream whose significance has been largely ignored in criticism of the novel:

> I dreamt I lay in the red-room at Gateshead. . . . The light that long ago had struck me into syncope . . . seemed . . . to pause in the centre of the . . . ceiling . . . the gleam was such as the moon imparts to vapours she is about to sever . . . then, not a moon, but a white human form shone in the azure, inclining a glorious brow earthward. It gazed and gazed and gazed on me . . . it whispered in my heart—
> "My daughter, flee temptation!"
> "Mother, I will." (p. 281)[16]

William Crimsworth, like Jane Eyre, had rediscovered the image of his dead mother at a crucial moment of his narrative. Befitting that realistic novel, the image came in the form of a framed portrait delivered by a porter. Brontë's second protagonist, the strangely mystical little governess, finds hers in a dream. The fact that Brontë aligns this dream to the red-room fantasy seems significant. There Jane had been terrified at the thought that the light was an emanation from the grave, that it came from Mr. Reed's corpse returning to comfort her. But that was only a childish illusion. Uncles do not love fiercely enough to crawl from the grave in search of their nieces. Only one's own mother would show that much love. And only a maternal spirit could possess the compassionate rigor to lead her daughter on a journey of expiation so strenuous as almost to kill her.

At any rate, the expiation for whatever crime is involved in Jane's existence seems successful. For Diana and Mary Rivers represent the last, benevolent variant of the evil stepsisters of the folk heroine. The purgative suffering which the heroine has undergone since her Whitcross experience has apparently laid the pattern of confrontation to rest. In the final section of the novel, at Ferndean, no stepsisters appear.

But one very striking distortion of the Cinderella myth does come to light at Ferndean. In Grimm's version of the tale, the evil stepsisters are punished twofold for their transgressions against their unfortunate sibling: their own greed leads them to mutilate themselves, and, at the wedding, the birds who represent Cinderella's dead mother peck out their eyes. In Brontë's version of the paradigm, that fate is reserved for precisely the male who comes closest to the figure of Cinderella's prince. When Jane returns to Rochester, she finds him mutilated and blinded. Brontë has condemned the prince to undergo the punishment of the evil stepsisters.

In order to explain this striking displacement of revenge, it is necessary to construct a theory concerning the relationship of the Cinderella configuration to Charlotte Brontë's psyche and to her life. In the first place, we should note the fact that, like Diana and Mary Rivers, Charlotte, Emily and Anne Brontë had been governesses and learned German in order to improve their teaching prospects. Indeed it seems quite reasonable to posit that the pastimes of the Rivers girls and Jane are close renderings of evenings spent in the Brontë home in the years before *Jane Eyre* was written. In all probability Emily and Anne provided part of the material out of which the Cinderella motif was fashioned.[17]

But Diana and Mary Rivers are ultimately the result of a transformation: they represent final, benevolent variants of a pattern which has been uniformly malign up to that point. And in a strange way Charlotte seems to force them to *will* themselves into benevolence, to participate in their own transformation from evil stepsisters into benevolent sisters. For when Jane comes upon them, they are reading aloud from Schiller's *Die Räuber*, a classic tale of sibling rivalry. Moreover, the passage they are reciting is strikingly relevant to the behavior of Cinderella's stepsisters. In that passage, Franz Moor, who has destroyed his brother and his father, is recounting a nightmare of divine retribution for his crimes against his family. A voice in the nightmare cries out to him: "Grace, grace to all sinners on earth and in the pit! Only you are abandoned!"[18] That is what happens to people who mistreat their siblings.[19] The warning seems sufficient: Diana and Mary will be uniformly kind to their little sister.

But I think we have to go further than that. To more fully understand the creative dynamics behind the novel's structure, it is necessary to return to a dream which was discussed in the first chapter, the dream about Maria and Elizabeth which Charlotte recounted to Mary Taylor. Mary writes:

> She told me, early one morning, that she had just been dreaming; she had been told that she was wanted in the drawingroom, and it was Maria and Elizabeth. I was eager for her to go on, and when she said there was no more, I said, "but go on! *Make it out.* I know you can." She said she would not; she wished she had not dreamed, for it did not go on nicely; they were changed; they had forgotten what they used to care for. They were very fashionably dressed, and began criticising the room, etc. (Gaskell, *Life*, p. 68)

It seems a safe assumption that one of the things they used to care for and are now criticizing is their younger sister Charlotte. Whether they actually criticized her in the dream or not, however, is of little moment. The fact remains that they were antagonistic to her surroundings and that this hurt her. Mary's plea—"Make it out. I know you can"— suggests that Charlotte was already trying to erase the dream, so destructive to her idealized picture of her sisters, from her memory. The content of the dream suggests a suppressed hostility to Maria and Elizabeth which, as we have seen in the first chapter, was not at all incompatible with her admiration of them. But the hostility has been projected from Charlotte onto her sisters. They have turned malicious.

If we turn back now to the vaguest, most mysterious appearance of the stepsister configuration in the novel, we can begin to see some possible connections between this dream and the novel. For Brocklehurst's daughters appear at Lowood, the fictional equivalent of the school where Maria and Elizabeth became fatally ill. They take no real part in the action of the novel. Like Maria and Elizabeth, they are beautifully dressed. They gaze at the humiliated little heroine, say "How shocking!" and drop from the novel entirely. They are, in other words, like the figures in the dream.

But one extremely important element has been added to the configuration in the novel: the disapproving girls have been joined by their mother. Art allows Brontë to penetrate her psyche to a depth which not even her dreamlife made manifest. For as we have seen, her fixation on the death of her older sisters served to veil the earlier, even more painful trauma of her mother's death. Art has the power to lift that veil, to bring the mother out into the open. When malicious stepsisters appear in *Jane Eyre*, whether they wear the masks of the Reeds, the Brocklehursts, or the Ingrams, they bring their mother with them. It is only when their hatred has softened, when stepsisters turn into sisters, that their implacable mother fades back out of sight. Diana's and Mary's mother is safely dead, her place taken by a harmless servant.

The difference between dream and art is instructive. In *Jokes and Their Relation to the Unconscious*, Freud states: "A dream is a completely asocial mental product; it has nothing to communicate to anyone else; it arises within the subject as a compromise between the mental forces struggling in him, it remains unintelligible to the subject himself and is for that reason totally uninteresting to other people."[20] The painful and inexplicable nature of her dream prevented Brontë from relating it fully even to her intimate friend. And yet nearly two decades later the material of the dream became the germ of one of the finest novels of the Victorian period. We cannot hope to explain the nature of the process through which the dream became transformed from asocial to eminently social product. But we can see several stages in the process, and they have to do with the power of myths to accrete to themselves unorganized, or painfully organized, mental energy.

It seems to have been necessary in the first place for the dream to become attached to, and ultimately metamorphosed into, a folk narrative which would allow the material of the dream, itself an early symptom of a profound obsession, to move into the less frightening, because less personal, realm of public myth. In this ability to attract to itself the private imaginings of its listeners lies the social importance of myth. With the passing of early childhood the dream becomes something to withhold from others, both because it reveals too much of the dreamer, and because it has not as yet taken on sequential meaning. It is egoistic and senseless, a product to be hidden or disguised from society, whose continuity demands at least a nominal adherence to altruism and sequential thought. But it is precisely these last two qualities which the tale of Cinderella provided for Charlotte Brontë. The public myth was more adequate as an image of her psychological dilemma than the structures her own dreaming mind could erect. And not simply because the public myth went deeper to resurrect a malicious maternal figure. Perhaps just as importantly, the fairy tale augments the dilemma of the dream in two crucial ways: it gives a set of quasi-rational explanations for the maliciousness of Cinderella's enemies, and it passes out fitting punishments and rewards. It is, in other words, a narrative rather than a puzzling set of juxtaposed symbols.

It would seem that Brontë's guilt feelings were too intense to be expiated simply by her surrogate's sufferings. The burden of guilt had to be transferred. Part of it was transferred to the shoulders of Jane's female antagonists. Thus the heroine is confronted at every turn by a triad of female enemies acting out of a nearly groundless malignity; they are guilty—not the lonely orphan.

But there is, if we search for it, a reason given for their

hatred. Jane's first and mightiest female antagonists are the Reeds. Mrs. Reed makes a deathbed confession of the grounds of her maliciousness: "I hated it the first time I set my eyes on it—a sickly, whining, pining thing! . . . Reed pitied it; and he used to nurse it and notice it as if it had been his own: more, indeed, than he ever noticed his own at that age" (pp. 203–204). Thus it is no wonder that the heroine is despised, no wonder that she is the butt of absurd accusations throughout the novel; she has stolen paternal love.

Yet the Cinderella motif is ultimately not a satisfying vehicle for the resolution of Brontë's dilemma. Though it expresses much, it has little to teach. Perhaps as a child Charlotte saw herself in daydreams as Cinderella, but she needed a more objective public vehicle than that particular fairy tale to produce adult and public art. Most importantly, the ending of the tale, although superficially it would seem to provide her with the unconscious satisfaction of seeing her psychic enemies punished, would simply reinforce the guilt and resultant anxiety she must have felt. For her rivals for paternal affection—her mother and her two older sisters—had already been fatally punished, while she had survived.

In this situation the Christian odyssey provided the perfect vehicle for the conflicting forces in the mind of the Protestant clergyman's daughter. Like *Cinderella, Pilgrim's Progress* moves from damnation to salvation, from subjugation to release and reward. Christian's guilt is as broad and existential (one is guilty and must be punished because one exists), his enemies as obnoxious, his reward as glorious as Cinderella's. But the religious work has two enormous psychic advantages over the folk tale. In the first place, its issues, far from hovering in the psychologically dangerous realm of family struggle, are eschatological and tropological in scope. Its eschatology, in particular, guarantees its status as a public myth of Protestant England. Its protagonist is an Everyman (or at any rate every Protestant untainted by false doctrine). And Everyman has a chance to be saved. No one need be irredeemably damned.

But of even greater psychic importance than its legitimacy is its seeming distance from the dilemma it interprets for Brontë. The enemies of Christian are male: his most ferocious antagonists are Apollyon and the Giant Despair, both viewed through the lens of knight-errantry. Thus males are free to take up a large portion of the guilt which, I would submit, belongs in the first place to Charlotte Brontë, guilt which in the context of the novel threatens to capsize Jane Eyre. Men become the truly monstrous enemies, huge louring creatures who attempt to devour the heroine.

The character who connects these two tales in the novel is Rochester. His disastrous position in the novel makes him both lover and enemy, the object of both undying love and divine retribution. We can perhaps better understand the precarious balance which Rochester is forced to maintain by turning back to another of Brontë's dreams. As was pointed out in the first chapter, Constantin Heger, Charlotte's adored teacher, became aligned with the dream pattern which recurred throughout much of her life. In one letter she had complained to him: "Day and night I find neither rest nor peace—if I sleep I suffer tormenting dreams in which I see you always severe, always somber, always angry with me. . . . If my master withdraws his friendship from me entirely I shall be altogether without hope—if he gives me a little—very little—I shall be satisfied—happy, I shall have a reason for living, for working" (Wise and Symington, *Correspondence*, 2: 21–22).

Nearly fifteen years after the dream of her sisters which Charlotte reported to Mary Taylor, another loved one has turned against her, appearing "always severe, always somber, always angry" with her. Charlotte herself, with her brilliant intuitive understanding of the human mind, recognizes elsewhere in the letter that the dreams are a result of repression, of the faculties' rebellion against the tyrannical grip of the conscience. But this time the loved one who has changed is a male, like Rochester, a man who is called "my master" by his forlorn admirer. It would be naive and simplistic to say that Rochester is a transcription of Heger, just as it would be misleading to call him a simple transformation of Zamorna. All three of them are images thrown up on the screen of Brontë's perception. But the case of Heger enables us to see a bit more clearly how this burden of guilt feelings, projected in the first place onto Jane, and from her onto the females of her fictional world, comes to rest finally on the shoulders of Jane's lover. For Rochester (and to a lesser extent John Reed, Brocklehurst, and St. John Rivers) bears the same relationship to the "stepsisters" as Heger in Brontë's dream life bears to Maria and Elizabeth.

The sex change involved in this transformation demands a leap across a seemingly wide psychic chasm; in our commonplace ideas about the world we like to feel that men are not women. Certainly Brontë consciously felt that men were almost of a different species from herself and all her friends. But her imagination seems to have solved the problem by building a bridge across the chasm. For at one point in the novel Rochester himself appears as a woman, an ugly old gipsy fortune-teller in a comic hoax.[21] The gipsy's opening words, and Jane's angry response to them, could serve as the emblem of the novel's entire pattern of accusation and denial:

> "You are cold; you are sick; and you are silly."
> "Prove it," I rejoined. (p. 173)

Rochester cannot prove it. Neither as man nor as woman can he defeat the little pilgrim travelling unescorted through a threatening world.

Taken together, then, the books Jane reads, the pictures she looks at and draws, the songs she listens to, as well as the adventures she undergoes, the novel can be seen as a sort of literary courtroom in which Brontë defends her heroine against an accusing world and proves her innocent.[22] Jane is not an alien to be banished from the family, but a true daughter worthy of inheritance. Thus in the course of the novel, the very meaning of Jane's last name undergoes a metamorphosis. *Eyre* no longer, after Sarah Reed's death, connotes a wandering sinner.[23] From the point in the tale where Jane receives the letter from her distant uncle asking her whereabouts, her name begins to take on the connotation of "inheritor."[24] Jane the Sinner slowly becomes Jane the Heiress.

But there is a profounder meaning to the novel than the question of guilt or innocence, punishment or vindication. For, as we have seen, guilt in the novel is in some suprarational way tied in with, somehow caused by, death. The metaphoric drift, if not the plot of the novel, demonstrates that connection.

If Jane were not guilty, if she were indeed existentially innocent, then the face of death could undergo a transformation, both for Jane and, in a sense, for Charlotte. And that is precisely what happens. Charlotte "proves" her heroine innocent, and for the first time in her art the nature of death undergoes a change. No longer, as in Angria, the result of a crime, it becomes a source of innocent opportunity for the survivor, almost a precondition of increasing maturity. Twice in the novel older women, threats to Jane's happiness, die. And their death leaves the way open for Jane Eyre to attain her goals in life.

Both Sarah Reed and Bertha Mason are maternal figures, images derived from Brontë's complex suspicion of mothers. Sarah Reed is the most vicious of all the women in the novel; her death provides the main turning point in the book, the event which divides the work essentially in half. It is the knowledge she gains at the deathbed of her stepmother, the information concerning her true family, which turns Jane from sinner to heiress.

Sitting beside the woman after her death, Jane contemplates the corpse like an Angrian mourner: "There was stretched Sarah Reed's once robust and active frame, rigid and still: her eye of flint was covered with its cold lid. . . . A strange and solemn object was that corpse to me. I gazed on it with gloom and pain" (p. 211). But not with guilt. The death of Mrs. Reed seems to break a pattern which had obtained since the earliest days of the Angrian cycle. For once, Brontë allows a protagonist to contemplate death without the accompaniment of guilt feelings.[25] Her heroine goes to some length to assure the reader that she will in no sense be responsible for Mrs. Reed's death. There had been, indeed, an undertone of aggression in her attitude toward her dying stepmother. Earlier, face to face with the woman, Jane had told us: "I felt pain, and then I felt ire; and then I felt a determination to subdue her—to be her mistress in spite of her nature and her will" (p. 203). But she conquers her enemy through Christian charity, not through violence. The energy of aggression is turned into fierce and Christian self-control, and when the stepmother dies, Jane can serve as a blameless mourner.

As critics have long noted, the second maternal figure, Bertha Mason, is Jane's Oedipal rival.[26] Jane cannot marry Rochester—who is, as Mrs. Fairfax complains, old enough to be her father—because he already has a wife, a brutal lunatic who lives on the third floor. When she finds out about this marriage, Jane runs away from Thornfield and the danger of bigamy. But a year later she is called back by the mystical voice of her lover.

As we have seen in Chapter 2, Charlotte had already used the theme of the voice of the distant lover calling the protagonist home. In "Albion and Marina," Albion had rushed back to his beloved's side only to find her dead. Jane too rushes back to a home she has left, and like Albion she fears to find her lover dead. But she is mistaken.

Brontë describes Jane's approach to Thornfield in a peculiarly roundabout manner, using an extended simile which seems to have little connection with the action of *Jane Eyre*:

> A lover finds his mistress asleep on a mossy bank; he wishes to catch a glimpse of her fair face without waking her. He steals softly over the grass, careful to make no sound; . . . he bends above her; a light veil rests on her features: he lifts it, bends lower; now his eyes anticipate the vision of beauty—warm, and blooming, and lovely, in rest. . . . He . . . grasps and cries, and gazes, because he no longer fears to waken by any sound he can utter—by any movement he can make. He thought his love slept sweetly: he finds she is stone-dead. (p. 373)

The passage is a vague reminiscence of "Albion and

Marina." But with a significant difference. For here it is
not the beloved whom the lover will find dead. Rochester
is still alive. The "mistress" whom Jane will find dead is
Bertha Mason, the insane older woman whose marriage to
Rochester stood in the way of the fulfillment of Jane's love.
In her lust for violence she had burned down the mansion
and plunged to her death from the roof.

If we try to deal with *Jane Eyre* from an ethical standpoint, then it must be admitted that the death of Bertha
Mason provides an almost ludicrously inadequate solution
to the problem faced by a woman in love with a married
man. But *Jane Eyre* is only superficially concerned with
ethics; at bottom it is concerned with the psychology of
survival. The deepest problem which confronted Charlotte
Brontë was the need to overcome the effects of death, and
this becomes in turn her heroine's task.

Moreover, it would be a mistake to treat Bertha's death
realistically. For she represents an aspect of a woman who
is already long dead, Mrs. Brontë. And there is ample evidence to indicate that metaphorically Bertha is a creature
from beyond the grave, the most tangible of all the figures
who call to Jane from the far side of death's portals.[27] Her
vengeful attacks on Jane do not cease until Jane has run
away from temptation, renouncing her love for Rochester.
Having carried out a severe penance, having run away from
Thornfield and remained chaste for a year, the protagonist
can then return to the manor and find her matriarchal
enemy safely locked in her coffin. The woman returned
from the dead has gone back to her home in the grave for
good. Bertha is the last figure in the novel who will threaten
the heroine from that other, supernatural world. With her
death, the grave closes its doors and Jane can concentrate
on this life.

Death has been overcome; the dead have no claim on the
living. And that is as it should be. People die every day,
and the world cannot always be mourning. The death of
her schoolmates at Lowood had given Jane her first taste
of this freedom. Wandering through the warm fields of
May, as her sisterly friend Helen lay dying, the young girl
had been struck with the thought that this life is really quite

pleasant. Years later, the death of Sarah Reed had provided no cause for bereavement. She too died in May, and the world grew green without her. Now, near the end of the novel, in another late spring, Jane receives the news of Bertha's death without a pang. Let the dead bury their dead. Jane has no time to mourn; she must move on to Ferndean and fruition.

Jane approaches Ferndean Manor like a knight riding toward an ultimate test: "I thought I had taken a wrong direction and lost my way. The darkness of natural as well as of sylvan dusk gathered over me. I looked round in search of another road. There was none: all was interwoven stem, columnar trunk, dense, summer foliage—no opening anywhere" (p. 379). Ferndean lies in the midst of an Eden gone strangely to seed. Nature's rank fecundity, unchecked by the human need for order, has run riot for years, piling stem on stem, engendering new life on the heaped-up bed of dead leaves. The cottage and the location are literary descendants of the Lodge of Rivaulx, the hidden love nest where Zamorna kept his youthful mistress Mina Laury safe from the jealousy of his wife. And in a metaphoric sense Ferndean plays that same role of haven from matronly jealousy. For Bertha Mason would have been unable to survive if she had come to Ferndean. Earlier, Rochester had told Jane: "I possess an old house, Ferndean Manor, even more retired and hidden than this, where I could have lodged [Bertha] safely enough, had not a scruple about the unhealthiness of the situation, in the heart of a wood, made my conscience recoil from the arrangement. Probably those damp walls would soon have eased me of her charge" (p. 264). Yet this sodden lodge will be Jane's home. Moreover, for all its threatening darkness she will find it a serpentless Eden. For she marries a broken man, and the sexual threat he presented in the earlier chapters will be softened into conjugal affection. The Beast fully tamed, the superficially plain little beauty leads him to their new home: "I took that dear hand, held it a moment to my lips, then let it pass round my shoulder: being so much lower of stature than he, I served both for his prop and guide. We entered the wood, and wended homeward" (p. 395).

Eluding the snares which had lurked in the shadows throughout the novel, Jane has found the way to her bourne. Helen Burns was wrong; we do not have to die to be saved. Grace can shower down its blessings on this life as well as the next. For the time being Charlotte Brontë has once again resolved the debate between the will to die and the will to live and has come down on the side of life. Jane Eyre has learned that death should be neither a welcome punishment nor a gentle release from martyrdom, but an enemy to be avoided.

Yet the novel ends with a peculiar coda which lies athwart the seeming optimism which Brontë's art has temporarily attained. The final paragraph of the book is a letter from the ailing St. John Rivers. Quoting a passage from the Apocalypse, St. John looks forward with triumphant joy to the end of life on this earth: "My master . . . has forewarned me. Daily he announces more distinctly,— 'Surely I come quickly!' and hourly I more eagerly respond, —'Amen; even so come, Lord Jesus!' " (p. 398). Brontë's novel celebrates life, but the last word is given to death.

Chapter Five
Emptiness: Shirley

FOR HER THIRD NOVEL Charlotte Brontë decided to widen her vision to a scope which seemed fitting and necessary for a contemporary novelist. It was 1848, the year of European revolution, and the world seemed on the verge of cataclysmic change. She would take that unrest into account. Using as her background the Luddite riots of the early nineteenth century, she would write a social novel.

Gifted with hindsight, the modern critic is tempted to see this shift of focus as an aberration from the author's natural line of development.[1] *Jane Eyre*, after all, had been the product of a sort of sublime tunnel vision, an intense concentration on the consciousness of a single individual to the near exclusion of the wider world. But Brontë's decision can be seen as a healthy one. For one thing, her view of reality had never been all that narrow. It should be kept in mind that she had already, in her adolescence, managed to create a complete social world. The construction of Angria had demanded the scope, if not the maturity, of a Walter Scott. *Jane Eyre* represented the conscious restriction of a vision capable of wider focus.[2]

And her second novel had accomplished its psychological task. In *Jane Eyre* Brontë had forced herself to come to terms with her childhood and the wounds it had left. She had faced the question of death honestly, and if she had not found answers, she had attained an equanimity on which she could now build. The novel was a stunning achievement, but it was also a work which she had to outgrow. It is quite possible that, given a few years of relative calm, Brontë would have developed along the lines of Dickens after *David Copperfield*. Certainly *Shirley* bears the same relationship to *Jane Eyre* that *Bleak House* bears to *David Copperfield*. Both novelists attempted to move away from the intense fictionalized examination of their own lives to an analysis of the society in which those lives were lived. Both *Shirley* and *Bleak House* represent a channeling of pain and resentment away from personal and toward social issues. The Victorians felt that personal wounds should be looked at, their causes examined, but that ultimately the cure lay in the transformation of pain into energy, the energy to carry out social action. And though the analysis was frequently hasty, the rush to action premature, the instinct itself was entirely healthy. In *Jane Eyre* Brontë had laid her childhood to rest. In *Shirley* she constructed a world of adults, a world beset with the problems which mature men and women face.

But she was not allowed those few years of calm which might perhaps have turned her into a more objective novelist. The traumas of her childhood came back to haunt her. *Shirley* was composed under almost impossible circumstances. Charlotte had barely completed the first third of the novel when Branwell died. She tried to return to the book, but the rapid deterioration of Emily's health made all thought of composition impossible. She took up *Shirley* again in the winter of 1849, after Emily's death, but her work was impeded by Anne's illness. Finally, in the weeks following Anne's death, she turned to her creative labor in an effort to maintain her sanity. With an admirable display of will power, she finished the novel in a matter of weeks.

She had managed to create artistic order in the midst of her chaotic reality. Yet there is little doubt that this new series of incursions of death into her life weakened the fabric of her novel.[3] As shock succeeded shock in the year in which *Shirley* was composed, Charlotte's feeling for the integrity of life seems to have faded somewhat. If Branwell and Emily and Anne could die so suddenly, then anything could happen. One result of the tragic absurdity which she was experiencing seems to have been a loss of any sense of inevitability in her fictional world. The relationship between cause and effect shows signs of breaking down. Whole chapters could be omitted, as G. H. Lewes pointed out, without disturbing the progress of the novel.[4] Characters appear out of nowhere at unexpected points

in the narrative and become major figures. Point of view
threatens to become fragmented as clumsy narrative tech-
niques, such as Shirley's devoir, are introduced. The author's struggle to complete the work is too frequently evident.

But the most important defect which the year's traumas
forced on *Shirley* was a temporary lapse in the maturity
of Brontë's vision of life. *Shirley* is at once the most and
the least mature of the four novels. It is the only one of her
novels which attempts to integrate personal and social considerations, the only one which gives the reader the sense
of a complete society. But, as we shall see, her grief over
the death of her sisters and brother forced Charlotte at one
point to abandon that society, to send one of her heroines
on a symbolic quest through the land of death in search of
her long-lost mother. The resultant mixture of realism and
romance, it seems to me, is the greatest defect of the novel.
Jane Eyre had inhabited a semi-gothic land where the
limits of credibility could be safely expanded. But Caroline
Helstone is a child of the industrial revolution, and her
quest is jarringly out of place in the practical world around
her. It becomes a childish if understandable excrescence in
an otherwise mature book.

There is nothing childish about the book's basic conception of life. *Shirley* is a much bleaker novel than its predecessors.[5] The bands of rebellious workers and squadrons
of cavalry which troop back and forth across the countryside do nothing to disturb the essential loneliness of the
landscape. *Shirley*'s settings are not, like *Jane Eyre*'s, symbolic. *Jane Eyre*'s landscape had implied a sense of the fit-
ness of things, of a providential arena in which obstacles
have been placed to test the strength of a traveller whose
destination is important. *Shirley* is a thoroughly secular
novel. God still exists, but He has retired to an awful distance and has no apparent concern for the fate of His
creatures.[6]

God certainly seems to have abandoned the working
class. The background of the novel is the Luddite riots
which took place in Yorkshire in the winter and spring of
1811–1812. Asa Briggs has described the movement, in

which factories were attacked, machinery broken, and mill owners ambushed, as "largely a protest against the introduction of the machine."[7] He adds: "Scarcity of work and high prices of provisions provided the impetus to action."[8] Labor unrest is important in the novel. Yet *Shirley* is no more about the struggle between labor and management than Dickens' *Hard Times* is about strikes and strikebreakers. The melodramatic form of the Victorian novel is in part the mirror and in part the cause of its individualist ideology. Even in the hands of Scott, the most historically minded of the great nineteenth-century British novelists, the novel is a genre which focuses on the struggle of people rather than epochs, individuals rather than classes. Brontë's novel shares that individualist bent. Set against the background of famine, industrial unemployment, and a torn social fabric, *Shirley* centers on a different form of unemployment. Its author had never been a factory worker, never experienced an industrial layoff. She chose to focus on a form of enforced idleness she had known at firsthand—the emptiness and isolation of a middle-class woman who can find no meaningful activity in a world controlled by men. The psychological hunger of the women of the novel serves as an individualistic metaphor for the collective hunger of the workers around them. Above all the novel concerns the attempt of two women, living in a chaotic, seemingly absurd world, to find or create meaning in their lives.

The condition which nearly all of the middle-class characters of the novel share is loneliness. Yet there seems to be a vast difference in the book between a man's loneliness and a woman's. The laws of the newly developed world of British capitalism dictate that a businessman remain aloof from his fellow men, but if Brontë deplores that form of social isolation, she also admires its strength. Robert Moore, the hero of *Shirley*, is a reworking of Edward Crimsworth, the villain of *The Professor*; his position in life and his pitiless treatment of his underlings are borrowed from William Crimsworth's tyrannical older brother. Robert's very loneliness is a precondition of his ruthless potency. He has no time to fret about his isolation:

the business which he owns provides him with the primary solution to the problem of emptiness, shaping his life and his consciousness. He can think of love if he wishes, dream of an end to his loneliness, but a man has a thousand other thoughts: "[Men's] discussions run on other topics than matrimony. . . . courtships, establishments, dowries: [we talk of] the cloth we can't sell, the hands we can't employ, the mills we can't run. . . . I believe women talk and think only of [love], and they naturally fancy men's minds similarly occupied."[9] But respectable women are society's ornaments, and thus denied any really meaningful solutions to the problem of emptiness. The loneliness of Caroline Helstone, one of the novel's two heroines, is desperate and seemingly hopeless. Her life is a blank. She tells Robert: "I should like an occupation; and if I were a boy, it would not be so difficult to find one" (p. 54). She is a girl, however, and she can only keep house for her uncle, or marry, or slide into the profession of spinsterhood. In each case her identity would be defined by her relationship to a man, or by the very lack of that relationship. Shut out from the masculine world of capitalist struggle, she cannot even think like a man, though at one point she tries: "Caroline . . . endeavoured to realise the state of mind of a 'man of business,' to enter into it, feel what he would feel, aspire to what he would aspire. Her earnest wish was to see things as they were, and not to be romantic" (p. 136). She cannot cross the line, even provisionally. Manhood, the guild which structures the events of the novel, is a closed corporation existing only for the benefit of its members, with by-laws and rituals which outsiders cannot fathom.

Caroline, the isolated woman questing for significance, is as much Brontë's surrogate as Jane Eyre had been. But the problems she has to work out are quite different from those of her predecessor. There had been no doubt in the second novel that a woman's life has meaning. If there were no meaning to life, then the question of guilt or innocence would have been thoroughly irrelevant. Jane's difficult task had been to fathom the moral nature of that meaning, to decide whether she was the child of God or the devil. *Shirley* moves beyond those essentially paranoid concerns to question the existence of meaning at all in the life of an unmarried woman. Charlotte Brontë was thirty-two years old when she began *Shirley*. She had attained professional success, but she was a very lonely woman. She had turned down two offers of marriage and saw no prospect of a third proposal. Before she came to the end of her third novel, her loneliness was to undergo a metamorphosis into a state of such thorough desolation that she would distort her book to escape from it. But in the first half of *Shirley*, at any rate, she forces her heroine to confront in a rational manner the prospect of a life of emotional emptiness.

Though in love with the aloof Robert, Caroline looks forward with despair to the comfortless state of spinsterhood. It is a peculiarly feminine form of loneliness. There are two groups of conspicuously single people in the book—the curates and the spinsters. The curates constitute a thoroughly gregarious, cheerful circle of slapstick mediocrities. One of their prime characteristics, indeed the trait they hold most in common, is precisely their need to join one another in quarrelsome conviviality. They could as easily have eaten alone, the narrator notes disapprovingly in the opening chapter. They would never think of that alternative, however, for the curates are essentially herd animals.

But the spinsters are strays. Ridiculed behind their backs by the males of the novel, they spend their lives constructing and maintaining protective walls between themselves and the emptiness of existence. Miss Mann has been hurt so badly and so often that her life consists as much as possible in dusting furniture, cutting flowers for her vases, dealing with objects which, if they provide little pleasure, at least impart no pain, for "to avoid excitement was one of Miss Mann's aims in life" (p. 141). Caroline, seeking a model for her own future life as an unmarried woman, is quickly able to break through the ice of Miss Mann's reserve: "Miss Mann felt that she was understood partly, and wished to be understood further; for however old, plain, humble, desolate, afflicted we may be, so long as our hearts preserve the feeblest spark of life, they preserve also, shivering near that pale ember, a starved, ghostly longing for appreciation and affection" (p. 143). Miss Mann, Caroline discovers, had been "a most devoted daughter and sister, an unwearied watcher by lingering deathbeds" (p. 143). Now there is no one left for Miss Mann to watch die, and she tends to her plants and her furniture, herself slowly stiffening into inanimate companionship with them. The spinster whose last name sounds so masculine must have seemed peculiarly close to Charlotte Brontë. Isolation is the bitter payment which fate deals out to a woman for her devoted service as a mourner.

Miss Mann attempts to escape the implications of her total isolation in a compulsive attention to the inanimate objects which prove her existence (if the dusted table is Miss Mann's, there must be a Miss Mann to whom the table belongs). Miss Ainsley, the novel's other elderly spinster, escapes her frozen self in "selfless" devotion to the poor and the sick. She ministers to the suffering of others in order to forget her own.

But selflessness is not a viable answer to emptiness in the secular world of *Shirley*. Caroline asks herself: "Is there not a terrible hollowness, mockery, want, craving, in that existence which is given away to others, for want of something of your own to bestow it on? I suspect there is. Does virtue lie in abnegation of self? I do not believe it" (p. 138). One must prove one's existence to oneself. Meaningful activity is as important to a woman as to a man. Thus Caroline asks: "What am I to do to fill the interval of time which spreads between me and the grave?" (p. 138). The corollary of this necessary activity is the earning of money, of one's "living." Caroline's provisional solution is to become a governess. She is dissuaded, however, by Mrs. Pryor, who recounts a statement by one of her former pupils which negates the humanity of the profession: "We need the imprudences, extravagances, mistakes, and crimes of a certain number of fathers to sow the seed from which we reap the harvest of governesses" (pp. 298–299). Thus the position of governess, as Charlotte Brontë knew so well, would represent the abnegation, not the maintenance, of the self.

Nor is there any other work which would give dignity and meaning to a woman's life. It is noticeable that the bachelors of the novel are not called bachelors. Mr. Malone, Mr. Donne, and Mr. Sweeting are defined through

their curacies, not through the secondary fact that they are
single. But Miss Mann and Miss Ainsley will never ac-
complish anything in their lives which will take primacy
over the fact that they have found no husband. They are
simply old maids. A woman cannot create a viable identity
through her productive activity or through her earnings.
Robert Moore can establish his humanity by following
William Crimsworth's old formula: by doing more, earning more, and possessing more, he can hope to be more.
To Caroline Helstone and to the other women in the world
of *Shirley*, however, that road is blocked.

But what if a woman were by nature an artist? If she
possessed the imagination to escape from the narrow world
of capitalist propriety and create an inner universe, at least
that inner world would be free. And internal freedom
would surely radiate out, create a psychological aura in
which a woman could attain a self-sufficiency that could
not be injured by the men around her.

As she watched her sister Emily die, Charlotte decided
to add such a character to her novel. Shirley Keeldar, she
told Elizabeth Gaskell, was her idea of what Emily would
have been "had she been placed in health and prosperity"
(Gaskell, *Life*, p. 277). Yet those advantages are not
enough to give Shirley the scope for meaningful activity.
Although she is rich, she is still faced with the problem
of what to do when one has been born a woman in a man's
world. And her powerful imagination does not solve the
problems of her feminine subordination; it simply mirrors it.

The products of Shirley's artistic flair are evident
throughout the novel. At one point she quarrels with Milton's conception of Eve. She professes her own love for
"my mother Eve, in these days called Nature," and envisions the first woman as a form outlined against the sky:
"I now see—a woman-Titan: her robe of blue air spreads
to the outskirts of the heath. . . . Her steady eyes . . . are
lifted and full of worship—they tremble with the softness
of love and the lustre of prayer" (p. 253).

Like Frances Henri's compositions and Jane Eyre's paintings, the myth which Shirley constructs around Eve seems
revelatory of the mind of its author—or rather its authors.

Eve's complex, contradictory reaction to male oppression highlights both Shirley Keeldar's and Charlotte Brontë's predicament as women in a man's world. Shirley's Eve is the daughter of Jehovah, and therefore, like all women, subject to masculine tyranny. Her response to tyranny is confused. On the one hand, Shirley envisions her in prayerful communion with her God—not the discourse of equals but the audience of a subject with her beloved ruler. On the other hand, Shirley's Eve was the mother of the Titans; she bore Prometheus: "The first woman's breast that heaved with life on this world yielded the daring which could contend with Omnipotence" (p. 253). Expelled by her mature knowledge or by the tyranny of the ruling male from the connectedness of the primal garden, the first woman faces a painful dilemma. She can adore the tyrant, thus reestablishing a pale version of her primal security at the expense of her self-worth, or she can rebel, asserting the autonomy of the self at the cost of eternal isolation. Eve seems unable to choose one path over the other, unable to reject either subservience or revolt. It is the same choice the industrial workers, locked out of their factories and forbidden access to the means of production, must face. They choose open revolt. But no woman in Charlotte Brontë's fiction is capable of that choice.

The middle-class men of the novel are the only characters spared Eve's dilemma. They see themselves as natural rulers of the world. The male form of isolation is, as the characters of this novel view it, both more extreme and at the same time more productive, more progressive than the female. We can see the difference in the characters' relationship to nature. At one point in the novel Caroline and Shirley agree to spend a day in Nunnwood. Caroline sees the excursion as an escape from the brutally active present: "We [are] going simply to see the old trees, the old ruins; to pass a day in old times, surrounded by olden silence, and above all by quietude" (p. 166). The most stringent requirement of the outing is that there be no men. If a man were to come along, "then Nature forgets us; covers her vast calm brow with a dim veil, conceals her face, and withdraws the peaceful joy with which, if we had been content to worship her only, she would have filled our hearts" (p. 166). Nature is a jealous mother who requires her daughters' affection for herself. What would the women obtain if they turned from the quiet love of nature to the love of men? "More elation and more anxiety: an excitement that steals the hours away fast, and a trouble that ruffles their course" (p. 167).

Women receive as compensation for their loneliness a calm connection with a maternal landscape. The men in the novel, whether or not they pay any attention to their surroundings, seem to lack this connectedness with the natural world around them. At the one extreme there is Peter Augustus Malone, "not a man given to close observation of Nature" (p. 12), who is more interested in a well-stocked inn than in the contrast of earth and sky. And at the other end of the spectrum, the end where most of the middle-class men seem bunched, is Louis Moore, Robert's brother. Shirley remarks to him: "You take a sort of harsh, solitary triumph in drawing pleasure out of the elements, and the inanimate and lower animal creation" (p. 359). Solitude and triumph, indeed, are inextricably mixed in Louis' feelings. He retorts: "With animals I feel I am Adam's son; the heir of him to whom dominion was given over 'every living thing that moveth upon the earth.' Your dog likes and follows me; when I go into that yard, the pigeons from your dove-cot flutter at my feet; your mare in the stable knows me as well as it knows you, and obeys me better. . . . No caprice can withdraw these pleasures from me: they are *mine*" (p. 359). The pleasure of dominion isolates the males of the novel from nature; they can never consider themselves part of that object which they claim to own. This change from an organic to a proprietary relationship with their surroundings seems to be both a cause and a result of the capitalist technology which structures the novel's social reality. For in their isolation from nature, the men feel free to improve on her, to introduce technological innovations, to create prosthetic extensions of their strength which will make them ever more powerful at the same time that they increase their isolation. Rather than live in the quiet cycles of the seasons, the men of the novel live for the news of recent inventions and the reports on the progress of the Peninsular War.

This exciting, unstable realm of technology, business, and warfare is closed to the women. Caroline accepts her exclusion from what might be termed the public domain of the novel, but Shirley's soul craves heroic activity, and she attempts to enter the alien world of masculinity. She will try her utmost to become a man. But a woman cannot do it; the chasm is too great to be leaped. She will in the end fall back into her femininity and accept a husband.

Shirley's androgynous nature begins with her name (in the early nineteenth century almost exclusively a man's name) and extends to her conception of herself and to much of her behavior. She tells Caroline: "They gave me a man's name; I hold a man's position: it is enough to inspire me with a touch of manhood, and when I see such people as . . . [Robert] Moore before me, gravely talking to me of business, really I feel quite gentleman-like . . . they ought to make me a magistrate and a captain of yeomanry" (p. 160). But her attempts to mimic a man are pitifully comic. On the night of the battle at Moore's mill, Mr. Helstone, Caroline's uncle, leaves Shirley to guard his niece at home while he goes off to fight. She sees herself as "the first gentleman of Briarfield" and carries a brace of pistols. But although the post entails some danger, she gets no chance to show her military prowess. She likes to call herself Captain Keeldar, but her only real opportunity to live the part is in the farcical march against the Nonconformists during the Sunday-school procession. Striding earnestly into battle she tells Caroline that she will pretend to be a Scottish Covenanter. The encounter, in which she is "ready . . . with her parasol, to rebuke the slightest breach of orders" (p. 240), is sad fare for such heroic hunger.

The world of significant action is closed to women. "Shirley Seeks to be Saved by Works" is the ironic title of one chapter. But no woman in the novel can be saved by her own works. Shirley can think of nothing more meaningful to do than getting up a charity. In a time of great poverty, the distribution of charity is obviously a useful activity, but the important point is that it is ultimately a peculiarly feminine preoccupation with a hint of futility about it. It will not change society, and it will not "save" Shirley or satisfy her desperate longing for a meaningful existence. Only men in this novel can be saved by works. Excluded from the world of deeds, condemned to triviality because of their gender and their rank in society, respectable women, if they are to be saved at all, must be saved by faith alone.

Earlier, Caroline had asked Shirley: "But are we men's equals, or are we not?" (p. 170). The oblique reply highlights the limits of the novel's feminism: "Nothing ever charms me more than when I meet my superior. . . . I should be glad to see him any day: the higher above me, so much the better: it degrades to stoop—it is glorious to look up. What frets me is, that when I try to esteem, I am baffled: when religiously inclined, there are but false gods to adore. I disdain to be a Pagan" (p. 171). It is not surprising that at the point in the novel where Shirley finally realizes that her good works have proven useless, an object for her faith should come on the scene—in the unlikely and unexpected guise of Louis Moore, Robert's brother.

Louis' character resembles that of his cousin Caroline. Both of them are essentially passive, depressed people who feel trapped in a lonely existence. But Louis holds the advantage of masculinity, and he projects his loneliness into a heroic myth, a romantic dream of emigration to North America: "I have such a thirst for freedom . . . her I will follow deep into virgin woods. . . . I know no white woman whom I love that would accompany me; but I am certain Liberty will await me, sitting under a pine: when I call her she will come to my loghouse, and she shall fill my arms" (pp. 484–485).

Shirley, his former pupil, sympathizes with Louis' amorous intentions toward that cold abstraction, Liberty. She had already told him: "I always think you stand in the world like a solitary but watchful, thoughtful archer in a wood; and the quiver on your shoulder holds more arrows than one" (p. 484). But Louis' masculine need for power will not allow him to return the favor by humoring Shirley's equally absurd vision of the Wild West. Earlier, burdened by her social duties, she had sighed: "Oh, for rest under my own vine and my own fig-tree! Happy is the slave-wife of the Indian chief, in that she has no drawing-room duty to perform, but can sit at ease weaving mats, and stringing beads, and peacefully flattening her picanniny's head in an unmolested corner of her wigwam. I'll emigrate to the western woods" (p. 367). Louis, gentleman that he is, tactfully ignores the awkward intrusion of the picanniny and his fig-tree into the wigwam, but he cannot resist taking note of Shirley's willingness to become a slave: "To marry a White Cloud or a Big Buffalo; and after wedlock to devote yourself to the tender task of digging your lord's maize-field, while he smokes his pipe or drinks fire-water" (p. 367). And, slowly gathering his psychological forces, Louis sets out to become Big Buffalo.

The would-be Captain Keeldar, aggressively searching for heroic action which would give meaning to her life, accomplishes nothing and becomes swiftly tamed. Louis is the tamer. When, in the days of her French lessons, she had threatened to get out of hand, Louis had forced her to recite *Le Cheval Dompté*—"the tamed horse." His reserved, polite manner, his decency and kindness aside, his mode of courtship is simple: "She must be scared to be won" (p. 490). His tactics work. Shirley reaches such a state of fawning submission that she can sigh to her lover: "I am glad I know my keeper, and am used to him. Only his voice will I follow; only his hand shall manage me; only at his feet will I repose" (p. 492). She need no longer search for a mode of existence which can console her for her femininity; her position is now fixed. When Louis tells her, "I am a dependent: I know my place," she answers: "I am a woman: I know mine" (p. 487).

The irony of Shirley's dream of meaningful activity is thus complete. The heroic Shirley, who wanted to be a man, the *bête fauve* ("wild beast") who dreamed of life in the western woods, ends caged in her mansion and liking it. She has done it of her own free will. She tells Caroline later: "Louis . . . would never have learned to rule, if [I] had not ceased to govern" (p. 504).

After viewing the exclusively masculine battle at the

mill, Shirley and Caroline had talked of the heroines of male novelists. Shirley had laughed at them with scorn: "The cleverest, the acutest men are often under an illusion about women: . . . their good woman is a queer thing, half doll, half angel. . . . Then to hear them fall into ecstasies with each other's creations, worshipping the heroine of such a poem—novel—drama, thinking it fine—divine!" (p. 278). Shirley's drive toward a meaningful existence had seemed to bar her from the easy acceptance of the doll-like status of the respectable women of her era. But in a repressive world passivity is rewarded and worshipped, aggressiveness tamed. Shirley had told Caroline that she would gladly love, but "there are but false gods to adore. I disdain to be a Pagan" (p. 171). She cannot, however, be a middle-class man and possess an autonomous self; she becomes instead a man's possession. Worshipping Louis, whose face "looks like a god of Egypt" (p. 489), Captain Keeldar dwindles into Mrs. Louis Moore, the lady of the manor.

The irony of Brontë's treatment of Shirley is at times bitter, but always adult. Her friend, the feminist writer Harriet Martineau, would later accuse her of a preoccupation with love which excluded the myriad other interests which a woman might have.[10] The charge seems rather unfair. The melodramatic Victorian novel, both through its form and through its history, was fated to that same overemphasis on romantic love. The novelist had no other frame on which to mount a work of fiction. But love is quite clearly a chimerical solution to Shirley's restlessness, and Brontë, I would assert, knew that full well. If anything, the accusation which a liberal critic like Harriet Martineau could more properly have levelled at the novelist was a pessimism which paralyzed social action, a hopeless and ironic conviction that meaningful action is impossible for a woman in a world owned and managed by men.

If Brontë is brilliantly adult, though bitter, in her treatment of Shirley, she is childish in her handling of Caroline Helstone. Yet even here it is not a question of naïveté, but of neurosis. For under the pressure of the series of deaths which occurred during the composition of the novel, she reverted, for the sake of her own psychological survival, to the level of childhood fantasy. In the summer of 1848 she had constructed a fully realized, mature set of problems for her heroine to confront. But then a new round of deaths began in Haworth Parsonage. Surrounded by death, desperate to envision a world in which obstacles are surmountable, Brontë suddenly awarded Caroline a childlike solution to the problems of life. She gave her back her mother.

In discovering that Mrs. Pryor is her long-lost mother, Caroline finds the remedy for her depression, the cure for all her doubts: " 'My own mamma,' then she went on, as if pleasing herself with the thought of their relationship, 'who belongs to me, and to whom I belong! I am a rich girl now: I have something I can love well, and not be afraid of loving' " (p. 351). Caroline is forced to undergo a sickness almost unto death in order to obtain this most valued possession. Robert can attain his most cherished goals through his own furious activity. But Caroline is a woman, and her closest approach to meaningful activity is to grow sick and attract maternal love to her bedside.

Yet her sickness is in itself a form of heroism. For it amounts to a conscious decision to die, to leave this meaningless world in search of something better. The chapter in which Caroline's illness is described is entitled "The Valley of the Shadow of Death," and it opens with this passage: "At . . . times [the] Future bursts suddenly, as if a rock had rent, and in it a grave had opened, whence issues the body of one that slept. Ere you are aware you stand face to face with a shrouded and unthought-of Calamity—a new Lazarus" (p. 329). Caroline is no Christ. Jesus was able to stand in front of the grave and summon Lazarus to come forth. Caroline has to take a more dangerous route to the fulfillment of her fondest dreams. She has to enter the grave herself, at least metaphorically, and fetch the beloved corpse. Not even Jane Eyre had had the courage to undertake such a journey. Jane had often wondered what the afterlife looked like, but had consistently refused to slake her curiosity. Caroline shows more audacity than her predecessor: "*Where is* the other world? In *what* will another life consist? . . . Great Spirit! . . . Sustain me through the ordeal I dread and must undergo! Give me strength! Give me patience! Give me—oh! *give me FAITH!"* (p. 334). She cannot visualize the place where her spirit will go, but the void does not terrify her as it had Jane Eyre. And she takes comfort in the thought that she knows full well where her body will lie. Like the Brontë family, the Helstones are buried inside the village church, and Caroline will join them there. Caroline's mind dwells on the graves she has grown up with. Like Charlotte Brontë, she needs to feel that they are well cared for:

> And does the [graveyard] look peaceful? . . . Can
> you see many long weeds and nettles amongst the
> graves; or do they look turfy and flowery? . . . I always
> like [the graves to be cared for]: it soothes one's
> mind to see the place in order: and, I dare say, within
> the church just now that moonlight shines as softly
> as in my room. It will fall through the east window
> full on the Helstone monument. When I close my eyes
> I seem to see poor papa's epitaph in block letters on
> white marble. There is plenty of room for other in-
> scriptions underneath. (p 336)

Only when Caroline has shown herself ready to die, when she has completed the mental preparations for the journey, taken leave of the living and pictured herself among the dead—only then does Mrs. Pryor admit that she is her mother. William Crimsworth and Jane Eyre had clung to this life with desperate ferocity. As a consequence of their avoidance of death, they had been allowed only symbolic glimpses of their mothers, William through a painting and Jane through a dream. In Charlotte Brontë's mental universe, finding a mother demands a full readiness to die.

But the prize is worth the agony. The girl who had looked forward to a life of total isolation has finally found a way to attain acceptance by the most important person in her life. And total acceptance will be followed by uncom-pounded bliss, by a paradisal return to infancy's warmth: "[Her mother] held her to her bosom: she cradled her in her arms: she rocked her softly, as if lulling a young child to sleep" (p. 339). And: "Caroline no more showed [any] wounding sagacity or reproachful sensitiveness now, than she had done when a suckling of three months old" (p. 350). Each woman accepts and affirms the other fully. Now Caroline need no longer play dead. She possesses the necessary proof that life is not empty but worthwhile: "But if you *are* my mother, the world is all changed to me. Surely I can live" (p. 339).

Brontë does not allow the lost mother to return without an explanation of the reasons behind her absence, however. Although Caroline expresses no resentment, and Charlotte insists that her heroine felt none, some apology for those years of maternal neglect must be offered. Mrs. Pryor's excuse is simple, absurd, and devastating: "I let you go as a babe, because you were pretty, and I feared your loveliness" (p. 342).[11] Caroline's only crime was that she was not as homely as her mother would have wished. The child was the image of her handsome father. Her mother transferred her hatred and fear of James Helstone to Caroline and ran from them both. She did not see her child again until she returned to the area as Shirley Keeldar's companion. Only then did she see that her daughter was no threat to her: "I soon saw you were diffident; that was the first thing which reassured me: had you been rustic, clownish, awkward, I should have been content" (p. 340). Caroline's beauty drove her mother away. Only by showing the full extent of her feelings of inferiority, only by demonstrating her willingness to die, has she been able to entice the woman to return. Now Mrs. Pryor, placated, cries: "James, your child atones" (p. 341). The crime of beauty and grace has been expiated. Caroline will go forth into life a new woman, her former passivity exchanged for an assurance which seems almost masculine in the context of this novel. Telling herself "I *will* alter this: this *shall* be altered" (p. 459), she will carry off Robert Moore as the prize of her assertiveness.

Brontë's solution to the problems faced by Caroline is, as many critics have pointed out, unbelievable. But it is an artistic error which is entirely understandable, seen in the light of the novelist's own life. In walking through the Valley of the Shadow of Death unscathed and finding her mother, Caroline has successfully completed a quest which Charlotte Brontë had in all likelihood thought of unconsciously since she was five years old. As we have seen, in her adolescent writings, she had tried various methods of resuscitating the dead. Moreover she had repeatedly forced her protagonists to find where the dead are located, to search them out and gaze at them. In other words, one or another portion of Caroline's task frequently appears in the Angrian writings. But here in *Shirley*, under the pressure of a new set of traumas, a new round of deaths, the outline of that old fantasy becomes disturbingly clear. At the root of a woman's depression is the loss of her mother. What must one do to regain her? Refuse all food, take to one's bed, come dangerously close to death. And *then* perhaps, on the brink of the grave, one's mother will return out of pity. That flirting with death will perhaps be punishment enough for whatever crime caused the mother to leave years before.

Quite understandably, given the situation in which the novel was composed, Brontë did not let any of *Shirley's* central characters die. Jane Eyre's career had been punctuated and even structured by the deaths of Helen Burns, Sarah Reed, and Bertha Mason. In *Shirley* the situation is different. Both Caroline and Shirley frighten their friends by deciding to die. They can feel themselves dying, but ultimately they change their minds and decide to live. And their approach to the grave brings them declarations of love. Six years after the composition of *Shirley*, Brontë made that same unconscious decision to die. Like Caroline, she refused all food and took to her bed. Her decision brought her only death.

But *Shirley* is a work of fiction, released from the inexorable rules of life. Caroline is allowed to find her mother and rescind her decision to die. The novel as a whole is the most realistic of Brontë's works, but the outcome of Caroline's story is escapist. Its author knew that. She said of the novel: "The occupation of writing it has been a boon to me. It took me out of dark and desolate reality into an unreal but happier region."[12] She was right, of course. The novel allowed her for once to escape from the real world it so convincingly portrays. Caroline's story carried the author out of the house of mourning, brought her to a land where lost mothers return to soothe away death like the nightmare of a little girl.

Chapter Six
Exile: Villette

Villette is Brontë's masterpiece, the culmination of her creative life. It combines the maturity of *Shirley*'s basic vision of life with the psychological penetration of *Jane Eyre* to form one of the finest, and at the same time one of the most painful, novels of its time. Its contemporary readers were profoundly moved and disturbed by the book. "There is something preternatural in its power," George Eliot claimed on first reading it, but she made no attempt to analyze what that something was.[1] Others tried to be more exact. Matthew Arnold read the book at a time when he was beginning to define just what was wrong with con-- temporary literature. He saw the novel as an example of the modern disease of subjectivity. He poses the question "Why is *Villette* disagreeable?" and then provides his own answer: "Because the writer's mind contains nothing but hunger, rebellion, and rage, and therefore that is all she can, in fact, put into her book. No fine writing can hide this thoroughly, and it will be fatal to her in the long run."[2] Arnold's prophecy was tragically accurate; the hunger so brilliantly projected onto the pages of *Villette* would indeed prove fatal to Brontë. *Villette* is at bottom the mirror of a wish to die. But as long as the artist could create, as long as she could transform personal pain into a fictional narrative, she could hold that death wish at bay. The inhabitants of her fictive world could take a portion of her own alienation onto their shoulders, thus relieving their creator. Lucy Snowe could move off into lonely exile, and Charlotte Brontë could remain at home.

As we have seen in Chapter 1, *Villette* was written in the midst of a black despondency. Brontë saw herself as an isolated survivor of the flood which had washed over her home. In one letter to W. S. Williams, her publisher's reader, she described the extent of her feeling of desolation: "Lonely as I am—how should I be if Providence had never given me courage to adopt a career—perseverence to plead through two long, weary years with publishers till they admitted me? How should I be with youth past— sisters lost—a resident in a moorland parish where there is not a single educated family? In that case I should have no world at all: the raven, weary of surveying the deluge and without an ark to return to, would be my type."[3] Her creativity, her career as a novelist, could protect her, she felt, from the fate of Noah's raven. But the characters of *Villette* are not creative. The homeless raven can indeed serve as an emblem of their condition.

Lucy Snowe, the protagonist of *Villette*, finds the evidence of her alienation wherever she looks. Even a bouquet reminds her of her misery: "I like to see flowers growing, but when they are gathered, they cease to please. I look on them as things rootless and perishable; their likeness to life makes me sad."[4] Rootlessness lies at the heart of *Villette*. *Shirley* had been a provincial novel, its characters seeking their destiny in Briarfield, or Nunnely, or Whinbury. Though they talked of emigration they stayed at home. But the characters of *Villette* wander over the face of Europe in hope of an experience or an illumination which will make life more bearable. Le Compte de Bassompierre, a Scotsman ironically named Home, recites "Auld Lang Syne" as he sits in wistful splendor in his foreign townhouse. The Brettons have been driven out of their homeland by financial disaster. Paul Imanuel travels to Guadeloupe without complaint simply because the people who run his life have told him that he should. Schoolgirls from England, France, and Germany congregate in Labassecour to acquire culture in a land which, according to Brontë, has none. Ginevra Fanshawe has travelled so much that she knows neither her language nor her religion: "I write English so badly—such spelling and grammar, they tell me. Into the bargain I have quite forgotten my religion; they call me a Protestant, you know, but really I am not sure whether I am one or not: I don't know well the difference between Romanism and Protestantism. . . . I was a Lutheran once at Bonn. . . . I was excessively happy at Bonn!" (p. 46). Ginevra's addled nostalgia is the expression of a world in which the pieces no longer fit together. Each of the main characters once lived an existence in which the center held. But a storm has washed away that world, and now each lives out his or her post-diluvial isolation, wandering in search of a new spot in which to strike root.[5]

Brontë had struggled for months in the midst of her own isolation before she was able to create *Villette*. Her mind was torn between the need to create, to establish yet another fictional world, and the need to mourn the dead. In her guilt-ridden frame of mind, she would begin to write only to be blocked by the onset of the symptoms of the disease which had killed her sisters and her brother. On New Year's Day 1852, she complained to Williams: "All the winter the fact of my never being able to stoop over a desk without bringing on pain and oppression in the chest has been a great affliction to me, and the want of tranquil rest at night has tried me much."[6] During this difficult period, she wrote two fragments which did not find their way into the finished novel. They have been overlooked in criticism of *Villette*, yet they add to our understanding of the tone and the underlying concerns of the novel itself.

The first fragment is a nostalgic description of the earlier, better time, the time before the flood waters rose and covered the land: "We came from a place where the buildings were numerous and stately, where before white housefronts there rose here and there trees straight as spires, where there was one walk broad and endlessly long, down which on certain days rolled two tides—one of people on foot, brightly clad with shining silks, delicate bonnets with feathers and roses, scarves fluttering, little parasols gay as tulips; and the other of carriages rolling along rapid and quiet. Indeed, all was quiet in this walk—it was a mysterious place, full of people but without noise."[7] The scene has all the bright and sinister formality of a schizoid vision. The dreamlike setting of the fragment is dignified and silent; the people, like the trees, seem to have no contact with one another. Life is manifested in movement and color, but the human voice is still. Even details like the fluttering scarves seem to accentuate that utter silence. It is as beautifully controlled a passage as Brontë ever wrote, and it sets a new tone for her work, a tone of icy detachment which has taken over from the impassioned excitement which characterizes nearly all of her earlier works.

The world described in the passage is one where human contact seems impossible. In another portion of the same fragment the narrator describes her attempts to overcome the loneliness of her existence: "My father . . . was the origin of all the punishments I had in those early days. I had an unreasonable wish to be always with him; and to this end, whenever the nurse who had charge of me turned her back, I was apt to escape from the nursery and seek the study. Then I was caught, shaken, and sometimes whipped, which I well deserved."[8]

The child has apparently, to judge from the last phase of the quotation, learned that one should not attempt to show affection so openly. Yet in the midst of her cool reserve, she can still think fondly of those times when she was actually allowed to touch her father: "How I liked to stroke his dark face with my hands, to stand on his knees and comb his hair, to rest my head against his shoulder and thus fall asleep!"[9] The fragment distills the essential hunger of *Villette*. That same burning and thwarted need for human contact appears throughout the novel. Separated from one another by the armor of their egos, the characters of the book would touch each other if they dared, but their pride and their fear hold them back. The adults of the novel have lost nearly all sense of touch, or rather they retain it only in the form of a fear of abrasive friction. They cringe when they come into unwelcome contact with a foreign skin. Having built up defensive spaces around their bodies, they allow no one to cross the line.[10]

They still retain the need for love, but it has been blocked up for so long that, in most cases, it has turned into a perverse urge to torment one another. Brontë's other fragment is a study of the twisted brutality which marks human relations. Its antagonists are a child named Rosa and the narrator, an older girl named Bessie Shepherd. Bessie com-

plains of Rosa's "exclusive attachment to a single plaything.
. . . An old wooden doll reigned supreme in her heart."[11]
In Charlotte Brontë's world, excessive attachment to anything is a defiance of the gods, an invitation to disaster.
Bessie has an unreasoning hatred of Rosa's doll. She teases
the child: "Rosa, that doll of yours is a great nuisance. . . .
it is a bore to look at—such an ugly thing! Where are its
mouth and nose? . . . Candacè is now good only for one
thing . . . To split into chips for firewood."[12] Rosa is horrified at Bessie's malicious suggestion. After all, she can remember a time when her doll was as beautiful as any other.
Ugliness is often a result of trauma, rather than a sign of
inner worthlessness. " 'It's a baby,' " she cries, " 'and used
to have red lips. I can remember them quite scarlet; but the
cradle was left on the window-seat one night, and the rain
rained into it. Its face was wet in the morning, and when
I wiped it the lips and cheeks came off. Poor Candathy!'
and she rocked it compassionately."[13] Rosa's compassion is
sporadic, however; she herself had knocked off the doll's
nose by striking its face on the floor once when she was
angry with it. But she loves the doll too much to let anyone
burn it. Bessie, she decides, is a witch, because "she's the
silentest, watchingest girl that ever lived."[14] The older girl
sets out to prove that Rosa's opinion of her is correct: "I
procured a smart new wax doll with pink cheeks, blue china
eyes, curled yellow hair, lilac kid arms, and dress of gauze
in the height of the mode. With equal secrecy I managed
to abstract Candacè from the little cupboard . . . and in
place of this dingy and hideous little idol I substituted my
purchase all fresh, fair, and glowing."[15] When Rosa discovers the trick she tells Bessie that she should be judged
by King Solomon for wishing to slice up a child. Finally
Bessie gives up her vicious game: "At last I restored her
the odious little gimcrack: and many a mother would
evince less rapture in receiving back a lost real child."[16]

The children are dancers in a strange ritual which illu-
minates Brontë's feeling of utter desolation in the period
during which she was trying to begin her novel. They are
playing out a sinister game of mother and child, a game
which in a very few years she herself would act out with

fatal consequences. Here, Bessie acts the part of the evil mother. Like the false mother in the tale of Solomon's judgment, she would allow a child to be chopped into pieces, simply because it belongs to another girl. Like the hag in "Hansel and Gretel," that classic myth of abandonment and destruction, Bessie would take the baby from the cupboard and throw it into the fire. Her silent, watchful nature proves her a witch; she has the power to murder with her eyes if she wishes, and though she does not kill she plays at killing.

Bessie is opposed by Rosa, a good mother who is quite willing to cuddle a homely baby. In fact she resents beautiful children. When she finds the new doll in the cupboard, she calls it rubbish, refuses to acknowledge its ownership, and gives it back to Bessie. She will cherish only those children who cannot threaten her with their beauty.[17]

In the second incident of the fragment the roles are reversed. Now it is Rosa who is the bad mother, while Bessie's maternal nature is admirable. Rosa has another favorite, a canary. Bessie hears a thump and enters the dining room to witness the following scene:

> I found the birdcage on the ground, its inmate with spread wings feebly fluttering in the bottom, and Rosa bending over, her cheeks white and eyes wide with anguish.
>
> "I have killed my own bird," she said, in *such* a tone, looking up with *such* a glance. . . .
>
> At first I thought Topaz was really killed, or at least dying. She had let the cage fall in attempting to unhang it, and for half an hour the bird lay half-paralysed with the shock. However, in due time, he came round; and ere long was pecking at his seeds and sugar as if nothing had happened. Rosa watched in perfect silence.
>
> "He is quite safe now," I said at last. "He will be sure not to die this time."
>
> "Sure not to die," she echoed.
>
> Two or three sobs escaped her little, relieved breast. The wild grief in her eye melted in a tear. She smiled, kissed the wires of the cage, watched me carefully

hang it up, and then without resistance permitted me
to carry her upstairs and lay her down for some repose
on my bed.
    She was an odd child.[18]

In attempting to feed her beautiful little pet, Rosa has
committed the unpardonable maternal sin of letting it fall
to the floor. The little mother's carelessness is almost fatal
to her child. But Bessie is more careful than her playmate.
She consoles Rosa, tells her that the bird will live, and then
carries her upstairs without dropping her a single time.
Bessie is a good mother.
    On one level the emotional contest between Bessie and
Rosa can be seen as a forerunner of *Villette*'s veiled struggle between Lucy Snowe and Paulina Mary Home. But the
relationship between the fragment and the novel is more
complex and ultimately more rewarding than that. The
emotional problems of the two girls are fascinating and
will be carried over on a more subtle plane into the novel.
But the plights of Candacè and Topaz really inform *Villette*. Though Lucy Snowe will borrow traits from Bessie
Shepherd, her strongest affinity will be to the doll and the
bird.
    Death can take many forms for those who are unfortu-
nate enough to depend for their survival on an unpredictable mother. And in Charlotte Brontë's world nearly all
mothers are unpredictable. Candacè's childhood consists of
a series of narrow escapes. Her mother has defaced her.
Now that she is ugly, she finds another, prettier doll in her
place, a tiny wax creature good for nothing but to be admired. Having survived the threat of death by flood, the
plain little creature faces death by fire. Luckily, her mother
intervenes and saves her.
    No sooner is the doll back in the safety of her cupboard
than the bird falls. Topaz experiences that most fearful of
infant mishaps, a mishap which, in a figurative sense, Caroline Helstone had already suffered in *Shirley*; he is dropped
by his mother. His reaction to the trauma is fright; he lies
on the floor as if dead, "half-paralysed by the shock."
    "And in catalepsy and a dead trance, I studiously held
the quick of my nature" (*Villette*, p. 39). Like Topaz,

Lucy Snowe has been dropped and lies stunned on the floor, afraid to move. Her catalepsy will last until someone takes the trouble to notice her and help her to her feet. The reader is never told the precise nature of Lucy's bereavement, but she describes its last stage metaphorically as a storm: "A heavy tempest lay on us; all hope that we should be saved was taken away. In fine, the ship was lost, the crew perished" (p. 30). Only Lucy is left, her features rather blurred and smeared in the flood, a plain, wooden girl beached alone in the post-diluvial world of adulthood.

In creating Lucy, Charlotte managed finally to plumb the depths of her own state of alienation. This is not to say that Lucy Snowe is a fictionalized Charlotte Brontë, any more than Mina Laury or Frances Henri or Jane Eyre had been. But like those earlier heroines, she does represent one aspect of her author's mind, the numbing depression which Brontë had fought against nearly all her life. The round of deaths in the Brontë household which had followed on the heels of *Jane Eyre*'s appearance had thrown her into a final state of depression from which she was never to recover, and the results of that mental pall are clearly evident in the characters of Caroline Helstone and Lucy Snowe. Caroline's existence before the return of her mother is described accurately in Rose Yorke's impassioned protests: "I am resolved that my life shall be a life: not a black trance like the toad's, buried in marble: nor a long, slow death like yours in Briarfield Rectory. . . . Might you not as well be tediously dying, as for ever shut up in that glebe-house— a place that, when I pass it, always reminds me of a windowed grave?"[19] Lucy Snowe is of course much stronger than Caroline Helstone, but her depression is even deeper than her predecessor's, manifesting itself in a dull resentment of nearly everything around her. Margot Peters claims that in Lucy "Charlotte had recorded the ambivalences of a neurotic mind. As psychological realism the novel has no equal in Victorian fiction."[20] Whether that is true or not, there can be little doubt that the delineation of Lucy's quiet resentment of the world, and her struggle against the numbing effects of that resentment, established a bench mark of psychological penetration which later novelists were hard pressed to match.

Psychologically paralyzed by the shock of abandonment, Lucy lives in a world in which to show the need for affection is to have the affection denied, removed, or destroyed. She exists in a perpetual state of exile—from England, from society, from herself. She stands out even among the isolated wanderers who float through *Villette*. Her very nostalgia is nearly rootless: "My godmother lived in a handsome house in the clean and ancient town of Bretton. . . . When I was a girl I went to Bretton about twice a year, and well I liked the visit" (p. 5). The others in the novel think fondly of the home and family they had before the storm; Lucy can only recall "the kinsfolk with whom was at that time fixed my permanent residence" (p. 6).

But the Bretton household was an island of calm contentment for the girl. Twice a year she could feel that she belonged somewhere: "One child in a household of grown people is usually made very much of, and in a quiet way I was a good deal taken notice of by Mrs. Bretton" (p. 5). With Graham Bretton away at school most of the time, Lucy could pretend that she was Mrs. Bretton's child. Even this tentative security, however, begins to melt away on the second page of the novel. Like the doll Candacè, Lucy watches as her place is usurped by a prettier plaything: "Seated on my godmother's ample lap, [Paulina Mary Home] looked a mere doll; her neck, delicate as wax, her head of silky curls, increased, I thought, the resemblance. . . Mrs. Bretton was not generally a caressing woman . . . but when the small stranger smiled at her, she kissed it" (p. 8).

The pretty new doll will become the object of everyone's attention. The godmother takes the waxen little thing on her lap and caresses it as she had never done to Lucy ("[she] was not generally a caressing woman"). One source of Lucy's pose of silent bystander lies in this arrival of Paulina. Lucy, thrust into the shadows by the bustling activity of the new girl, will no longer be seen; the poor doll with her deformed nose and smudged lips will become invisible, feeling both the resentment and the relief of a homely child no longer on display.

The natural concomitant of Lucy's invisibility is voyeurism. No longer the object of anyone's attention herself, the girl stares with repressed jealousy at her usurper. Her disgust reaches its climax when Paulina's father returns to visit her: "I—watching calmly from the window . . . saw her caught up, and wrapt at once from my cool observation. . . . It was not a noisy, not a wordy scene: for that I was thankful. . . . He kissed her. I wished she would utter some hysterical cry, so that I might get relief and be at ease" (pp. 12–13). Paulina has already captured the affections of Lucy's godmother. Now she goes further, commandeering the only father in the neighborhood. It is no relief to Lucy's shocked jealousy to realize that the man is Paulina's own father. The puns involved in Mrs. Bretton's and Mr. Home's names have been noticed before, but not the full function of the puns.[21] Mrs. Bretton is Britain, the motherland; Mr. Home is the homeland, the fatherland. In capturing the love of both figures, Paulina has made Lucy an expatriot before she ever leaves England. Exile, like charity, begins at home.

Banished from the attention of her elders, Lucy is continually dismayed at the lack of judgment shown by adults. They simply cannot estimate true worth: "Candidly speaking, I thought her a little busybody; but her father, blind like other parents, seemed . . . wonderfully soothed by her offices" (p. 14). This frustration at the blindness of others, reiterated throughout the novel, is the natural accompaniment to Lucy's feelings of invisibility. She is there and might be worth something if someone could only see her. But at the same time she would be extremely embarrassed if she were seen. Her misery has penned her into a closed circle of discomfort.

Within three days of her father's departure for the Continent, Paulina turns her attentions to Graham Bretton, serving him his tea and fawning over him in a shy but persistent courtship which will end in their marriage. Lucy's reaction to Paulina's behavior is illuminating: "I often wished she would mind herself and be tranquil; but no—herself was forgotten in him: he could not be sufficiently well waited on, nor carefully enough looked after: he was more than the Grand Turk in her estimation" (p. 21). Later she will think of Paulina as a Turkish slave-girl. To forget the self in one's adoration of another is the great danger which threatens all of Charlotte Brontë's heroines, both in her juvenilia and in her mature fiction. All of them love, and the emotion looms as a menace to their sense of self. Bereft of parental support, the Brontë heroines must develop a precarious sufficiency within themselves. The departed parents have carried a great portion of the child's love with them. The tiny mite of remaining love is necessary to counter the child's own self-hatred; if she worshipped another, she would capsize and drown in selfloathing. Paulina is an Oriental slave without a self, and she seems to enjoy it. Lucy tries to take the other road— to "mind herself and be tranquil"—but her tortured selfconsciousness achieves only the tranquility of numbness after great pain. "I, Lucy Snowe, was calm," she says (p. 19), watching Paulina suffer, and the formulation captures wonderfully the essence of Lucy's quiveringly taut concentration on the self, an excruciating introversion disguised as cool detachment. From her hiding place in the soul she watches those others, all of them, acting, loving, alive and unaware, and can only burrow deeper into her molten calm.

As Fanny Ratchford points out, Paulina Mary Home is a literary descendant of Marian Hume and Mary Percy, the unfortunate heroines of the Angrian cycle. But it would be more fully adequate to say that all three women are avatars of Charlotte's complex rivalry with her oldest sister Maria. Paulina represents, however, only one aspect of Maria. From her entrance into the novel until the last mention of her name, she will serve as the heroine's successful rival, the usurper of love. Yet she will never be punished for her theft, and Lucy will never bring herself to hate the beautiful girl who takes up so much of everyone's attention. In part, she comes off unscathed because, as Robert Bernard Martin points out, *Villette* is a novel informed with a highly adult sense of the inscrutable nature of divine justice.[22] Paulina is a charmed creature who can sail calmly through life, untroubled by storm.

But it is important to examine the psychological reasons behind Brontë's need to award Paulina a fortunate existence. Throughout the Angrian cycle as well as in *Jane Eyre*, Brontë had punished the fictional avatars of her sibling rival. There is nothing fortunate about the lives of Marian Hume, Mary Percy, and Helen Burns. They die and are left behind. In the novels written after the deaths of Branwell, Emily, and Anne, however, a change occurs in the pattern of aggression which had occupied so much of the earlier fiction. We can see this change quite clearly in *Shirley*. Caroline Helstone and Shirley Keeldar are polite rivals, though they treat each other like sisters. The contest which seems on the surface to center on Robert Moore turns out on closer examination to be a latent struggle over Mrs. Pryor. For Caroline's mother had entered the novel as Shirley's matronly companion. In a sense, then, Caroline lures a mother away from her sister. But her method is exceedingly dangerous: she plays at the game of dying. It is as if for once in Brontë's fiction remorse *preceded* aggression and turned it inward, as if the prize of maternal affection could only be won by a daringly masochistic act.[23] Aggression has turned back upon the self.

In other words, the death of her brother and her two younger sisters seems to have blocked one channel of aggressive self-assertion in Charlotte Brontë's later novels. Caroline and Lucy have the same compelling need to discover themselves, to grow and mature, as her earlier protagonists, but growth can no longer come at the expense of one's rivals. In *Shirley* the author is forced into the clumsy device of rushing Louis Moore onto the stage to compensate Shirley for the loss of Robert Moore and Mrs. Pryor. And in *Villette* Paulina can take everyone's attention away from Lucy with full impunity. Lucy may smolder with jealousy, but her rival cannot be touched. If Lucy is to grow, she must mature at her own expense, not through the pain of her rivals.

Thus she cannot even admit to herself that she is angry at Paulina. Her jealousy can find no outlet except in increased masochism. Frustrated in her timid attempt to seek love from her godmother, Lucy waits eight more years before establishing a relationship with another human being. Then she becomes Miss Marchmont's nurse.

Maria Marchmont is a rheumatic cripple whose paralysis is the physical equivalent to Lucy's repression. The relationship between the two women is a caricature of a bond which neither Lucy nor Charlotte Brontë had ever known: "Even when she scolded me—which she did, now and then, very tartly—it was in such a way as did not humiliate, and left no sting; it was rather like an irascible mother rating her daughter, than a harsh mistress lecturing a dependent" (p. 31). Lucy has finally found a surrogate mother—one whose name, like Charlotte's mother's, is Maria—who is so sick, so disagreeable, and so isolated that there is no danger of usurpation; no one would wish to take her place in the gravelike atmosphere of Miss Marchmont's home. Lucy joins her dying companion in a neurotic game of suffering in which the nurse imitates the patient: "Two hot, close rooms thus became my world. . . . I forgot that there were fields, woods, rivers, seas, an ever-changing sky outside the steam-dimmed lattice of this sick-chamber; I was almost content to forget it" (p. 31). Lucy has turned away with relief from the possibility, however painful, of experience, to a form of neurotic innocence, from the garish, implacable world outside to the thin grey antisepsis of Miss Marchmont's closed room.

But innocence is a state which cannot be maintained for long. Maria Marchmont dies, leaving Lucy once more isolated and alone. The homely wooden doll has been abandoned by yet another mother. This time she will act out her sense of exile. She will go to Labassecour.

Lucy sees herself as a specially chosen victim of a jealous divinity, and she exults in her suffering. Her conception of her relationship to God is visible in the voice she hears driving her toward Labassecour: "Leave this wilderness . . . and go out hence" (p. 37). The words echo Jehovah's command to Abraham. But Lucy's divinely appointed journey is an exile, not a mission. Many of the myriad Oriental references in the novel refer to the Babylonian Captivity of Israel. Daniel, Vashti, Nebuchadnezzar, Babylon—the metaphors which are used for people and places in Labassecour point to a journey into foreign captivity, to an exile from the chosen land which is the result of divine anger.

For one bright moment during the channel crossing, Lucy imagines herself as God's favorite: "In my reverie, methought I saw the continent of Europe, like a wide dream-land, far away. . . . For background, spread a sky, solemn and dark-blue, and—grand with imperial promise, soft with tints of enchantment—strode from north to south a God-bent bow, an arch of hope" (p. 48). And then she takes it back: "Cancel the whole of that, if you please, reader. . . . Becoming excessively sick, I faltered down into the cabin" (p. 48). Lucy would like to be Noah, God's chosen servant who has survived the deluge to be faced with the divine rainbow, the sign of a new Covenant. But she cannot sustain her vision; exile will not turn into pilgrimage. Not every victim of a flood can be Noah.

Labassecour is not only the site of Lucy's Oriental captivity, however; in a deeper sense it is the world of death. The novel's heavy theological and psychological gloom is evident in the description of Lucy's departure from the London dock: "Down the sable flood we glided; I thought of the Styx, and of Charon rowing some solitary soul to the Land of Shades."[24] And the city itself is aligned with the dead. Villette, as befits a metropolis situated on the far side of the River Styx, is ruled over by a king who "had looked on the visits of a certain ghost" (p. 183). Indeed wherever Lucy looks, she finds a necrophiliac concentration on the spirits of the dead. Almost all of the city's adult inhabitants seem to have lost either a spouse or a lover.

Labassecour is a kingdom where English rationality seems to have little place, where dream visions and drugged trances take the place of clear-sighted reason. Ghosts can be seen in Villette. And one of the most important of those ghosts is, in a sense, Mme. Beck: "She would move . . . on her *souliers de silence* ['slippers'], and glide ghostlike through the house, watching and spying everywhere, peering through every key-hole, listening behind every door" (p. 62). Lucy's description of her first meeting with the matron is significant: "No ghost stood beside me, nor anything of spectral aspect; merely a motherly, dumpy little woman" (p. 55). In Charlotte Brontë's prose, people receive part of their definition through negatives. The description of Mme. Beck as "no ghost" leaves the aura of ghostliness clinging to her. Thus, having been replaced in the affections of the motherly Mrs. Bretton, the heroine has moved in the first eight chapters of the novel to the bedside of a dying mother-figure and then to the employ of a matron who can be compared to a ghost. The progression recapitulates the course of Charlotte Brontë's own development, the construction of her own neurosis.

The section from Lucy's arrival in Villette to her rediscovery of the Brettons, comprises a discrete segment of the novel.[25] Throughout this section the girl is still made of wood: "[Dr. John] laid himself open to my observation, according to my presence in the room just that degree of notice and consequence a person of my exterior habitually expects: that is to say, about what is given to unobtrusive articles of furniture, chairs of ordinary joiner's work" (pp. 83–84). She remains an isolated onlooker of life in the school, watched over herself in turn by her ghostly maternal warder, Mme. Beck. As long as Lucy can force herself to play the homely, neglected doll, as long as she can remain in her self-imposed trance, she will need only that one maternal presence to guard her. But when she begins to break out of her psychological prison, mother-figures will multiply until Lucy's world seems full of malevolent older women who would banish the young girl back to her lonely cell.

One measure of the difference between the mood of Brontë's first novel and her last can be seen in the way the two books treat the landscape of the Brussels school. Lucy's favorite spot in Mme. Beck's establishment is the *allée défendue*, a feature which Charlotte borrowed from the Heger *pensionnat* and had used in *The Professor*. In her first novel it had provided the opportunity for psychological growth. William Crimsworth had overheard his *petite maman* chatting with her lover beside the path one evening and realized her true nature. In *Villette*, too, the garden is a parental area, a forbidden paradise where strange things are liable to occur in the darkness. Indeed "something had happened on this site which, rousing fear and inflicting horror, had left to the place the inheritance of a ghost story" (p. 90). But for Lucy the sexual overtones of the garden are forceably subdued, sublimated into the safer idea of marriage: "There was a large berceau, above which spread the shade of an acacia; there was a smaller, more sequestered bower, nestled in the vines which ran all along a high and gray wall, and gathered their tendrils in a knot of beauty, and hung their clusters in loving profusion about the favoured spot where jasmine and ivy met, and married them" (p. 91). The French word *berceau* means both arbor and cradle; the garden contains metaphorically both a married couple and a child's bed.[26] So the forbidden garden, which in *The Professor* had been almost blatantly sexual, takes on here—at least for Lucy—the aura of parental succor and protection. Babies are rocked here,[27] and Lucy feels strangely comfortable. She sits in her garden for hours on end like a doll in a child's nursery, and staves off her rage for experience and real adulthood.

Indeed when sex comes to the garden in the form of a love letter thrown from a window of the adjoining boys' school, the area temporarily loses its charm for Lucy: "That casement which rained billets, had vulgarized the once dear nook it overlooked; and elsewhere, the eyes of the flowers had gained vision, and the knots in the tree-boles listened like secret ears. Some plants there were, indeed, trodden down by [Graham] in his search, and his hasty and heedless progress, which I wished to prop up, water, and revive; some foot-marks, too, he had left on the beds" (p. 99). Let sex invade Lucy's parental garden even once, and the result is destruction and paranoia. In a sense, the thing which is *défendu* in the garden is sexuality. Lucy is fascinated by the garden's legend. Between the roots of a giant pear tree is a slab which is supposedly the portal of a vault, "imprisoning deep beneath that ground . . . the bones of a girl whom a monkish conclave of the drear middle ages had here buried alive, for some sin against her vow" (p. 90). One can assume with relative assurance that the sin was sexual. But it need not have been. For in this novel the very wish for experience deserves punishment like a foreign invader: "This longing, and all of a similar kind, it was necessary to knock on the head . . . after the manner of Jaël to Sisera, driving a nail through their temples" (p. 93). Lucy has, after all, gone the medieval nun one better:

she has buried herself before she can sin. Thus the conscience punishes to forestall punishment, and the circle of Lucy's repression is complete.

The closed circle is broken by the rude entrance into Lucy's life of Paul Imanuel, the fictional representative of Charlotte Brontë's beloved Constantin Heger. Like his real-life counterpart, Imanuel drives the young Englishwoman out of her neurotic childhood and, ultimately, into the pain of adulthood. He demands that Lucy act in a play.

Acting presents a twofold threat to Lucy's neurosis. In the first place, it forces her to move out of her cataleptic trance, however temporarily. And second, she has to exhibit herself before a large, eager audience. Everything to which she has unconsciously devoted her life is threatened by her appearance on the stage. To her horror, she will have to play a lover. In *Shirley*, the world of action was the exclusive province of males. Here, when Lucy mimics the part of a lover, she turns temporarily masculine: her name becomes, in Imanuel's joke, "M. Lucien." If Lucy cannot refuse to act, she can at least rebel against this attempt to steal her femininity: "To be dressed like a man did not please, and would not suit me. . . . Retaining my women's garb without the slightest retrenchment, I merely assumed in addition, a little vest, a collar, and cravat, and a paletôt of small dimensions" (pp. 119–120).

With this strange little emblem of masculinity supplementing her normal female identity, the now androgynous heroine walks onstage. For a few moments her longing for activity and self-assertion takes command. Not only does she now want to be seen and to be active, she goes so far as to become, for a moment, a man, capable of fierce competition: "I put my idea [of Ginevra's flirtation with Dr. John Graham Bretton] into the part I performed; I threw it into my wooing of Ginevra. In the . . . sincere lover [of the play], I saw Dr. John . . . I know not what possessed me either; but somehow, my longing was to eclipse . . . Dr. John" (p. 121).

Lucy, so long in the shadow, now radiates light. The masculine, assertive side of her self has suddenly come into sharp focus, distorting the rest of the play and terrifying the player: "What I felt that night, and what I did, I no more expected to feel and do, than to be lifted in a trance to the seventh heaven. . . . I took a firm resolution never to be drawn into a similar affair . . . it would not do for a mere looker-on at life" (p. 121). The language with which Lucy describes the experience turns quickly passive. She attempts to divorce herself from responsibility for her actions; she was drawn, she was lifted. She swears again her nun's vow of retirement from the active life, but it is too late. Her punishment comes quickly.

Charlotte Brontë's transformation into Currer Bell, her decision to become a novelist capable of competing with Dickens and Thackeray, had been followed with devastating suddenness by the deaths of her brother and her two sisters. She had feared that she would go blind if she tried to create, but the punishment had been visited on her loved ones, rather than on her. She must have felt that in some way her success had caused their deaths. At any rate, her feelings of guilt increased enormously as she watched Branwell, and Emily, and Anne die. And for several years, after completing *Shirley* in a furious rush of activity, she was unable to create, caught in a neurotic if understandable concentration on the dead.

Lucy's reluctant entry into the world of creative action brings on a similar punishment. She too becomes trapped in a psychological cage, accompanied by projections of her guilt. Significantly enough, the aftermath of Lucy's audacity leads Brontë back to a heightened awareness of her own Brussels experience, to the long vacation she had spent in isolation, to her need to confess her guilt before a priest.

Three pages after the day of Lucy's acting debut, the long vacation begins for the pupils of Mme. Beck's school. In the logic of the novel's form, then, the agony of the vacation is a punishment for Lucy's crime of activity. Her situation is deplorable: "The house was left quite empty, but for me, a servant, and a poor, deformed and imbecile pupil, a sort of crétin whom her stepmother in a distant province would not allow to return home" (p. 134). Like Helen Burns in *Jane Eyre*, the cretin cannot even return during vacation to the distant province where her father lives. This twisted, ugly young girl bears the significant name of Marie; she is yet another version of Charlotte's older sister, Maria. Lucy cannot escape from her: "The hapless creature had been at times a heavy charge; I could not take her out beyond the garden, and I could not leave her a minute alone. . . . A vague bent to mischief, an aimless malevolence made constant vigilance indispensable . . . it was more like being prisoned with some strange tameless animal, than associating with a human being" (p. 136). A wild beast has silently entered Lucy's parental garden, one who makes strange, malevolent faces at the poor girl. Lucy sits like a mouse in a snake's grotto, watching the cretin watch her.

Nor can Marie Broc be placated. Later, Lucy will defend her treatment of the cretin to Paul Imanuel: "I washed her, I kept her clean, I fed her, I tried to amuse her; but she made mouths at me instead of speaking" (p. 175). Imanuel will not be impressed: "Yours are not the qualities which might constitute a Sister of Mercy" (p. 174). Perhaps Lucy would not make a good Sister, but, like Charlotte Brontë, she tries. Nevertheless, she is tortured by a dream of the return of the dead, a dream which had tormented Brontë herself: "Methought the well-loved dead, who had loved *me* well in life, met me elsewhere, alienated: galled was my inmost spirit with an unutterable sense of despair about the future. Motive there was none why I should try to recover or wish to live; and yet quite unendurable was the pitiless and haughty voice in which Death challenged me to engage his unknown terrors" (pp. 137–138).[28]

Lucy's dream presents the clearest version in all of Brontë's fiction of the paradigm connecting survivor's guilt and suicidal impulse. It is a connection which, as we have seen, had been implicit throughout her writings, one which came closer to the surface with each successive novel. For each of the orphaned protagonists (except perhaps Shirley Keeldar) the welling up of the need to live, to thrive and grow, had been accompanied by a seductive urge to die.[29] After all, in the guilt-ridden mind of the survivor, her death would be simple justice, the restoration of the world to a state of balance which had been lost when the others died and she lived on.

Lucy's dream has suggested a possible escape from her dilemma, a way to redress the balance. She has played at being dead throughout the novel. Now she must either make the decision to kill herself, thus completing the process begun years before, or break out of the prison of her mind and struggle into life.

Following a path which Charlotte Brontë had taken during the extremity of her Brussels depression, Lucy escapes first to the confessional. In answer to the priest's question on the nature of her sins, Lucy tells the reader: "I reassured him on this point, and, as well as I could, I showed him the mere outline of my experience" (p. 139). But then, Lucy's "sin" is the fact of her experience, the fact that she exists at all.

Père Silas knows a path that would take Lucy out of the storm: "A mind so tossed can find repose but in the bosom of retreat, and the punctual practice of piety" (p. 140). She should become a Catholic nun. But Lucy hates Catholicism; in fact her disgust with the creed arises precisely from its easy claim to exculpate its communicants: "The Church strove to bring up her children robust in body, feeble in soul, fat, ruddy, hale, joyous, ignorant, unthinking, unquestioning. 'Eat, drink, and live!' she says. 'Look after your bodies; leave your souls to me'" (p. 109). The Church is an indulgent but ultimately untrustworthy mother, allowing her fat children to romp and snuggle without thought of their guilt. At this point only Calvinism can satisfy Lucy's hunger for exclusion—and an inverted, romantic Calvinism at that, in which the true chosen ones are those who like Cain become wanderers out of guilt.[30] A bit earlier in the novel Ginevra had claimed that mentioning a lover to Lucy "is like showing poor outcast Cain a far glimpse of Paradise" (p. 126). Lucy herself had answered a question with Cain's formula: "Am I her keeper?" (p. 128). Her certainty of her exclusion is after all her only proof of God's parental attention, and she will not give it up by submitting to the care of Mother Church. She would rather remain in the cold, following her own conscience. She leaves the confessional and submits herself to the storm which is raging outside. Fainting from exposure, she experiences a foretaste of death: "Where my soul went during that swoon I cannot tell. . . . She may have gone upward, and come in sight of her eternal home . . . an angel may have warned her away from heaven's threshold, and, guiding her weeping down, have bound her, once more, all shuddering and unwilling, to that poor frame, cold and wasted, of whose companionship she was grown more than weary. I know that she re-entered her prison with pain" (p. 142).

The metaphors which control Charlotte Brontë's fiction reach their most extended range here: existence itself is a prison, the body its walls, and eternity has become the real home. In Lucy's formula—a formula which almost certainly echoes Brontë's own—life is a form of exile; the pain of individual consciousness resolves finally into the ache of the soul's homesickness for death. If she could only die, then the walls of her repression would become windows and her spirit would soar out into the afterlife.

But the shining air of her homeland is denied her, and she is led once more down into exile and captivity, forced to grow, not die. She awakens in a bedroom in Graham Bretton's villa, La Terrasse, not in a timeless afterlife.

The new friendship with the Brettons will turn into a strange replay of the drama of exclusion which had occurred in Lucy's adolescence. For like an avenging spirit in a dream, Paulina Mary Home will reenter the novel and lure affection away from Lucy once more. There are dilemmas in life which cannot be run from, which will track a woman down even though she flees to a foreign country. But this time exclusion from love will provide Lucy with an opportunity for growth. For this time she will express her pain, not repress it. As Charlotte Brontë had done years before in her letters to Constantin Heger, Lucy will write to a man who does not love her. And the very act of expression will force open the door of her prison.

There are maternal forces in Lucy's mind which attempt to block that growth. Her most vicious enemy is given the deceptive name of Reason. Having left La Terrasse and returned to her school, Lucy sits pondering an exchange of letters with Graham, while "Reason still whispered me, laying on my shoulder a withered hand, and frostily touching my ear with the chill lips of eld" (p. 196). This hag, who sounds strangely like William Crimsworth's dangerous guest, Melancholy, tries to restrain Lucy from participation in human relationships: "Hope no delight of heart— no indulgence of intellect: grant no expansion to feeling— give holiday to no single faculty: dally with no friendly exchange: foster no genial intercommunion" (p. 196).

Above all Lucy must not write. Talk is good discipline for the girl since she is a clumsy and halting speaker: "While you speak, there can be no oblivion of inferiority— no encouragement to delusion: pain, privation, penury stamp your language" (p. 196). But these symptoms of inferiority might be hidden if she wrote. Lucy complains: "But . . . where the bodily presence is weak and the speech contemptible, surely there cannot be error in making written language the medium of better utterance than faltering lips can achieve?" (p. 196). "*Never!*" is the answer. Writing would be a form of release. The hesitation, the stammering would be gone, and only the kernel of pure expression would remain, the nugget of meaning which could be seen after the accidents of ugliness were burned away. Moreover, Lucy's method of composition would be peculiarly consoling to a girl whose loved ones had died. For the act of writing is a means of resurrection. Later in the book Lucy describes her procedure: "I got books, read up the facts, laboriously constructed a skeleton out of the dry bones of the real, and then clothed them, and tried to breathe into them life, and in this last aim I had pleasure" (p. 339). If Lucy were, like Charlotte Brontë, to transform reality's dry bones into the shining life of the literary artifact—a letter to a loved one, or a novel perhaps—then the shackles of her mind would fall away and for a moment she could exult in her natural strength.

Lucy will of course not become a novelist. She will settle for being a teacher. But she does write her letters, does express the depth of her emotion, though she refuses to mail them. If in this section of the novel she has not yet achieved communication, she has at least overcome her repression enough to express herself, to put her emotion down on paper where she herself is forced to see it.

The most important concomitant of Lucy's movement out of her cataleptic trance is a shift in the nature of seeing. In the first half of the book, chained within her tacit conception of herself as a homely wooden doll, a nearly inanimate little creature staring out at the world with unblinking eyes, she had been a voyeur. Now the act of seeing becomes more objective; her sight is no longer so severely distorted by her smoldering resentment of her isolation.[31] Nevertheless, "seeing" is still the most important activity in her life. In *Villette*, significant action is no longer, as in *Jane Eyre*, the prime vehicle of change. In her final novel Charlotte Brontë is beginning to follow out the implications of her concentration on the psyche to their logical conclusion, and action is beginning to fall away, to be replaced by sheer perception. Thus where Jane was a knight on a pilgrimage, Lucy must attempt to find meaning in mere tourism. Like the author in the years after her brother's and sisters' deaths, Lucy escapes from her blank prison in bouts of sightseeing. The possible objects of quest have been drained of significance, the grails have turned into ordinary cups, and the shrines of meaning are the art galleries and the concert halls where society's old symbols are exhibited.

Lucy finds what she is looking for in these cultural warehouses. Thus when she visits an art gallery, she is inevitably drawn to contemplation of a painting of Cleopatra: "She lay half-reclined on a couch: why, it would be difficult to say . . . she could not plead a weak spine, she ought to have been standing, or at least sitting bolt upright. She had no business to lounge away the noon on a sofa. . . . Then, for the wretched untidiness surrounding her, there could be no excuse" (p. 171).[32] The lady of the painting exists in a state of rapt self-contemplation, with no interest in the world around her. She is not sick, her spine is not weak, she ought to get up. Cleopatra—like a mother who has fallen inexplicably ill—lies on the couch in the middle of the day, half dressed, her body and her surroundings slovenly, taking no notice of the crowd of gaping onlookers who surround her reclining form.[33]

Lucy sits enthralled and disgusted by the voluptuous queen. But Graham Bretton is not impressed: "Pooh! My mother is a better-looking woman" (p. 177). A bit later he will take his young friend to the theater to see another Oriental queen: "What I saw was the shadow of a royal Vashti: a queen, fair as the day once, turned pale now like twilight, and wasted like wax in flame" (p. 220).

In a sense, both Cleopatra and Vashti represent facets of Lucy's own mind, projections onto the external world of internal threats to her own hard-won sense of selfhood. In the first place they serve as images of Lucy's sense of being hemmed in by older women who threaten her desire for fulfillment—in other words projections of the Oedipal trap in which Lucy lives. She has already interacted with three women whose relationship with her is clearly maternal: Mrs. Bretton, Miss Marchmont, and Mme. Beck. In this third section of the novel, as Lucy tries to struggle out of her depressive mental prison, maternal threats proliferate. Her quest for full adulthood takes her through a gamut of menacing older women. But they are not, like the male enemies of Jane Eyre, monsters in human form.[34] Rather, they are mental abstractions—the stepmother Reason, the slovenly hag Human Justice—or paintings, or an actress in a play. Significant action has become almost fully internalized; though Lucy has external enemies who live in the world around her, her most important antagonists reside in her own psyche. The dialogue of the mind with itself controls the novel.

The threatening aspect of the painting and the actress can be seen more clearly if we view them as two facets of what might be called the Oriental Queen. We have seen already that Lucy views her European journey through the metaphoric lens of Israel in exile. The land in which she resides seems to be ruled over—again metaphorically—by a sensuous older woman. The painting of Cleopatra represents the queen in voluptuous and indolent power; Vashti represents the queen in anguished decline. Like Cleopatra, the biblical Vashti was an egocentric woman who paid no attention to the wishes of others. Summoned by Ahasueris, her royal husband, to show her beauty before the men of the court, she had refused disdainfully. The king, angered by this insult, replaced her with a foreign orphan, Esther. This story of a young orphaned girl languishing in Babylonian captivity, whose beauty and virtue enabled her to replace the disobedient queen in the king's affections, serves as a mirror of Lucy's situation and her tacit dream. In the midst of her own exile, while consciously thinking of her ugliness and her loneliness, Lucy would still be Esther if she could.

The painting, and particularly the actress, then, become metaphoric reinforcements not only of Lucy's situation, but perhaps also of Brontë's vision of her own traumatic year in Brussels. At the same time, they seem to mirror the novelist's own complex image of her mother's sickness and death. As was pointed out, Cleopatra pretends that she is ill. Vashti's illness is real, but she will not let it defeat her without a struggle: "Suffering had struck that stage empress; . . . she stood locked in struggle, rigid in resistance. . . . white like . . . Death. . . . Pain, for her, has no result in good; tears water no harvest of wisdom: on sickness, on death itself, she looks with the eye of a rebel" (p. 221).[35]

Yet if the painting and the actress serve as monitors of Lucy's behavior, blocks to her—and perhaps to the author's —maturation, they must also be seen at the same time as representatives of the protagonist's need for a less ascetic existence. In the art gallery, the voluptuous Cleopatra had formed one extreme of which the opposite was a series of paintings depicting the Catholic ideal of piety. Like Georgiana and Eliza Reed in *Jane Eyre*, Cleopatra and the saccharine religious paintings represent alternative ideals which Lucy must reject in her search for a viable existence. And Vashti presents yet a third alternative reaction to the problems of life—enraged rebellion. Like *Jane Eyre*'s Bertha Mason, Vashti is a soul on fire. In the midst of her performance the very theater in which she is appearing catches fire. Rebellion and unbridled sensuality are latent aspects of the self which Lucy will do well to avoid.

But if Lucy is fascinated and repulsed by these images

of licence, she is not driven back into her shell by them. The process of emergence has begun. And it takes a form which her Victorian audience found rather shocking. Contemporary readers of *Villette*—including George Smith, Brontë's publisher, on whom the character of Graham Bretton was based—complained of Lucy's shift from her love for Graham to her love for Paul Imanuel.[36] But this transferral of affection is a necessary and fitting transition in the novel, a major factor in the book's psychological profundity. For as the "masculine" side of her nature begins to grow and flourish, she outgrows Graham Bretton. She begins to notice that there is something rather feminine about him. The scene in Chapter 20 where he tries unsuccessfully to exchange the lady's headdress he has won in a raffle for the cigar-case which is Lucy's prize, is only the most obvious point in a long struggle between the two of them. Like the earlier Brontë heroines, Lucy has given away important parts of the self by constructing, out of her unconscious need to remain inadequate herself, a gorgeous dream of male potency with which she can fall in love. In conquering her love for Graham, Lucy is, in effect, taking back those aspects of the self she had given away— those "masculine" aspects—and recognizing them as her own. If to be potent is to be a man, and if effectiveness is necessary in a world of struggle, then Lucy must become, at least metaphorically, a man. One of the crucial vehicles for this development in Lucy's psyche is Ginevra Fanshawe. As we have seen already, during the school play Lucy had, under the guise of "M. Lucien," courted her foolish classmate. Throughout the novel, light, mocking forms of that courtship continue. Finally, when Lucy's character has emerged enough to show its quiet effectiveness, Ginevra metaphorically recognizes the change in her friend: "Who *are* you, Miss Snowe? . . . If you really are the nobody I once thought you, you must be a cool hand" (p. 262), and takes her by the arm like a man. Lucy complains: "When she took my arm, she always leaned upon me her whole weight; and, as I was not a gentleman, or her lover, I did not like it" (p. 262)—but strides along like a courtier all the same. Once again the negative metaphor becomes a valuable device in Brontë's fiction. The denial of masculinity cannot erase its assertion.

Taking into account these gestures of androgynous courtship, then, we can say that Lucy has three love relationships, not two. Her love for Imanuel has been preceded by the infatuation for Graham and the role-playing banter with Ginevra. Only after the interlude with Ginevra, after she has taken back the alienated "masculine" portions of the self, can she approach Imanuel as a whole woman.

It would be esthetically and ethically satisfying to be able to claim that Lucy's love for Imanuel is fully adult. However, that claim would be false to the experience of the novel. Brontë was never able to portray a fully believable sexual relationship between equals, perhaps because she had never seen one. The problem with Lucy's love for the Belgian teacher can be seen in his very name. Imanuel means "God with us." A man with that name would seem to be more an object of worship than of sexual companionship.

Their love, like all other Brontëan relationships, is for a time a struggle for power. M. Paul's recognition of Lucy's power is hinted at all through the novel. The connection of that power with masculinity can be seen clearly in his complaint: "Ah . . . if it came to that—if Miss Lucy [meddled with my hat]—she might just put it on herself, turn garçon for the occasion, and benevolently go to the Athénée in [my] stead" (p. 277).

Lucy, however, simply cannot compete successfully without being attacked by the paranoid guilt which is part of her mind. And her sense that she loves Imanuel, that she might even be loved by him, leads her into a new stage of Oedipal difficulties. Part of the difficulty is realistic. Mme. Beck is frightened by Lucy's effectiveness. Like her forerunners, *The Professor*'s Mlle. Reuter and Brontë's own antagonist, Mme. Heger, Lucy's employer turns actively malevolent. Together with Père Silas (the parental pun involved in the priest's title is perhaps important), she will plot successfully to keep Lucy and Paul Imanuel apart.

But the extent of the maternal threat which the novelist

sees looming over her protagonist's head is too great to be embodied in a normal woman, realistically portrayed. Belgium had been the land where Brontë's own Oedipal complex had come to a traumatic climax. The figure of Lucy's maternal enemy must be backed up by a monster, Malevola. And Malevola becomes a central figure for the understanding of Brontë's own mind.

The chapter in which the old hag appears is a fairy tale. Lucy is preparing to go on a shopping expedition when "Madame, running into the little salon, brought thence a pretty basket, filled with fine hothouse fruit, rosy, perfect, and tempting, reposing amongst the dark green, wax-like leaves, and pale yellow stars of, I know not what, exotic plant" (p. 326). Mme. Beck tells Lucy to take this pretty basket to a certain grandmother, Mme. Walravens, who lives at Numéro 3, Rue des Mages. We have been thrust into the midst of "Little Red Riding Hood." As in *Jane Eyre*, Brontë is using a fairy tale to convey her deep sense of the threatening nature of reality. The wolf does not appear as a separate animal, and, indeed, he has no need to do so. For in Lucy's mind, grandmother and wolf, old woman and devourer are one.

After being rebuffed by a servant, Lucy is shown into an upper room by a priest who is later revealed to be Père Silas. Left alone there, she gazes at a painting: "Imperfectly seen, I [took] it for a Madonna; revealed by clearer light, it proved to be a woman's portrait in a nun's dress. . . . it was not beautiful; it was not even intellectual; its very amiability was the amiability of a weak frame, inactive passions, acquiescent habits" (p. 330–331). "A weak frame, inactive passions, acquiescent habits." The girl could be *Jane Eyre*'s Helen Burns seen in an unfavorable light. Brontë has led us into a dimly lit cavern of the mind where her neurosis can be shown almost brazenly. The subject of the painting is a dead girl who is still worshipped by Paul Imanuel. The deceased virgin, who looks from afar like Mary, but on closer examination turns out to be merely a normal bourgeoise, bears the name Justine Marie. Like the cretin Marie Broc, her name is the French equivalent of

Maria. Both are, in one sense, fragmented images of Charlotte's sister Maria. But like the girl whose death was so traumatic for Charlotte, the picture of Lucy's dead rival is ultimately merely a screen which hides an older, more dangerous woman. The house at Rue des Mages ("Street of the Magi") contains wizardry enough to remove the screen image and show the woman behind it: "By-and-bye, the picture [of Justine Marie] seemed to give way; to my bewilderment, it shook, it sank, it rolled back into nothing; its vanishing left an opening arched, leading into an arched passage, with a mystic winding stair; both passage and stair were of cold stone, uncarpeted and unpainted. Down this donjon stair descended a tap, tap, like a stick; soon, there fell on the steps a shadow, and last of all, I was aware of a substance" (p. 328).

The passage acts out the material of Charlotte Brontë's neurosis. For the reality behind the image of the dead Marie is an older woman, a threatening hag named Mme. Walravens, "Malevola":

> She might be three feet high, but she had no shape. . . . Her face was large, set, not upon her shoulders, but before her breast; she seemed to have no neck; I should have said there were a hundred years in her features, and more perhaps in her eyes—her malign, unfriendly eyes . . . How severely they viewed me, with a sort of dull displeasure! . . . Hunchbacked, dwarfish, and doting, she was adorned like a barbarian queen. (p. 329)

The "real" queen, the figure who pulls together Cleopatra, Vashti, and the other regal women of Labassecour, has finally arrived. Like the hag Bertha of "The Green Dwarf" or *Jane Eyre*'s Bertha Mason, the wrinkled crone has emerged from her hiding place so that the heroine can confront her.

Earlier in the novel, Lucy had seen herself as Cain, whose sacrifice was not acceptable. Now, as Red Riding Hood, she succeeds in delivering her present to the wolfish grandmother, but Malevola receives the offering with disdain and impoliteness:

> "Is that all?" she demanded.
> "It is all," said I. (p. 329)

There is no way that Lucy can propitiate the hag, no gift which will find favor in Malevola's staring, disapproving eyes.[37] The old woman is the ultimate vampire, living from the blood of the man Lucy loves, and the young girl will never be able to overcome her. Lucy has finally begun to understand the full nature of the forces aligned against her, the vast extent of the power, seemingly magical, of her maternal enemies: "Just as [Mme. Walravens] turned, a peal of thunder broke, and a flash of lightning blazed broad over salon and boudoir. The tale of magic seemed to proceed with due accompaniment of the elements. The wanderer, decoyed into the enchanted castle, heard rising, outside, the spell-wakened tempest" (p. 329). The metaphorical storms which began before the novel's opening and which will end only when the novel ends have been tracked to their source in the malign magic of an ugly old woman who lurks behind the image of a dead young girl.

Lucy's striking vision of the woman behind the painting is followed by an even more surrealistic revelation. Malevola and her allies, Père Silas and Mme. Beck, succeed in playing on Paul Imanuel's sympathy enough to banish him to Guadeloupe. In the interval before his departure they attempt to keep the lovers apart, at one point going so far as to administer an opiate to Lucy. But the drug is too strong to work as a soporific, and Lucy's awareness is heightened, not depressed. As she wanders through the city, the narcotic becomes the agent of revelation, and the woman sees the shape of her own neurosis projected onto the world.

More than any other Brontë novel, more perhaps than any other novel of its period, *Villette* concentrates on the act of seeing. Lucy's adventures are minimal. The epidemics, the begging journeys, the battles for factories which had entertained the audience in the two previous novels are gone. What is left is a woman's consciousness and a

woman's eyes, open to the full enormity of a neurotically
threatening world. One of the marvelous effects of *Jane
Eyre*, perhaps its most lasting contribution to the English
novel, is Brontë's demonstration to her contemporaries of
just how threatening the world can look to a lonely child.[38]
Villette is even more audacious than its great predecessor.
Working in the tradition of De Quincey and Poe, Charlotte
shows her audience just how vast and how shifting, how
incisive and surreal, an adult's powers of sight can be. De
Quincey had talked in *The Confessions of an English
Opium-Eater* of "the creative state of the eye,"[39] but for
him as for Charlotte's brother Branwell, creative vision is
something induced by drugs. For Charlotte, as for Sigmund
Freud, it is ideagenic, the result of the tension between
conflicting ideas of the self. Lucy's visions culminate in her
drug-induced wanderings through the park, the most famous episode of the novel, but drugs only complete the
process of neurotic revelation which has been slowly building throughout the novel.[40]

Lucy's narcotic wanderings begin regressively, as an attempt to escape from the dangerous world of time in which
people collide painfully against her. Under the influence
of the opiate, her imagination would lead her away from,
not toward, revelation: "Imagination. . . . lured me to leave
this den and follow her forth into dew, coolness, and
glory. . . . she showed the park, the summer-park, with its
long alleys all silent, lone and safe; among these lay a huge
stone-basin, brimming with cool water, clear, with a green,
leafy, rushy bed. . . . once within, at this hour the whole
park would be mine—the moonlight, midnight park!" (p.
380). Loneliness and safety are still nearly cognates for
Lucy, silence the medium in which her inadequacy longs
to exist. The moonlit park of her deranged vision is calm
with the numbed serenity of death-in-life.[41] The shadowed
basin seems to provide both the wetness and the dark of
the womb without its warmth or intimacy. With the knowledge that her lover is leaving for the Caribbean, Lucy's
sense of desolation has increased. Throughout the book
she had felt herself to be a survivor in a post-diluvial existence. She had seen Labassecour as a kingdom of death.

That metaphor extends now to take in all of life: "To me the face of that sky bears the aspect of a world's death" (p. 381). The entire world is dying; to the distant sound of military music it strolls serenely to its grave. Lucy's narcotic derangement projects her misery onto the universe.

It is no wonder that the sky over Villette should mirror death, for Imanuel, Lucy believes, has already departed; in a manner befitting his Christlike last name, he has, she thinks, already descended to Basseterre (literally, "the world below") to create order in the estates of the Evil Woman, Malevola. Like his namesake he has gone to harrow Hell, and he is to stay there three years, not three days.

But Lucy and the upper world receive a postponement if not a reprieve. As she wanders in search of the dark loneliness of the stone-basin, she hears music which sounds divine: "Choiring out of a glade to the right, broke such a sound as I thought might be heard if Heaven were to open—such a sound, perhaps, as *was* heard above the plain of Bethlehem, on the night of glad tidings" (p. 383). Imanuel is alive and in Labassecour, and escape turns quickly into revelation. Lucy moves through a park in which all is changed utterly—at least to her mind. It is alive now, thronged with a celebrating populace. The town is observing its day of deliverance; it has heard the Te Deum sung, and has gathered in the park.

The world may be joyous, but Lucy is still doomed to a bitter form of suffering. For when Imanuel appears, he walks in the midst of a Catholic trinity of Oedipal evil: Père Silas, Mme. Beck, and Malevola surround him. Moreover, like Christ before the tomb of Lazarus, he seems to have brought back a corpse. A girl walks beside him. Lucy exclaims:

> So strange a feeling of revelry and mystery begins to spread abroad, that scarce would you discredit me, reader, were I to say that she is like the nun of the attic, that she wears black skirts and white head-clothes, that she looks the resurrection of the flesh, and that she is a risen ghost.

> All falsities—all figments! We will not deal in this
> gear. Let us be honest, and cut, as heretofore, from
> the homely web of truth. . . . A girl of Villette stands
> there. (p. 392)

Once more Charlotte has made fruitful use of the negative
metaphor as the mediator between vision and rationality.
The girl is, but then again is not, a resurrected virgin.
Justine Marie Sauveur—again the name Marie stands out—
has, in Lucy's narcotic vision, climbed out of whatever
obscure tomb she inhabits to block Lucy's road to love. The
redeemer is more interested in the dead than in the living.
Lucy denies her assertion quickly, but she cannot erase the
impression that the homely web of realistic truth is merely
a thin veil covering a more frightening, surrealistic vision
of experience.

This mixture of levels of vision is the crowning achievement of Brontë's final novel. Lucy may be haunted by the
return of the dead, she may dream of them, see them in
pictures, even be confronted with their shadows walking
in the park, but she fights her way through to sanity again
and again. On her return from her nocturnal wanderings,
she destroys one of the worst of her fears.

Her most frightening visitor from the land of the dead
has for most of the novel been the nun who haunts Mme.
Beck's school. The use of this nun is ultimately highly
ironic: far from representing a symbol of chastity sent from
the world of death, the ghostly figure is in reality a young
fop in search of a sex life.[42] Lucy's tortured reflections on
self-control have been carried on in the midst of a crowd
of healthy young females all too ready to wax and multiply.
Within a few pages of her opiate vision, Lucy returns to
her dormitory to find the nun there to haunt her once
more. She flies into a fury: "I defied spectra. In a moment,
without exclamation, I had rushed on the haunted couch;
nothing leaped out, or sprang, or stirred; all the movement
was mine, so was all the life, the reality, the substance, the
force; as my instinct felt. I tore her up—the incubus! I held
her on high—the goblin! I shook her loose—the mystery!

And down she fell—down all round me—down in shreds and fragments—and I trod upon her" (pp. 396–397). It is merely a shabby nun's costume. Ghosts are not figures from the world beyond the grave. However real they may seem, however inhibiting their effect, they are emanations of the living mind, figures out of a neurotic pantomime.

Lucy has escaped for the last time from the shadows of irreality. She will reside in a realistic world now, one which will quickly become drab and gloomy. But before that happens, she is awarded a moment of illumination whose afterglow will allow her to survive.

Imanuel finds Lucy on the day following her nocturnal wanderings. It is a fitting day for a lover to come to a Brontë heroine: August 15, the Feast of the Assumption. On this day Mary, the Virgin Mother, left her earthly children behind and was received into Heaven. M. Paul, a transfigured version of Constantin Heger, is in a sense a replacement for that departed mother: "He took my hand in one of his, with the other he put back my bonnet; he looked into my face, his luminous smile went out, his lips expressed something almost like the wordless language of a mother who finds a child greatly and unexpectedly changed, broken with illness, or worn-out by want" (p. 404).

Imanuel has come to redeem his follower, to transform her from a wooden doll into a human being in need of love. Her guilt still exists, but it has become, for once, irrelevant: "I was full of faults; he took them and me all home" (p. 413). For one day she experiences the primordial world of connectedness: "We walked back to the Rue Fossette by moonlight—such moonlight as fell on Eden—shining through the shades of the Great Garden, and haply gilding a path glorious, for a step divine—a Presence nameless. Once in their lives some men and women go back to these first fresh days of our great Sire and Mother—taste that grand morning's dew—bathe in its sunrise" (p. 413). Only for one day, however. *Jane Eyre* had ended metaphorically in the Earthly Paradise, Beulah, where the marriage of the soul and its saviour is consummated; its final chapter is a panegyric on connectedness. But Brontë was older now and had achieved a bitter maturity. One cannot marry the Hegers of this life; one can only learn from them and then move on.[43] Lucy, when Imanuel has left for the underworld, must remain alone on the earth through the long night of three years, the faithful steward of her departed lord.[44]

Villette's morality is more adult than *Jane Eyre*'s. The attainment of a second innocence does not result in a return to paradise; or, rather, the return is a momentary epiphany in which the soul sheds its isolation, huddles in the womb of love, and falls again to the dark earth, having known and remembering the nature of love. Yet Lucy, like Charlotte Brontë, can live and work without the presence of a loved one, as long as she knows she is loved: "Reader, they were the three happiest years of my life" (p. 414). There are natures which are used to separation, which can fool themselves into thinking that they thrive on it.

Imanuel dies at sea. The promise of a second coming with its concomitant resurrection of the dead remains unfulfilled. The dead will not awake for Lucy Snowe any more than for Charlotte Brontë. They are creatures of the storm, doomed to live alone in exile, in Hell, and await their own death as the event which will connect them once again with the people they have lost. Earlier, Lucy had described what waiting is like:

> I waited my champion. Apollyon came trailing his
> Hell behind him. I think if Eternity held torment, its
> form would not be fiery rack, nor its nature, despair.
> I think that on a certain day amongst those days which
> never dawned, and will not set, an angel entered
> Hades—stood, shone, smiled, delivered a prophecy
> of conditional pardon, kindled a doubtful hope of
> bliss to come, not now, but at a day and hour un-
> looked for, revealed in his own glory and grandeur
> the height and compass of his promise; spoke thus
> —then towering, became a star, and vanished into his
> own Heaven. His legacy was suspense—a worse boon
> than despair. (p. 376)

Lucy remains in Labassecour and awaits her death. By

the time of her writing she has been there a long time. Referring to the action of the novel, Lucy tells the reader: "I speak of a time gone by: my hair, which till a late period withstood the frosts of time, lies now, at last white, under a white cap, like snow beneath snow" (p. 38). Her family, her lover, even her enemies are long dead. Lucy lives on, alone, exiled, waiting. Whether she waits in despair or suspense is a question she does not answer.

Epilogue

THE FINALITY OF last novels appears only in hindsight. Brontë did not give up writing when she completed *Villette*. Life without composition was unthinkable, unbearable to her, and she continued until her death to follow the calling which was part of her religion. She left behind her two fragments which are known to scholars as "Willie Ellin" and "Emma." Thematically, they center on the concerns which had fascinated the author throughout her life.

"Willie Ellin" represents a return to the material of *The Professor*'s opening chapters; it is yet another version of the sibling struggle which Brontë had been writing out in story after story since her teens. But this time the oppressed younger brother is a mere child, tortured and nearly killed by an overpowering adult. He has no means to defend himself. Nor is the heroine of "Emma" able to struggle against her victimization. She has been left at a boarding school under false pretenses by a man who then disappears, and she quickly becomes the object of jealousy and suspicion. The story breaks off before the mystery of the shy, awkward girl's identity is solved. Fittingly enough, this last story thus centers around a girl who seems to belong to no one, a lonely little waif too strange to find acceptance.

Abandonment, brutalization, the search for identity. And a degree of helplessness which had been absent from her earlier fiction. *Jane Eyre* had opened with the orphan's revolt against her oppressive surroundings. The heroine of "Emma" would not have rebelled, we may be sure, if the story had continued. The strange sense of motionlessness, of suspended existence, which had characterized the end of *Villette* is carried over in varying forms into "Willie Ellin" and "Emma." There seems only one real exit from the victimization of life.

Ultimately, both "Willie Ellin" and "Emma" are too short and too fragmentary to be of more than historical interest as narratives. But one facet of Brontë's late work is of central importance to our understanding of the author. She made three attempts to get "Willie Ellin" underway, each time using a different narrator. One of those narrators is a creature whose only relationship is with death.

The speaker is "an essence bodiless and incomplete, yet penetrative and subtle."[1] It inhabits a mansion from which every human being has departed except the aged housekeeper, and it professes to be quite contented with its isolation. It has no understanding of human beings, no need to be near them. Sitting alone in the parlor of Haworth Parsonage through the long summer evenings of 1853, Brontë imagines a being which can look on the departure of the people around it without the emotion which a girl or a woman would be forced to feel when her loved ones went away: "Whoever in my early days were the inmates of the house, on me they made no impression. . . . At last, I suppose, [they] forsook retirement and went permanently away. . . . This departure made no difference to me, except that I remember looking at the sun and listening to the wind with a new holiday feeling of unconstraint."[2] The spirit's faulty memory looks suspiciously like the result of repression: it can recall nothing about the people who surrounded it in its earlier days. But of course spirits are not human; they are not burdened by rage, or guilt, or even loneliness when they are abandoned, and so have no need for repression. It must have simply forgotten those with whom it once lived.

The spirit does have one memory, though, the recollection of its birth. Interestingly enough, it seems to have risen from the grave: "The short, green, flower-bearing turf around [the mansion] covered an ancient burying-ground—so ancient that all the sleepers under the flowers had long ago ceased to be either clay or bone, and were become fine mould. . . . I came to consciousness at a moment within the rim of twilight. I came upward out of earth—not downward from heaven."[3] The narrator is a projection of Brontë's neurosis, of a nearly crippling, ultimately fatal depression disguising itself as an analytic, detached, loveless consciousness which hovers about the grave which is its past and future home. And in a sense, it represents the end point in the curve of its author's development as an artist.

Brontë had begun her novelistic career with a deeply rooted faith in the human ability to find meaning in life on this earth. Like Arnold, Eliot, Ruskin, and the other leading writers of her generation, she had started with a belief in salvation through work. In her early novels, human activity was in the profoundest sense significant, a reflection of an ultimately meaningful universe. William Crimsworth and Jane Eyre had literally worked their way to their goals in life, struggling over obstacles in a landscape which was rooted in part in the traditions of Protestant allegory.

The deaths of Branwell, Emily, and Anne did not make Charlotte lose her faith in an orderly universe, but they presented the bereaved woman with the final proofs that the principles of that order are not accessible to the human mind, that God's justice is not man's. In the second half of her short career, human activity has lost its metaphysical significance, has been set free to drift randomly in a mechanical age where God is ominously silent. Work has become a matter of "filling the time which spreads between me and the grave," as Caroline Helstone puts it (*Shirley*, p. 138). Like the finest of her literary peers, Brontë had to come to terms with a new world drained of religious meaning—secularized, industrialized, urban Europe. After putting the absurdities of *The Professor* behind her, she became a pioneer in the fictionalized description of that new world. We forget too easily how few industrial novels were written before *Shirley*, how few purely urban novels existed in the English language before *Villette*.

Work, activity, movement are still life in her last two novels. But there is hardly any space left in the society she imagines for moderate, constructive activity. The world of affairs, cut loose from all religious sanctions, has become the arena of open class warfare, a struggle in which all too many clerics serve as conservative captains. Brontë's imaginative universe had always contained cruelty. But in her late novels, brutality is no longer simply explainable as a manifestation of a twisted psyche. It is the way of the world now, a conscious weapon for maintaining an oppressive status quo.

And in the shadows, immured from the bustling, truculent marketplace are the secluded loners, the Miss Manns, Miss Ainsleys, Miss Marchmonts, waiting with painful dignity for something to occur. But it is not simply a matter of a few minor characters. The heroines of the last two novels struggle against a numbed passivity which had been absent from the earlier work. Caroline Helstone suffers a decade of suspended animation in her tomblike home before her mother returns to call her back into life. And Lucy Snowe is frozen in a cataleptic trance throughout half of her narrative, stunned by her losses into a state in which any movement at all demands a conscious act of will. Caroline and Lucy overcome their dangerous passivity; they struggle or are hauled back into life. Yet entropy has become an important factor in Brontë's imaginative world. The body is heavy, wooden, listless.

The main polarity of the fragments which come after *Villette* is between corporeality and release from the body. The tortured little boy and the abandoned little girl of the last stories are encumbered by their bodies. Flesh is there to be beaten, to be embarrassed; limbs are painful in "Willie Ellin," ungainly in "Emma." Relief is only found in states where the mind is unaware of its prison—in fainting, in sleepwalking.

Unlike the protagonists of the last two stories, the ghostly narrator of "Willie Ellin" is disembodied and thus free. Human life with its pain, its brutality, its possible ultimate meaninglessness is irrelevant to it, a transient nuisance obtruding for a moment on its airy serenity. The spirit has no curiosity about life at all; its only interest is in the grave.

The woman who had written all her life about human passion quickly realized that she could not write a novel from this new standpoint, and she broke off the experiment. Yet the death-centered persona was part of her, just as

Charles Wellesley and Jane Eyre and the other narrators were part of her. The ghost was a projection of a potentially fatal aspect of its author's mind. Given the right conditions, the life-denying spirit could flourish at the expense of the more creative aspects of that mind, and the passionate desire for experience, which no trauma of Brontë's life had quite been able to extinguish, would turn into an irresistible need for rest.

Those conditions were reached before long. A year and a half after the composition of "Willie Ellin," Charlotte found herself pregnant, at the age where her mother had died of pregnancy's complications. A black core of depression had existed within her for thirty-three years. That dark mass began to spread like a cancer now, consuming the frame in which it resided. In her final moment of consciousness, she saw death as an event imposed from without, as a judgment pronounced on her by God, but she was wrong. The need to die had come from deep inside her. The time and the manner of her dying were an organic outgrowth of the life she had lived.

Notes

Introduction

1. Marjorie Editha Mitchell, *The Child's Attitude to Death*, p. 106.
2. John Bowlby, "Childhood Mourning and its Implications for Psychiatry," *American Journal of Psychiatry* 118 (1961): 487.
3. Arnold Gesell and Frances L. Ilg, *The Child from Five to Ten*, pp. 429–432.
4. Bowlby, "Childhood Mourning and Its Implications for Psychiatry," p. 485.
5. Charlotte Brontë, *Shirley* (London: J. M. Dent, 1965), p. 342. All quotations from *Shirley* will be taken from this edition.
6. Ibid, p. 350.
7. To Ellen Nussey, undated. *The Brontës: Their Lives, Friendships, and Correspondence*, ed. T. J. Wise and J. A. Symington, 1: 143.
8. See Philip Momberger, "Self and World in the Works of Charlotte Brontë," *English Literary History* 32 (1965): 349–369.
9. Brontë, *Shirley*, p. 511.
10. Margot Peters, *Charlotte Brontë: Style in the Novel*, p. 128.
11. Charlotte Brontë, *The Professor and Emma: A Fragment*, p. 10.

One. Silence and Language

1. Elizabeth Cleghorn Gaskell, *The Life of Charlotte Brontë*, p. 82. This work was originally published in 1857.
2. In the village of Haworth, where the Brontës lived for most of Charlotte's lifetime, the mortality rate was appalling. In *The Brontës and Their Background: Romance and Reality*, p. 32, Tom Winnifrith points out that "between 1838 and 1849 41.6 per cent of the population died before reaching the age of six." Margot Peters, in *Unquiet Soul: A Biography of Charlotte Brontë*, pp. 247–248, expands on Winnifrith's point. She notes: "Brief as their lives were, [Branwell, Emily, and Anne Brontë] bettered the 25.8 years' average life expectancy of Haworth residents. . . . [When the Superintending Inspector of the General Board of Health visited Haworth in 1850, he] found 316

houses . . . sharing 69 privies . . .; in one case twenty-four families used the same privy. One privy 'perched upon an eminence commanding the whole length of the main street'; underneath festered a cesspool that could and did overflow. He found an open channel running down the steep main street, a sluice for refuse of all descriptions. There were no sewers. He found 50 middensteads, one in the West Lane behind the parsonage [where the Brontës lived] heaped with entrails, slaughterhouse refuse, and 'green meat.' He found 23 manure piles. He found 11 pumps (2 out of order) that gave up impure water. Fastidious villagers walked half a mile to the Head Well to draw their water, which nevertheless was scanty in the summer and occasionally so green and putrid that cattle refused to drink it. The parsonage boasted a pump in the kitchen—the well sunk in ground just yards from the cemetery. [The inspector] shook his head over the graveyard that crowded the parsonage, a site that had seen 1,344 burials in the last ten years alone." The source of Winnifrith's and Peters' information is *The Report to the General Board of Health of a Preliminary Inquiry into the Sewerage, Drainage and Supply of Water and Sanitary Condition of Haworth* (Benjamin Herschel Babbage, 1850).

3. Dr. Philip Rhodes, "A Medical Appraisal of the Brontës," *Brontë Society Transactions* 16, 2 (1972): 102. *Brontë Society Transactions* will be abbreviated hereafter as *BST*.

4. To the Rev. John Buckworth, Nov. 27, 1821. Wise and Symington, *Correspondence*, 1: 59.

5. As was brought out in the Introduction, the inability to become conscious of the pain involved in loss is central to the formation of pathological symptoms. Helene Moglen, in *Charlotte Brontë: The Self Conceived*, p. 21, suggests: "The fact that Charlotte speaks only once of Mrs. Brontë in her copious correspondence and journals does not confirm the idea that the memory of her death and dying was so trivial that it could be easily dismissed, but rather suggests that it was so painful that it had to be repressed."

6. There is evidence that Branwell thought of his aunt as a mother, but no corresponding evidence for his sisters. During his aunt's terminal illness, Branwell wrote: "I am attending at the death-bed of my aunt, who has been for twenty years as my mother." To Francis H. Grundy, Oct. 25, 1842. Wise and Symington, *Correspondence*, 1: 273.

7. John Lock and Canon W. T. Dixon, in *A Man of Sorrow: The Life, Letters and Times of the Rev. Patrick Brontë*, the fullest treatment of Brontë's life, stress his love and understanding for children. Still, it seems clear that, at least after the death of his wife, he was never in truly close communion with any of his children.

8. Wise and Symington, *Correspondence*, 1: 69n.

9. "Ellen Nussey's Narrative," Wise and Symington, *Correspondence*, 1: 97. These recollections had first appeared as "Reminiscences of Charlotte Brontë," in *Scribner's Monthly*, vol. 2 (1871).

10. Of all the Brontës, it was Branwell who was most crippled in later life by his need to idealize his oldest sister. In *Branwell Brontë*, p. 11, Winifred Gérin writes: "The logical outcome of this sense of severance from [Maria,] his too-perfect sister and the consciousness of his own unworthiness was almost to provoke and certainly to exaggerate every failure in life, until his morbid imagination had made a pariah of him."

11. "Ellen Nussey's Narrative," Wise and Symington, *Correspondence*, 1: 98.

12. See Robert B. Heilman, "Charlotte Brontë's 'New' Gothic," in *From Jane Austen to Joseph Conrad*, ed. R. C. Rathburn and Martin Steinmann, Jr., pp. 118–132. The essay is reproduced in *The Brontës: A Collection of Critical Essays*, ed. Ian Gregor.

13. Winifred Gérin, in *Charlotte Brontë: The Evolution of Genius*, p. 286, writes: "*Not* to be loved had been Charlotte's ultimate dread since childhood. The nightmare of her schooldays, as Mary Taylor recalled, was the vision of her beloved dead sisters, returned, but changed towards her; unloving and censorious. The impression lasted all her life, and in *Villette* it haunted her again with a recurrent horror."

14. Quoted in Gérin, *Evolution of Genius*, pp. 103–104. I have quoted Gérin's transcription of the Roe Head Journal passages rather than that of Wise and Symington because she *appears* to reproduce Brontë's unique punctuation more accurately than do Wise and Symington. Winnifrith, in *The Brontës and Their Background*, pp. 1–27, discusses the inadequacy of published transcriptions of Charlotte Brontë's unpublished writings. Until a full and definitive edition of Brontëana appears, critics without access to the original manuscripts will have to operate with the knowledge that the texts they are using might be inaccurate.

15. To Ellen Nussey, undated. Wise and Symington, *Correspondence*, 1: 143.

16. Ibid.

17. To Ellen Nussey, February 20, 1837. Wise and Symington, *Correspondence*, 1: 153.

18. Robert Southey to Charlotte Brontë, March, 1837. Wise and Symington, *Correspondence*, 1: 155.

19. To Robert Southey, March 16, 1837. Wise and Symington, *Correspondence*, 1: 157.

20. To Ellen Nussey, August 4, 1839. Wise and Symington, *Correspondence*, 1: 184.

21. Gérin, *Evolution of Genius*, p. 145.

22. To Ellen Nussey, June 30, 1839. Wise and Symington, *Correspondence*, 1: 181.
23. Lucy Snowe, the protagonist of *Villette*, will experience the same quiet anguish as she watches Paulina Mary Home petted by the Brettons. See below, Chapter 6.
24. To Ellen Nussey, May 4, 1841. Wise and Symington, *Correspondence*, 1: 231.
25. To Ellen Nussey, May, 1842. Wise and Symington, *Correspondence*, 1: 260–261.
26. To Ellen Nussey, Nov. 10, 1842. Wise and Symington, *Correspondence*, 1: 282.
27. To Branwell Brontë, May 1, 1843. Wise and Symington, *Correspondence*, 1: 297.
28. To Emily Brontë, May 29, 1843. Wise and Symington, *Correspondence*, 1: 299.
29. To Emily Brontë, September 2, 1843. Wise and Symington, *Correspondence*, 1: 303.
30. Ibid, p. 304.
31. Ibid, p. 303.
32. Wise and Symington, *Correspondence*, 1: 307.
33. Charlotte told Ellen: "[M. Heger] wanted me to take one of his little girls with me [as a pupil], but I refused. I was surprised also at the degree of regret expressed by my Belgian pupils, when they knew I was going to leave." To Ellen Nussey, Jan. 3, 1844. Wise and Symington, *Correspondence*, 2: 3.
34. For example Lucile Dooley, in "Psychoanalysis of Charlotte Brontë, as a Type of the Woman of Genius," *American Journal of Psychology* 31 (1920): 250, states: "M. Heger answered every requirement of the father fixation." This little-read, much-maligned article seems to have been the first, and remains one of the best, attempts to deal with Charlotte Brontë through the use of the psychoanalytic method.
35. To Constantin Heger, July 24, [1844]. Wise and Symington, *Correspondence* 2: 10–11. I have translated this and subsequent excerpts from the Heger letters from the original French.
36. To Ellen Nussey, January 23, 1844. Wise and Symington, *Correspondence*, 2: 3.
37. To Constantin Heger, January 8, [1845]. Wise and Symington, *Correspondence*, 2: 21–23.
38. To Constantin Heger, November 18, 1845. Wise and Symington, *Correspondence*, 2: 67.
39. Ibid, p. 69.
40. M. Heger seems to have treated all of Charlotte's correspondence in this manner. But his prudent wife retrieved what she could from the wastebasket and pieced it back together in order to retain proof of her foreign student's unrequited infatuation.

41. "Vous me direz peut-être—Je ne vous porte plus le moindre intérêt Mademoiselle Charlotte—vous n'êtes plus de ma Maison—je vous ai oubliée." *De ma maison* can be translated either "part of my household" or "one of my family," but in normal French usage the latter is the more common nuance. Charlotte was not the first to use the language of family connection to refer to her relationship with the Hegers. When Charlotte and Emily returned home after the death of their aunt, Heger wrote a letter to their father in which he stated: "Nous sommes affligés parce que cette brusque séparation vient briser l'affection presque paternelle que nous leur avons vouée ... vous me pardonnerez si nous vous parlons de vos enfants ... comme si elles faisaient partie de notre famille; leurs qualités personnelles, leur bon vouloir, leur zèle extrême sont les seules causes qui nous poussent à nous hasarder de la sorte" [We are pained because this sudden separation comes to sever the almost paternal affection we have felt for them ... you will forgive us for talking about your children ... as if they were a part of our family; their personal qualities, their good nature, their intense zeal are the only reasons which impel us to be so audacious]. Constantin Heger to Patrick Brontë, [1842]. Wise and Symington, *Correspondence*, 1: 279–280.
42. This idea, and the applicability of the passage to the dreams of children in *Jane Eyre*, were suggested to me by my colleague, Lee Edwards.
43. Brontë, *Shirley*, p. 382.
44. Charlotte Brontë, *Jane Eyre*, ed. Richard J. Dunn, p. 193.
45. Charlotte Brontë, "Biographical Notice of Ellis and Acton Bell," in Emily Brontë, *Wuthering Heights*, ed. V. S. Pritchett, pp. xvii–xviii.
46. Rhodes, in "A Medical Appraisal of the Brontës," p. 106, conjectures: "Could one or other of the sisters have picked up a further dose of tubercle bacilli [in London] which when they returned to Haworth they handed on to Branwell and to Emily? This seems a most likely supposition. Almost certainly one or other of them introduced a new pathogenic element into the closed community of Haworth Parsonage, which wreaked so much havoc so quickly."
47. Since his return in disgrace from the Robinsons', Branwell had been filling his correspondence with melodramatic wishes for death. He had entertained his friends with sketches of himself as a martyr at the stake, as a hanged criminal, as a corpse on a bier, etc.
48. To W. S. Williams, Oct. 2, 1848. Wise and Symington, *Correspondence*, 2: 261–262.
49. Moglen in *The Self Conceived* stresses the idea that Branwell's downfall allowed Charlotte to develop psychologically

to the point of becoming a professional writer. She writes: "It is not inappropriate that this woman, whose masochistic dependence and passivity had evolved within the strictures of a patriarchal Victorian family, should find the sources of freedom in the moral and physical disintegration of her brother and in the growing blindness of her father. Only thus could her ego survive at all" (p. 78). I am inclined to agree. But Brontë paid a heavy price for her freedom. It is one of the ironies of her life that every increase in maturity and in freedom brought with it an increase in the level of her guilt feelings.

50. To W. S. Williams, June 4, 1849. Wise and Symington, *Correspondence*, 2: 338.
51. To W. S. Williams, June 13, 1849. Wise and Symington, *Correspondence*, 2: 340.
52. To W. S. Williams, June 25, 1849. Wise and Symington, *Correspondence*, 2: 348–349.
53. To W. S. Williams, September 21, 1849. Wise and Symington, *Correspondence*, 3: 24.
54. To W. S. Williams, July 26, 1849. Wise and Symington, *Correspondence*, 3: 9.
55. To W. S. Williams, [November 20, 1849]. Wise and Symington, *Correspondence*, 3: 40.
56. To Ellen Nussey, June 12, 1850. Wise and Symington, *Correspondence*, 3: 118.
57. To Ellen Nussey, January 19, 1853. Wise and Symington, *Correspondence*, 4: 35.
58. To Ellen Nussey, September, 1850. Wise and Symington, *Correspondence*, 3: 166.
59. To George Smith, February 5, 1851. Wise and Symington, *Correspondence*, 3: 207.
60. To Ellen Nussey, January 24, 1852. Wise and Symington, *Correspondence*, 3: 310.
61. To Elizabeth Gaskell, February 6, 1852. Wise and Symington, *Correspondence*, 3: 312.
62. To Ellen Nussey, June 6, 1852. Wise and Symington, *Correspondence*, 3: 336.
63. To Ellen Nussey, December 15, 1852. Wise and Symington, *Correspondence*, 4: 29.
64. To Ellen Nussey, December 18, 1852. Wise and Symington, *Correspondence*, 4: 30.
65. To Ellen Nussey, January 2, 1853. Wise and Symington, *Correspondence*, 4: 32.
66. To Ellen Nussey, May 27, 1853. Wise and Symington, *Correspondence*, 4: 69.
67. To Ellen Nussey, April 11, 1854. Wise and Symington, *Correspondence*, 4: 112–113.
68. To Ellen Nussey, August 9, 1854. Wise and Symington, *Correspondence*, 4: 145.

69. Ibid, pp. 145–146.
70. Rhodes, in "A Medical Appraisal of the Brontës," was the first to suggest the possibility of a neurotic basis for Brontë's death. Since then the idea has begun to gain currency. Two studies published since I completed this chapter have dealt with the question of a willed death. Peters, *Unquiet Soul*, p. 405, asks: "Was her death to be in a sense voluntary—an unconscious solution to an unresolvable conflict—as she felt—between her art and her marriage?" Moglen, *The Self Conceived*, p. 241, states: "[Several months] after her marriage, Charlotte Brontë conceived a child and fell ill of the conception: sickened, apparently by fear. It was the last of her neurotic illnesses; the last of her masochistic denials.... On March 31, 1855, at thirty-eight years of age, in the early months of pregnancy, Charlotte Brontë died. She could not bring to birth the self she had conceived." Other biographers, however, are content to accept without reservation Gaskell's account of the reasons for Charlotte Brontë's death. Brian Wilks, for example, in *The Brontës*, writes: "Charlotte . . . became pregnant, and a chill which she caught after walking on the moors in a rainstorm compounded complications of the pregnancy which made her seriously ill" (p. 137). Yet the chronology of events as they are mirrored in Brontë's correspondence does not support this traditional view of her last months. She had caught the chill on November 28, 1854, and by December 7 could announce: "I am better now, but not quite well" (To Ellen Nussey. Wise and Symington, *Correspondence* 4: 165). On January 19, she wrote to Ellen: "My health has been really very good ever since my return from Ireland till about ten days ago, when the stomach seemed quite suddenly to lose its tone—indigestion and continual faint sickness have been my portion ever since. Don't conjecture—dear Nell—for it is too soon yet though I certainly never before felt as I have done lately" (Wise and Symington, *Correspondence*, 4: 171). As late as January 21, she was still feeling well enough to contemplate a trip to visit Ellen within the fortnight (see the letter to Amelia Taylor, Wise and Symington, *Correspondence*, 4: 172). The chill, in other words, must have occurred before the onset of pregnancy and, at least as far as she was concerned, had no more than very minor lingering aftereffects. It was only after she had learned that she was pregnant that she feared there was anything wrong.
71. Her opinion of the effect of her mother's pregnancies is probably mirrored in the language of a letter by Elizabeth Gaskell, written after Charlotte had told her in rough outline the story of her life: "[Mrs. Brontë] had 6 children as fast as could be; & what with that, & the climate, & the strange half mad husband she had chosen she died at the end of 9 years" (To Cath-

erine Winkworth, [August 25, 1850]. *The Letters of Mrs. Gaskell*, ed. J. A. V. Chapple and Arthur Pollard, p. 124).

72. To Margaret Wooler, August 30, 1853. Wise and Symington, *Correspondence*, 4: 83.

73. Rhodes, "A Medical Appraisal of the Brontës," p. 107.

74. I would conjecture that the concatenation of two factors—the attainment of her mother's life span and the onset of pregnancy—formed the basis on which Brontë's death wish could finally overcome her will to live. It is entirely possible that she could have survived pregnancy at any other age, or that if she had not become pregnant she could have survived beyond the significant age of thirty-eight. But the two factors coming together must have caused her to identify with her mother more strongly than she had ever done before. And that was dangerous, for identification is a two-edged sword. If on the one hand it is a means of unconsciously denying loss, on the other hand it can be a way of punishing one's self. One takes on the personality traits and at the same time the fatal symptoms of the departed loved one. In "Identification as a Defence against Anxiety in Coping with Loss," *International Journal of Psychoanalysis* 46 (1965): 312, George R. Krupp points out that identification "may occur when the death wish is strongest." The symptoms of her disorder bore a strong resemblance to the nausea and abdominal pain which her mother had experienced in her final illness. Thus Brontë's pain served as a form of retribution for her survival. As Krupp puts it, " 'Justice' results when the survivor punishes himself with the same kind of suffering that had been endured by the dying" (pp. 311–312).

Two. Death and Art

1. The importance of the Byronic hero for the development of Charlotte Brontë's vision of life, and her need to wean herself away from that conception of masculinity, are discussed in Moglen, *The Self Conceived.*

2. Peters, in *Unquiet Soul*, discusses Charlotte's attraction for Zamorna: "Gradually her old idol, the white-haired, fatherly Duke of Wellington, faded from her imagination to be replaced by his magnificent son, Arthur Augustus Wellesley. ... [He] in turn gradually lost his filial aspect, evolving into the Duke of Zamorna, dark, cruel, sexually magnetic, and sinning. Unconsciously she turned from her father to his son to a stranger. The new branches shot from the old tree, however: her male idol continued to be masterful, domineering: she could not separate sexuality from domination since she could not free herself from the powerful authority of her

father" (p. 34). Peters continues a few pages later: "The figure of Zamorna loomed gigantic over her life. . . . He was all she longed to be—rich, despotic, adored, sinning, and masculine. From this deep well of imagination she thus slaked her sexual and creative thirst" (p. 43).

3. Fannie Ratchford, *The Brontës' Web of Childhood*, p. 102.

4. Sigmund Freud, *Beyond the Pleasure Principle*, trans. James Strachey, p. 33.

5. Ibid, p. 35.

6. *The Miscellaneous and Unpublished Writings of Charlotte and Patrick Branwell Brontë*, ed. T. J. Wise and J. A. Symington, 1: 32. Unless otherwise indicated, all quotations from Charlotte Brontë's juvenilia will be taken from this edition. The reader should be warned that since T. J. Wise, who controlled the juvenilia for decades, has been proven a forger, we cannot be certain that Charlotte, and not Branwell, wrote all of the stories attributed to her. Thus I have rested my argument on a general pattern discernible throughout the juvenilia, rather than on any one story. For more information on this difficulty, see Winnifrith, *The Brontës and Their Background*, p. 16 and p. 225, notes 43 and 44, where he calls into question the authorship of "The Foundling" on the basis of a larger than normal signature and some rather coarse stanzas in the story. Although his evidence is unconvincing on this point, I do not mean to rule out the possibility that he may just be correct.

7. Gérin, *The Evolution of Genius*, p. 17, notes: "The effect of the successive deaths of their mother and sisters was to drive them far from all thought of mortality—as far as the wings of invention could bear them—towards the creation of an existence of which they held the key and of whose permanence they themselves could be the guarantors. It was not for mere love of magic that, for years after, in their games and dramatized stories, they claimed to 'make alive again' the casualties of the day."

8. Brontë, *Jane Eyre*, p. 72.

9. Ratchford, *Web of Childhood*, p. 75.

10. Quoted from the Roe Head Journal by Gérin, *The Evolution of Genius*, p. 107.

11. 2: 286. My italics.

12. "The Green Dwarf," *Legends of Angria*, ed. Fannie E. Ratchford and William C. DeVane, p. 90. All quotations from "The Green Dwarf" will be taken from this edition.

13. Ratchford, *Web of Childhood*, p. 62.

14. "A Peep into a Picture Book," *The Twelve Adventurers and Other Stories*, ed. Clement Shorter and C. W. Hatfield, pp. 168–169.

15. "Mina Laury," *Legends of Angria*, ed. Ratchford and DeVane, p. 173.

16. Moglen, *The Self Conceived*, pp. 49ff., discusses Charlotte's treatment of the later heroines of the Angrian cycle insightfully and intelligently. Readers may also wish to consult Margaret Blom's discussion of Brontë's juvenilia in *Charlotte Brontë* (Boston: Twayne, 1977). Unfortunately I was not able to obtain a copy of this book before my own study was completed.

17. "Mina Laury," *Legends of Angria*, ed. Ratchford and DeVane, p. 206.

18. Ratchford, *Web of Childhood*, Chapter 26, discusses the correspondences between the characters of Charlotte Brontë's novels and those of her juvenilia.

19. On April 12, 1850, Brontë told Williams: "[Jane Austen's] business is not half so much with the human heart as with the human eyes, mouth, hands and feet; what sees keenly, speaks aptly, moves flexibly, it suits her to study, but what throbs fast and full, though hidden, what the blood rushes through, what is the unseen seat of Life and the sentient target of death—*this* Miss Austen ignores" (Wise and Symington, *Correspondence*, 3: 99).

Three. Possession

1. Charlotte Brontë, *The Professor and Emma: A Fragment*, p. 45. All quotations from *The Professor* will be taken from this edition.

2. This is not to say that Brontë is consciously writing a story about life and death. She is consciously writing a tale about one man's attempt to get ahead in the world. But the novel would be much more boring than it is if her unconscious were not coloring the novel, not reverting from time to time to the darker side of William Crimsworth's psyche. There has been very little valuable criticism of this novel. One of the most useful examinations of the novel is M. M. Brammer, "The Manuscript of *The Professor*," *Review of English Studies* 11 (1960): 157–170.

3. The problems Brontë encounters through the use of a masculine narrator have been intelligently examined by, among others, Earl A. Knies, *The Art of Charlotte Brontë*.

4. Moglen, *The Self Conceived*, discusses the androgynous aspects of William Crimsworth's character and the ambiguities involved in the novel's concerns.

5. Terry Eagleton, *Myths of Power: A Marxist Study of the Brontës*, p. 44, writes: "At one level, *The Professor* could be said to be an inversion of *Jane Eyre*: whereas that novel showed a bourgeoise elevated to the gentry, this one shows an aristocrat transformed into a bourgeois. Yet the difference, for all

the striking imaginative distance between the two works, is purely superficial, a question of two variations of a single categorical structure. The point about both Jane and Crimsworth is that they are socially 'impure'—exiles, hybrids, outcasts, ambiguous figures trapped at a point of tension between alternative classes and competing ideologies."

6. Of course it might also be said to move it closer to struggle with a brother, and therefore to the complex of sibling rivalry between Charlotte and Branwell. It was much easier during this period of her life for Charlotte to acknowledge to herself her ambivalence toward Branwell than it would have been to recognize that there was also an ambivalence toward Maria and toward her other sisters.

7. Ratchford, *Web of Childhood*, p. 199, states: "Mademoiselle Reuter's name . . . is carried over from Zorayde, the heroine of 'A Leaf from an Unopened Volume.'" This is true, but her function is that of Zenobia Ellrington.

8. Much of the criticism which has appeared in the *Brontë Society Transactions*, both before and after the appearance of Ratchford's study of the juvenilia (*Web of Childhood*), has insisted on the correspondences of Brontë's fictional characters with her real-life acquaintances.

9. Moglen (*The Self Conceived*) writes: "Given the odd blurring of identity boundaries, . . . discussions [between Crimsworth, Henri, and Hunsden] are dramatized interior debates in which one aspect of Brontë's personality seeks ascendancy over the others" (p. 88).

10. The Protestant Cemetery is the site Brontë visited on the day she confessed to a Catholic priest.

11. "Editor's Preface to the New Edition of *Wuthering Heights*," in Emily Brontë, *Wuthering Heights*, ed. V. S. Pritchett, p. xxviii.

12. William has gained M. Vandenhuten's favor by rescuing his son from drowning. He has proven his heroism by thwarting death.

Four. Innocence

1. Charlotte Brontë, *Jane Eyre*, ed. Richard J. Dunn, p. 11. All quotations from *Jane Eyre* will be taken from this edition.

2. "Author's Preface," *The Professor*, p. xi.

3. Recognizing the danger inherent in Helen's example, M. A. Blom, in "'Jane Eyre': Mind as Law Unto Itself," *Criticism* 15 (1973): 353, writes: "Jane is incapacitated for Christian faith by her reliance on her vital, autonomous imagination which forces her to conceive of death not as a prelude to an eternity of rewards or punishments, but as a doorway to noth-

ingness." I would argue that it is precisely the otherworldly rewards and punishments that she fears. She does not avoid death because she sees it as nothingness, but because she sees it as unknowable and fearsome.

4. Laurence E. Moser, S. J., "From Portrait to Person: A Note on the Surrealistic in *Jane Eyre*," *Nineteenth-Century Fiction* 20 (1965): 279. Thomas Langford, in "The Three Pictures in *Jane Eyre*," *Victorian Newsletter* 31 (1967): 47, asserts that "the pictures may represent the three major sections of Jane's life." He sees the sections as Lowood ("childhood and adolescence"), Thornfield ("womanly instincts"), and Marsh End ("ascetic austerity"). M. B. McLaughlin, in "Past or Future Mindscapes: Pictures in *Jane Eyre*," *Victorian Newsletter* 41 (1972): 23, writes: "Both [the first and the second] pictures tell . . . of a traumatic loss and abandonment—the first symbolizing the consequences of Mr. Reed's death, the second that of Miss Temple's loss through marriage. . . . The martyr imagery of the third painting can, I think, be related to Helen Burns."

5. The motif of drowning is one which Brontë had used before, in Zamorna's fantasy of Maria Henrietta Percy's death. William Crimsworth had shown his valor in *The Professor* by saving a boy from drowning.

6. Moglen, *The Self Conceived*, p. 110, notes the connection of the pictures with death, but not with guilt. She writes: "They are images of isolation and despair, of death and infinity. They are images of the sublime and suggest the kinsmanship of human feeling with a larger mysterious world that exists beyond the self, accessible and yet threatening because it cannot be ordered or contained."

7. Wilks, in *The Brontës*, writes: "Branwell's morbid sense of humor made him susceptible to the kind of illustration that Charlotte found disturbing. Many of his scribbled drawings show the Bewick 'fiend'" (p. 47).

8. G. Armour Craig, "The Unpoetic Compromise: On the Relation between Private Vision and Social Order in Nineteenth-Century British Fiction," in *Jane Eyre*, ed. Richard S. Dunn, p. 476, states: "In every relationship Jane rises from inferiority to superiority. Her inferiority is expressed again and again as imprisonment; her superiority appears as the narrative confirmation of her rightness in resisting imprisonment." Craig's essay originally appeared in *Self and Society in the Novel*, ed. Mark Schorer (New York: Columbia University Press, 1956), pp. 30–41.

9. Charles Burkhart, in *Charlotte Brontë: A Psychosexual Study of Her Novels*, p. 67, notes the five-part structure of the novel. Elsewhere he mentions in passing the resemblance of Jane to Cinderella, and the relevance of *Pilgrim's Progress* to the

novel but does not offer any discussion of these motifs. Moglen, *The Self Conceived*, Chapter 3, discusses the two motifs at some length in the course of her brilliant treatment of the romance structure of the novel. Because of the nature of her discussion, she combines the two motifs. I have kept them apart, because I have tried to stress the fact that they represent separate if overlapping levels of thought, two stages in Brontë's attempt to distance herself from the complex of ideas which the novel works out for her.

10. There is more than a hint of danger in Rochester's song. It makes a rather ominous claim: " 'My love has sworn, with sealing kiss, / With me to live—to die' " (p. 240). Jane has made no such fatal compact.

11. R. E. Hughes, "*Jane Eyre*: The Unbaptized Dionysos," *Nineteenth-Century Fiction* 18 (1964): 364, states: "The Christianity of the novel is an overlay on the primary pattern, which pre-dates Christianity."

12. Craig concludes: "I know no other work that so effectively demonstrates the demon of the absolute" ("The Unpoetic Compromise," p. 478).

13. Winnifrith, *The Brontës and Their Background*, p. 52, points out that *Jane Eyre* preaches universal salvation.

14. The *Kinder- und Hausmärchen* of the Brothers Grimm, in which *Cinderella* appeared, was introduced to the English public as *German Popular Stories* [trans. Edgar Taylor], 2 vols. (London, 1824–1826), with illustrations by George Cruikshank.

15. On leaving the room soon after this conversation, Jane loses her slipper, thus allowing Rochester to catch up to her.

16. Moglen, *The Self Conceived*, p. 131, comments: "The authority which Jane has sought is female; the moon, maternal nature, the mother within herself—a cosmic and personal principle of order and control."

17. I would assume that Charlotte saw the Rivers sisters as a complimentary portrait of Emily and Anne, just as she viewed Helen Burns as a portrayal of Maria.

18. Act V, scene 1, my translation. Friedrich Schiller, *Die Räuber* (Stuttgart: Reclam, 1969), pp. 122–123.

19. Of course at the same time it can be viewed as a lesson for Jane, too, a warning that she should treat all siblings kindly.

20. Sigmund Freud, *Jokes and Their Relation to the Unconscious*, trans. James Strachey, p. 179.

21. Rochester's sex change is part of an interesting pattern which runs throughout Brontë's fiction. Robert Bernard Martin, in *The Accents of Persuasion: Charlotte Brontë's Novels*, p. 158n, writes: "[A Freudian psychologist] might . . . be interested in the frequency with which Miss Brontë describes male characters in female terms, and in the fact that Rochester, Lucy, de

Hamal, and Dr. John all assume the clothing of the opposite sex. . . . The narrator of her first novel is a man, and she fought to keep the masculine anonymity of her penname, Currer Bell. Shirley Keeldar, of course, constantly refers to herself in masculine terms. What significance, if any, there is in all this is probably a matter for the biographer, not the critic."

22. Peters, *Style in the Novel*, p. 130, notes the frequency in the novel of legal terminology.

23. The key to one meaning of Jane's name occurs in a conversation between Rochester and Jane:

> "Dread remorse when you are tempted to err, Miss Eyre: remorse is the poison of life."
> "Repentance is said to be its cure, sir." (p. 120)

I do not mean to negate the more traditional argument that the name connotes air. See Eric Solomon, "Jane Eyre, Fire and Water," *College English* 25 (1964): 215–217; and David Lodge, "Fire and Eyre: Charlotte Brontë's War of Earthly Elements," *The Language of Fiction*, pp. 114–143, reprinted in *The Brontës: A Collection of Critical Essays*, ed. Gregor, pp. 110–136.

24. Her primary inheritance is of course the £20,000 she receives from her uncle, John Eyre. St. John Rivers would have her receive a more mystical inheritance. He reads her a passage from the first chapter of Revelation: "He that overcometh shall inherit all things; and I will be his God, and he shall be my son. But . . . the fearful, the unbelieving, &c. shall have their part in the lake which burneth with fire and brimstone, which is the second death" (p. 367).

25. William Crimsworth's destruction of the dog had involved guilt feelings, although those feelings were quickly transferred to his son.

26. See, for example, Wayne Burns, "Critical Relevance of Freudianism," *Western Review* 20 (1956): 301–314.

27. As Moglen, in *The Self Conceived*, points out, Bertha is seen metaphorically as a vampire. Rochester tells Bertha's brother to "think of her as someone dead and buried" (p. 187).

Five. Emptiness

1. In his chapter on *Shirley*, Knies (*The Art of Charlotte Brontë*) discusses Brontë's problems with the third-person point of view of the novel. Eagleton (*Myths of Power*, p. 80) makes an interesting point: "If *The Professor* conceals a third-person narration beneath its autobiographical form, *Shirley*, a third-person novel, secretes a tacitly first-person narration—that of Caroline Helstone—within it. The choice of the third-person

form is logical enough for a novel which offers itself in part as a kind of social documentary; but it is the lack of structural symmetry between this aspect of the work and the 'first-person' Romance woven into it which accounts for a good deal of the book's formal diffuseness."

2. As has often been pointed out, *Jane Eyre* possesses an important dimension of social protest. The author's social anger can be seen in Jane's cry: "Who blames me? Many, no doubt; and I shall be called discontented. . . . It is in vain to say human beings ought to be satisfied with tranquillity: they must have action; and they will make it if they cannot find it. Millions are condemned to a stiller doom than mine, and millions are in silent revolt against their lot. Nobody knows how many rebellions besides political rebellions ferment in the masses of life which people earth" (pp. 95–96).

3. Moglen, *The Self Conceived*, p. 156n, divides critics of *Shirley* into two strictly opposed camps, those who believe the book lacks unity and those who believe it has "principles of unity." Among the former she cites Ivy Holgate, "The Structure of *Shirley*," *BST* 14, 2 (1961): 27–35; J. M. S. Tompkins, "Caroline Helstone's Eyes," *BST* 14, 1 (1961): 18–28, and several other less important essays. Among the defenders of the novel's coherence, she cites only Jacob Korg, "The Problem of Unity in *Shirley*," *Nineteenth-Century Fiction* 12 (1957): 125–136; Arnold Shapiro, "Public Themes and Private Lives: Social Criticism in *Shirley*," *Papers on Language and Literature* 4 (1968): 74–84; and Carol Ohmann, "Charlotte Brontë: The Limits of Her Feminism," *Female Studies* 6 (1972): 152–163. Moglen, who sees a high degree of unity in the book, recognizes Hiram Yorke's importance in the novel, but mistakes his function. She writes: "In the first chapter of *Shirley*, Brontë demonstrates her resolution of purpose by launching immediately into an attack on the Church—the church of which Patrick Brontë was minister. . . . Its spine broken, the organism must collapse. . . . In two of their rectors—the Reverends Matthew Helstone and Hiram Yorke—the curates' symptoms become more pronounced, made virulent by class and status" (pp. 159–160). Yorke, far from being a clergyman, is a stridently anticlerical manufacturer who is "without the organ of Veneration—a great want, . . . which throws a man wrong on every point where veneration is required. . . . he spoke of 'parsons' . . . with a harshness, sometimes an insolence, as unjust as it was insufferable" (Brontë, *Shirley*, pp. 34–35). The most important clergyman in the book aside from Matthew Helstone is Cyril Hall, Vicar of Nunnely, whom Brontë clearly sets off against Helstone in order to show that there are good clergymen as well as bad, understanding males as well as misogynists. Moglen's reading makes the novel's social vision

seem less troubled, more optimistic and single-minded than it really is.

I would agree with Moglen that the novel contains strong "principles of unity." But that does not mean the book is unified to anything like the extent claimed by some critics. Moglen's need to stress the book's ideological and esthetic unity leads her into a methodological mistake, I think. She writes: "Ruthlessly shunting the tragedies aside, we are able to find the principle of unity which reconciles what for so long have been seen as disparate themes, dissonant chords" (p. 158). A biographical critic cannot temporarily shunt aside the central facts of the subject's life. In her chapter on *Villette*, she discusses the importance of bereavement to Charlotte's final novel. But the deaths of Branwell, Emily, and Anne occurred during the composition of *Shirley*. Therefore, if the deaths are relevant to Brontë's art, they are relevant to *Shirley* as well as to *Villette*.

4. G. H. Lewes' review of *Shirley* appeared in the *Edinburgh Review* (January, 1850). It is reprinted in *The Brontës: The Critical Heritage*, ed. Miriam Allott, pp. 160–170.

5. Martin, *The Accents of Persuasion*, p. 118, writes: "It has been customary to group *The Professor* and *Shirley* as examples of an attempt at realism in the novel, with *Jane Eyre* and *Villette* as triumphs of the imagination. It would be equally valid to speak of her first two novels as exemplifying Miss Brontë's early optimism and hope, with *Shirley* showing her growing doubt and pessimism, followed by the autumnal resignation of earthly hope in *Villette*."

6. Martin, *The Accents of Persuasion*, p. 115, writes: "If there is a presiding god in *Shirley*, it is the shining golden power of money, frustrating those who are deprived of it, keeping them from love and human companionship, even confining its possessors behind a barrier that frightens off intruders into their isolation. . . . In no other novel of Charlotte Brontë is there so much talk of churches, parish schools, clergymen, and the religious affiliations of characters, and in no other is there so little sense of Christianity having any effect upon its adherents."

7. Asa Briggs, "Private and Social Themes in *Shirley*," *BST* 13 (1958): 208.

8. Ibid, p. 208.

9. Brontë, *Shirley*, pp. 16–18.

10. "I do not like the love, either the kind or the degree of it; and its prevalence in [*Villette*], and the effect on the action of it, help to explain the passages in the reviews which you consulted me about, and seem to afford *some* foundation for the criticisms they offered." Harriet Martineau to Charlotte Brontë, undated. Wise and Symington, *Correspondence*, 4: 41.

11. In a letter to Mrs. H. M. Jones, quoted in E. M. Delafield, *The Brontës: Their Lives Recorded by Their Contemporaries*, p. 184, Sara Coleridge wrote: "The worst fault [of the novel] by far is the development of the story. Mrs. Pryor's reason for putting away her daughter is absurdly far-fetched and unnatural." G. H. Lewes was even more disturbed. In his review of *Shirley*, published in the *Edinburgh Review* (January, 1850), he wrote: "Currer Bell! if under your heart had ever stirred a child, if to your bosom a babe had ever been pressed,—that mysterious part of your being, towards which all the rest of it is drawn, in which your whole soul is transported and absorbed,—never could you have imagined such a falsehood as that!" (I am indebted to Peters, *Unquiet Soul*, pp. 260 and 273, for the quotations from Coleridge and Lewes.) But Currer Bell's experience was far different from that of Sara Coleridge and G. H. Lewes, and she could indeed imagine absurd reasons for leaving a defenseless daughter behind.

12. To W. S. Williams, August 29, 1849. Wise and Symington, *Correspondence*, 3: 15.

Six. Exile

1. George Eliot to Mrs. Charles Bray, February 15, [1853]. *The George Eliot Letters*, ed. Gordon S. Haight, 2: 87.

2. Matthew Arnold to [his sister,] Mrs. Forster, April 14, 1853. *Letters of Matthew Arnold*, ed. George W. E. Russell, 1: 33–34.

3. To W. S. Williams, July 3, 1849. Wise and Symington, *Correspondence*, 3: 6.

4. Charlotte Brontë, *Villette*, ed. Geoffrey Tillotson and Donald Hawes, p. 286. All quotations from *Villette* will be taken from this edition.

5. See Herbert R. Courser, "Storm and Calm in *Villette*," *Discourse* 5 (1962): 318–333.

6. To W. S. Williams, January 1, 1852. Wise and Symington, *Correspondence*, 3: 304.

7. "Two Unpublished MSS., Foreshadowing 'Villette,'" *BST* 7 (1931): 278. Hereafter cited as Fragment.

8. Fragment, p. 278.

9. Fragment, p. 279.

10. Mrs. Bretton, as we shall see, is "not . . . a caressing woman" (p. 8). Mme. Beck is much colder: "If the youngest, a puny and delicate, but engaging child, chancing to spy her, broke from its nurse, and toddling down the walk, came all eager and laughing and panting to clasp her knee, Madame would just calmly put out one hand, so as to prevent inconvenient concussion from the child's sudden onset: 'Prends garde, mon

enfant!' she would say unmoved, patiently permit it to stand near her a few moments, and then, without smile or kiss, or endearing syllable, rise and lead it back to [its nurse]" (p. 79).

11. Fragment, p. 279.
12. Fragment, pp. 279–280.
13. Fragment, p. 280.
14. Fragment, p. 281.
15. Fragment, p. 281.
16. Fragment, p. 282.
17. Rosa's mistrust of beautiful children is similar to Mrs. Pryor's in *Shirley*.
18. Fragment, pp. 282–283.
19. Brontë, *Shirley*, p. 316.
20. Peters, *Unquiet Soul*, p. 354.
21. See Georgia S. Dunbar, "Proper Names in *Villette*," *Nineteenth-Century Fiction* 15 (1960): 77–80.
22. See the chapter on *Villette* in Martin, *The Accents of Persuasion*.
23. One of the concepts which inform Moglen's *The Self Conceived* is the idea of feminine masochism and Brontë's need to overcome it. See also Kate Friedländer, "Charlotte Brontë: Zur Frage des masochistischen Charakters," *Internationale Zeitschrift für Psychoanalyse und Imago* 26 (1941): 32–49.
24. P. 42. On her arrival at the ghostly ship, the heroine is nearly denied entrance by a disapproving older woman who treats her as an intruder. The woman is bothered by the news of trouble at home: "She professed to be writing a letter home,— she said to her father; she read passages of it aloud, heeding me no more than a stock—perhaps she believed me asleep: several of these passages appeared to comprise family secrets, and bore special reference to one 'Charlotte,' a younger sister, who, from the bearing of the epistle, seemed to be on the brink of perpetrating a romantic and imprudent match" (p. 43). The insolent keeper of the gate to the afterlife has a foolish younger sister named Charlotte. In that respect she seems to resemble Charlotte Brontë's conception of her older sister Maria. But Lucy claims that the woman is about thirty-nine or forty years old, i.e., roughly the age of Mrs. Brontë at her death.
25. E. D. H. Johnson, in " 'Daring the Dread Glance': Charlotte Brontë's Treatment of the Supernatural in *Villette*," *Nineteenth Century Fiction* 20 (1966): 326, divides the novel into four parts: Chapters 1–6 (introduction), 7–15 (Lucy as solitary onlooker), 16–27 (Lucy's love for Graham Bretton), and 28 to the end (Lucy's love for M. Paul).
26. In a chapter entitled "The Use of the French Language and Stylistic Echoes of French in the Novels," Enid L. Duthie, *The Foreign Vision of Charlotte Brontë*, discusses the problem of

Brontë's frequent novelistic recourse to French. She concludes: "The artistic utilisation of the French language made an important contribution to Charlotte Brontë's art, but so perfectly was it assimilated in [her] work . . . that English readers accepted it without question" (p. 199). I, for one, find the intrusive linguistic exercises disturbing. But there can be little doubt that *at times,* Brontë is able to attain meanings through the use of French which would be impossible in English.

27. Later, in one of Brontë's metaphors, a baby will be born next to the *berceau*: "Dark as it was, it seemed to me that something more solid than either night-shadow, or branch-shadow, blackened out of the boles [of the tree]. At last this struggle ceased. What birth succeeded this travail? What Dryad was born of these throes?" (p. 311).

28. Gérin, *The Evolution of Genius*, p. 286, connects this dream to Charlotte's dream of Maria and Elizabeth, discussed earlier in Chapter 1.

29. Even Shirley, bitten by a possibly rabid dog, decides to die at one point in the novel.

30. Winnifrith, *The Brontës and Their Background*, p. 54, points out that "the philosophy of St. John Rivers is supported in *Shirley* and *Villette.* His gloom and his Calvinism, but not his confidence, affect these books, which do not contain the unorthodox doctrine of salvation outlined in *Jane Eyre.*"

31. There is still, however, a residue of unexpressed anger and self-loathing. Lucy's reaction to the sight of herself in a large mirror is striking: "For the first, and perhaps the only time in my life, I enjoyed the 'giftie' of seeing myself as others see me. No need to dwell on the result. It brought a jar of discord, a pang of regret; it was not flattering, yet, after all, I ought to be thankful; it might have been worse" (pp. 179–180).

32. Gustave Charlier, in "Brussels Life in 'Villette,' " trans. Phyllis Bentley, *BST* 12 (1955): 388, suggests that the painting is Charlotte's memory of a painting of a young dancing girl which she had seen in a salon in 1842. It is typical of Brontë's imagination that she would transform the threatening sensuality of a young dancer into the heavier voluptuousness of an older woman, a queen.

33. Cleopatra's slovenly housekeeping resembles that of an allegorical figure described by Lucy later in the novel. "Human Justice," as the heroine sees it, is a slovenly mother who pays no attention to the cries of her neglected children: "I saw her in her house, the den of confusion: . . . a swarm of children, sick and quarrelsome, crawled round her feet and yelled in her ears appeals for notice, sympathy, cure, redress. The honest woman cared for none of these things" (p. 340). To be ignored by one's mother is for Lucy the archetypical form of injustice.

34. In the final section of *Villette*, Malevola will appear as a monster.

35. In his letter on the final illness of his wife, Mr. Brontë had written: "During many years she had walked with God, but the great enemy, envying her life of holiness, often disturbed her mind in the last conflict" (see Chapter 1, note 4). Vashti's reaction to illness might well be similar to Mrs. Brontë's.

36. For Smith's reaction, see Peters, *Unquiet Soul*, p. 353.

37. Lucy's fear of being stared at resembles a characteristic of earlier Brontë heroines. Jane says of the vision of her mother: "It gazed and gazed and gazed on me" (p. 281). The novelist herself was horrified at the idea of people watching her. And it will be recalled that a major part of the discomfort of her dreams of returned loved ones lay in the fact that they stared at her with such disapproval.

38. Dickens' *David Copperfield* was written under the influence of *Jane Eyre*. In *Novels of the Eighteen-Forties*, p. 114n, Kathleen Tillotson notes: "The sequence of incidents in *Jane Eyre*, chs. i–v, and *David Copperfield*, chs. iv–v, is similar; both children defy their substitute-parents, are physically ill treated by them, half-crazed by solitary confinement, and then sent away to severe and inefficient schools, where they form their first friendships." But there is even more to the relationship of the two novels than this. A comparison of the psychological subtlety of *David Copperfield* with the cruder psychology of Dickens' earlier works would show just how much Dickens learned from his obscure contemporary.

39. De Quincey notes the connection between his drug-induced trances and his dreams. He asserts that "as the creative state of the eye increased, a sympathy seemed to arise between the waking and the dreaming states of the brain in one point—that whatsoever I happened to call up and to trace by a voluntary act upon the darkness was very apt to transfer itself to my dreams" (*The Confessions of an English Opium-Eater*, p. 233). But he does not understand that both trance and dream are motivated by his own wishes and fears.

40. Although Brontë had seen the effect of drugs on her brother's mind, she had never herself experienced the effects of an opiate. She told Elizabeth Gaskell that in composing the opium vision of *Villette*, "She had followed the process she always adopted when she had to describe anything which had not fallen within her own experience; she had thought intently on it for many and many a night before falling to sleep,—wondering what it was like, or how it would be,—till at length, sometimes after the progress of her story had been arrested at this one point for weeks, she had wakened up in the morning with all clear before her, as if she had in reality gone through

the experience, and then could describe it, word for word, as it had happened" (Gaskell, *Life*, p. 386).

41. Lucy's vision of the lonely stone-basin bears a strong psychological resemblance to the vision of her home recounted by the narrator of the Fragment quoted earlier in this chapter.

42. See Johnson, "'Daring the Dread Glance,'" for an intelligent critical discussion of *Villette*. Two other particularly valuable discussions of the novel are Robert A. Colby, "*Villette* and the Life of the Mind," *PMLA* 85 (1960): 410–419; and W. A. Craik, *The Brontë Novels*.

43. I am speaking here of Brontë's idealized conception of Heger, not of the real man. She learned a great deal from her French teacher, but she learned even more from her interaction with her ideal conception of the man, a conception which she had to outgrow.

44. Lucy tells Imanuel: "I will be your faithful steward.... I trust at your coming the account will be ready" (p. 410).

Epilogue

1. Charlotte Brontë, "'The Story of Willie Ellin.' Fragments of an Unfinished Novel by Charlotte Brontë," *BST* 9 (1936): 7.

2. "Willie Ellin," pp. 7–8.

3. "Willie Ellin," p. 6.

Bibliography

Works by Charlotte Brontë

The Brontës: Their Lives, Friendships, and Correspondence. Edited by T. J. Wise and J. A. Symington. 4 volumes. Oxford: Shakespeare Head Press, 1932.

"Editor's Preface to the New Edition of *Wuthering Heights.*" In Emily Brontë's *Wuthering Heights,* edited by V. S. Pritchett. Boston: Houghton Mifflin, 1956.

Jane Eyre. Edited by Richard J. Dunn, New York: Norton, 1971.

Legends of Angria. Edited by Fannie Elizabeth Ratchford and William C. DeVane. New Haven: Yale University Press, 1933.

The Miscellaneous and Unpublished Writings of Charlotte and Patrick Branwell Brontë. Edited by T. J. Wise and J. A. Symington. 2 volumes. Oxford: Shakespeare Head Press, 1936–1938.

The Professor and Emma: A Fragment. London: J. M. Dent, 1972.

Shirley. London: J. M. Dent, 1965.

"'The Story of Willie Ellin.' Fragments of an Unfinished Novel by Charlotte Brontë," *Brontë Society Transactions* 9, 1 (1936): 3–22.

The Twelve Adventurers and Other Stories. Edited by Clement Shorter and C. W. Hatfield. London: Hodder and Stoughton, 1925.

"Two Unpublished MSS., Foreshadowing 'Villette.'" *Brontë Society Transactions* 7 (1931): 277–283.

Villette. Edited by Geoffrey Tillotson and Donald Hawes. Boston: Houghton Mifflin, 1971.

Other Works

Allott, Miriam, editor. *The Brontës: The Critical Heritage.* London and Boston: Routledge and Kegan Paul, 1974.

Arnold, Matthew. *Letters of Matthew Arnold.* Collected and arranged by George W. E. Russell. 2 volumes. London: Macmillan, 1895.

Blom, M. A. "'Jane Eyre'; Mind as Law Unto Itself." *Criticism* 15 (1973): 350–364.

Blom, Margaret. *Charlotte Brontë*. Boston: Twayne, 1977.

Bowlby, John. "Childhood Mourning and Its Implications for Psychiatry." *American Journal of Psychiatry* 118 (1961): 481–498.

Brammer, M. M. "The Manuscript of *The Professor*." *Review of English Studies* 11 (1960): 157–170.

Briggs, Asa. "Private and Social Themes in *Shirley*." *Brontë Society Transactions* 13 (1958): 203–219.

Burkhart, Charles. *Charlotte Brontë: A Psychosexual Study of Her Novels*. London: Victor Gollancz, 1973.

Burns, Wayne. "Critical Relevance of Freudianism." *Western Review* 20 (1956): 301–314.

Charlier, Gustave. "Brussels Life in 'Villette.'" Translated by Phyllis Bentley. *Brontë Society Transactions* 12, 5 (1955): 386–390.

Colby, Robert A. "*Villette* and the Life of the Mind." *Publications of the Modern Language Association* 85 (1960): 410–419.

Courser, Herbert R. "Storm and Calm in *Villette*." *Discourse* 5 (1962): 318–333.

Craig, G. Armour. "The Unpoetic Compromise: On the Relation between Private Vision and Social Order in Nineteenth-Century British Fiction." In *Jane Eyre*, edited by Richard J. Dunn. New York: Norton, 1971.

Craik, W. A. *The Brontë Novels*. London: Methuen, 1968.

Delafield, E. M. *The Brontës: Their Lives Recorded by Their Contemporaries*. London: Hogarth Press, 1935.

De Quincey, Thomas. *The Confessions of an English Opium Eater*. London: J. M. Dent, 1960.

Dooley, Lucile. "Psychoanalysis of Charlotte Brontë, as a Type of the Woman of Genius." *American Journal of Psychology* 31 (1920): 221–272.

Dunbar, Georgia S. "Proper Names in *Villette*." *Nineteenth-Century Fiction* 15 (1960): 77–80.

Duthie, Enid L. *The Foreign Vision of Charlotte Brontë*. London: Macmillan, 1975.

Eagleton, Terry. *Myths of Power: A Marxist Study of the Brontës*. London: Macmillan, 1975.

Eliot, George. *The George Eliot Letters*. Edited by Gordon Haight. 6 volumes. London: Oxford University Press, 1954.

Freud, Sigmund. *Beyond the Pleasure Principle*. Translated by James Strachey. New York: Bantam Classic, 1959.

———. *Jokes and Their Relation to the Unconscious*. Translated by James Strachey. New York: Norton, 1960.

Freidländer, Kate. "Charlotte Brontë: Zur Frage des masochistischen Charakters." *Internationale Zeitschrift für Psychoanalyse und Imago* 26 (1941): 32–49.

Gaskell, Elizabeth Cleghorn. *The Letters of Mrs. Gaskell*. Edited by J. A. V. Chapple and Arthur Pollard. Cambridge, Mass.: Harvard University Press, 1967.

————. *The Life of Charlotte Brontë*. London: J. M. Dent, 1960.

Gérin, Winfred. *Branwell Brontë*. London: Thomas Nelson and Sons, 1961.

————. *Charlotte Brontë: The Evolution of Genius*. London: Oxford University Press, 1967.

Gesell, Arnold and Ilg, Frances L. *The Child from Five to Ten*. New York: Harper and Brothers, 1946.

Gregor, Ian, editor. *The Brontës: A Collection of Critical Essays*. Englewood Cliffs, N.J.: Prentice-Hall, 1970.

Heilman, Robert B. "Charlotte Brontë's 'New' Gothic." In *From Jane Austen to Joseph Conrad*, edited by R. C. Rathburn and Martin Steinmann, Jr. Minneapolis, Minn.: University of Minnesota Press, 1958.

Holgate, Ivy. "The Structure of *Shirley*." *Brontë Society Transactions* 14, 2 (1961): 27–35.

Hughes, R. E. "*Jane Eyre*: The Unbaptized Dionysos." *Nineteenth-Century Fiction* 18 (1964): 347–364.

Johnson, E. D. H. "'Daring the Dread Glance': Charlotte Brontë's Treatment of the Supernatural in *Villette*." *Nineteenth-Century Fiction* 20 (1966): 325–336.

Knies, Earl A. *The Art of Charlotte Brontë*. Athens, Ohio: Ohio University Press, 1969.

Korg, Jacob. "The Problem of Unity in *Shirley*." *Nineteenth-Century Fiction* 12 (1957): 125–136.

Krupp, George R. "Identification as a Defense against Anxiety in Coping with Loss." *International Journal of Psychoanalysis* 46 (1965): 303–314.

Langford, Thomas. "The Three Pictures in *Jane Eyre*." *Victorian Newsletter* 31 (1967): 47–48.

Lock, John, and Dixon, Canon W. T. *A Man of Sorrows: The Life, Letters and Times of the Rev. Patrick Brontë*. London: Thomas Nelson and Sons, 1965.

Lodge, David. "Fire and Eyre: Charlotte Brontë's War of Earthly Elements." *The Language of Fiction*. London: Routledge and Kegan Paul, 1966.

Martin, Robert Bernard. *The Accents of Persuasian: Charlotte Brontë's Novels*. London: Faber and Faber, 1966.

McLaughlin, M. B. "Past or Future Mindscapes: Pictures in *Jane Eyre*." *Victorian Newsletter* 41 (1972): 22–24.

Mitchell, Marjorie Editha. *The Child's Attitude to Death*. New York: Schocken Books, 1967.

Moglen, Helene. *Charlotte Brontë: The Self Conceived*. New York: Norton, 1976.

Momberger, Philip. "Self and World in the Works of Charlotte Brontë." *English Literary History* 32 (1965): 349–369.

Moser, Laurence E., S. J. "From Portrait to Person: A Note on the

Surrealistic in *Jane Eyre.*" *Nineteenth-Century Fiction* 20 (1965): 275–280.

Ohmann, Carol. "Charlotte Brontë: The Limits of Her Feminism." *Female Studies* 6 (1972): 152–163.

Peters, Margot. *Charlotte Brontë: Style in the Novel.* Madison, Wisc.: University of Wisconsin Press, 1973.

———. *Unquiet Soul: A Biography of Charlotte Brontë.* Garden City, N. Y.: Doubleday, 1975.

Ratchford, Fannie Elizabeth. *The Brontës' Web of Childhood.* New York: Columbia University Press, 1941.

Rhodes, Dr. Philip. "A Medical Appraisal of the Brontës." *Brontë Society Transactions* 16, 2 (1972): 101–109.

Shapiro, Arnold. "Public Themes and Private Lives: Social Criticism in *Shirley.*" *Papers on Language and Literature* 4 (1968): 74–84.

Solomon, Eric. "Jane Eyre, Fire and Water." *College English* 25 (1964): 215–217.

Tillotson, Kathleen. *Novels of the Eighteen-Forties.* London: Oxford University Press, 1954.

Tompkins, J. M. S. "Caroline Helstone's Eyes." *Brontë Society Transactions* 14, 1 (1961): 18–28.

Wilks, Brian. *The Brontës.* London: Hamlyn, 1976.

Winnifrith, Tom. *The Brontës and Their Background: Romance and Reality.* London: Macmillan, 1973.

Index